Efficient Accounting with Xero

The definitive guide to optimizing your accounting with proven techniques and best practices

Jay Kimelman

BIRMINGHAM—MUMBAI

Efficient Accounting with Xero

Copyright © 2023 Packt Publishing

All rights reserved. No part of this book may be reproduced, stored in a retrieval system, or transmitted in any form or by any means, without the prior written permission of the publisher, except in the case of brief quotations embedded in critical articles or reviews.

Every effort has been made in the preparation of this book to ensure the accuracy of the information presented. However, the information contained in this book is sold without warranty, either express or implied. Neither the author, nor Packt Publishing or its dealers and distributors, will be held liable for any damages caused or alleged to have been caused directly or indirectly by this book.

Packt Publishing has endeavored to provide trademark information about all of the companies and products mentioned in this book by the appropriate use of capitals. However, Packt Publishing cannot guarantee the accuracy of this information.

Group Product Manager: Rohit Rajkumar

Publishing Product Manager: Vaideeshwari Muralikrishnan

Senior Editor: Keagan Carneiro

Senior Content Development Editor: Debolina Acharyya

Technical Editor: Simran Ali

Copy Editor: Safis Editing

Project Coordinator: Sonam Pandey

Proofreader: Safis Editing

Indexer: Pratik Shirodkar

Production Designer: Vijay Kamble

Marketing Coordinator: Nivedita Pandey, Namita Velgekar, and Anamika Singh

First published: April 2023

Production reference: 1210423

Published by Packt Publishing Ltd.

Livery Place

35 Livery Street

Birmingham

B3 2PB, UK.

ISBN 978-1-80181-220-7

www.packtpub.com

To my wife Wendy Kimelman and my daughter Abigail for keeping me going and encouraging me to keep writing on weekends after putting in long hours each week. Thank you for your patience and for being my biggest cheerleaders.

– Jay Kimelman

Foreword

Finding people in life to inspire you is a challenge. Finding people to both inspire and challenge your perceptions is even more difficult. Finding people to inspire, challenge, teach, and support you is the hardest. Jay Kimelman is one of the rare humans that has the ability to do all of those things. Jay's passion shines through in his incremental innovations within the accounting world. He foundationally understands the industry, the technology, the mindsets of the people, and the needs of the small business world.

I first met Jay at a Xerocon almost 10 years before the publishing of this book. I was a young, queer, female business owner in my late 20s challenging everyone in sight for any reason. I lived the part of the "I know tech better than you" because I could program a basic API integration. I was strong-headed, arrogant, and skeptical – the worst combination. Jay had been around the Xero ecosystem longer than me. He was a **Certified Public Accountant** (**CPA**) long before me. He looked like a more traditional accountant, and I discounted him based on appearances. Boy, was I wrong. He took every challenge I gave in his stride and thoughtfully provided insight into a different perspective. He was genuine. He was authentic. He was kind in his approach. A few years later, I was asked to become a Xero National Ambassador and work alongside Jay in that role. He reintroduced himself humbly with, "I'm not sure if you remember meeting me, but…." Jay and I built a rapport based on mutual respect, an innovative mindset, and an underlying understanding that the tech we employed could do more. Fast forward a few years, and Jay and I now work side by side on the same team, building High Rock Accounting together.

Jay regularly finds ways to use the tools at his disposal, Xero being one, to build efficient practices. He challenges assumptions and builds logical solutions for firms to better service clients. Reading this book will provide the insights of an understated badass in our industry who brings massive value with his approach.

Liz Mason

Founder and CEO, High Rock Accounting

Contributors

About the author

Jay Kimelman is a CPA and is the director of technology and e-commerce industry lead for High Rock Accounting. Before joining High Rock Accounting in January 2022, Jay was the founder and **chief executive officer** (**CEO**) of The Digital CPA from its inception in November 2011.

Jay is a workflow process and workflow automation expert. Jay enjoys working with other accounting and tax professionals in building automation to create efficiency in processes.

Jay received the Xero Most Valued Professional award in 2016 due to his support of the cloud accounting movement. He has also served as a National Xero Ambassador since 2016.

I want to thank the people who have been close to me and supported me, especially my wife Wendy and my daughter Abigail.

About the reviewer

M.D. Khurshid Alam is a Xero partner, Pro-Advisor, and senior bookkeeping manager for a renowned bookkeeping firm in London, UK. He manages the firm's accounting clients and businesses to provide cloud accountancy, VAT, payroll, tax, and year-end accounts. Khurshid graduated from Jagannath University, Bangladesh with a bachelor's degree in business administration, management, and accounting and completed an MBA from the same university. He has served clients ranging from small to limited companies for the last 5 years. He is also the founder and CEO of Khurshid Accountancy, a cloud accountancy firm. He currently provides consultancy to different cloud accounting apps and works as a reviewer.

Table of Contents

Preface — xiii

Part 1: Hitting the Ground Running

1

Xero Basics – Subscriptions and When to Use Them — 3

A bit about Xero	3	Partner subscription plans	6
Business subscription plans	4	Partner subscription plan comparisons	6
Business subscription plan comparisons	4	Summary	7

2

Exploring Bank Feeds – the Heart of Xero — 9

Why bank feeds?	9	Balancing the bank feed	19
Setting up your bank feeds	10	Summary	22

3

Setting Up Your Organization's Financial Settings in Xero — 23

Why are settings in Xero so important?	24	Maneuvering through the Chart of accounts screen	33
Your first major Xero decision – the COA	24	Tracking categories	34
Importing your chart of accounts	30	Setting up tracking categories	34

Other settings that require attention	36	Subscription and billing	42
Organizational details	36	Financial settings	43
Let's add a user	39	**Summary**	**44**

4

Restarting with the Fresh Start Method — 45

When to use Fresh Start	45	Importing using the COA	48
Where do we find our beginning balances?	46	Data entry using conversion balances	56
		Bank feed time	56
Importing your beginning balances	47	**Summary**	**56**

5

Conversion to Xero Made Easy — 57

When to convert versus using The Fresh Start method	57	Preparing your QBDT file	58
		Preparing your QBO file	59
Automating your Xero conversion with Jet Convert	58	**Time to start the conversion**	**59**
		Converting your QBDT file	60
Preparing for conversion by looking into the prerequisites	58	Converting your QBO file	62
		Summary	**65**

Part 2: Handling the Day-to-Day Processes

6

Recording and Reconciling the Bank — 69

The bank feed basics	69	Using Xero to your advantage	79
No bank feed? Not a problem – import it	73	Cash coding	81
		Reconciling that account	82
Rules, rules, rules	76	**Summary**	**84**

7

Invoicing and the Sales Process — 85

Products and services	85	Edit	100
Setting up invoices (and other forms)	88	Add Credit Note	100
Quoting your opportunities	92	Share invoice	101
Time to send the invoices	97	**Getting paid in Xero**	**103**
Repeat	98	Applying payments from the bank feed	104
Void	99	**Summary**	**107**
Copy to	99		

8

Managing Bills and Purchases with Procure-to-Pay in Xero — 109

Exploring the Purchase Order	109	Paying bills is super easy	118
Processing bills and the purchase process	114	Summary	122

9

Using Xero on the Go — 123

Xero mobile on the go	123	Battle of the apps in different operating systems	135
Xero features on the go	124	Summary	135

Part 3: Closing Out the Accounting Period

10

Managing Fixed Assets in Xero — 139

Exploring fixed assets	139	Disposing of assets	147
Adding assets to Xero	143	Summary	149
Depreciating those assets	145		

11

All You Need to Know about Manual Journals in Xero — 151

The manual journal	151	The repeating journal entry	157
Xero's rules for creating manual journals	152	Importing your journal	159
Getting into the manual journal	153	Summary	160
Creating manual journals	153		

12

Correct Your Mistakes with Find and Recode — 161

The basics of Find & Recode	161	Correcting mistakes with Recode	166
Find, the ultimate Xero search tool	163	Summary	169

Part 4: Reporting – Knowing About the Performance of Your Business (KPIs)

13

Running and Customizing Basic Reports in Xero — 173

Reporting in Xero	173	Summary	184
Saving reports in Xero	183		

14

Business Analytics with Business Snapshot and Short-Term Cash Flow — 185

Analytics in Xero	185	Business snapshot	190
Short-term cash flow	185	Summary	193

15

Creating Custom Reports in Xero Using the layout editor — 195

Exploring the layout editor	195	Saving your reports	207
Customizing the basic report	197	Summary	207
Starting from a blank slate	203		

Part 5: For the Advisor

16

Run Your Practice with Xero HQ — 211

What is Xero HQ?	211	What is Ask, you ask?	226
Clients in Xero HQ	214	Staff in Xero HQ	237
Explorer details in Xero – what is it exactly?	222	Practice	243
		Summary	243

17

Exploring Practice-Wide Report Templates — 245

What are Report templates?	245	Using Report templates	254
Editing Report templates	250	Summary	255
Assigning report codes	252		

18

Exporting Your Data and Reports Out of Xero — 257

Exporting Xero reports to expand their role	257	Using Trial Balance apps to make tax time easier	266
Exporting accounting data to make your life easy	259	Summary	268
The Schedule C report for sole proprietors	262		

19

Increasing Your Powers with Apps and Xero — 269

What are apps that are built for Xero?	269	Connecting apps to Xero	273
		What apps should I use with Xero?	275
Why use apps with Xero?	273	Summary	276

Index — 277

Other Books You May Enjoy — 282

Preface

Efficient Accounting with Xero is the ultimate how-to guide to get started using Xero for your small business or using Xero as an anchor in building your bookkeeping or accounting practice. I have used Xero since the early days in the US, starting my Xero journey in 2012. I have watched Xero grow since then and have been a participant in guiding the direction of the product. I can say without a doubt Xero is the best accounting software for your **small to medium business** (**SMB**) or your accounting/bookkeeping practice servicing SMB clients.

Who this book is for

This book was written to guide SMB owners in performing their own bookkeeping and accounting professionals who will build or expand their businesses using Xero. There are no technical prerequisites, but I assume you have a basic understanding of accounting and bookkeeping principles if you are performing services for clients.

What this book covers

Chapter 1, *Xero Basics – Subscriptions and When to Use Them*, is a primer on Xero subscriptions, the costs, and when to use each one.

Chapter 2, *Exploring Bank Feeds – the Heart of Xero*, discusses what bank feeds are and how central they are to Xero operations.

Chapter 3, *Setting Up Your Organization's Financial Settings in Xero*, talks about setting up the basics in Xero and is a good foundation for a fast start.

Chapter 4, *Restarting with the Fresh Start Method*, explores the best conversion method in most cases.

Chapter 5, *Conversion to Xero Made Easy*, discusses how you can fully convert to Xero from QuickBooks if you need transactional history.

Chapter 6, *Recording and Reconciling the Bank*, explores reconciling the bank, the core process in Xero.

Chapter 7, *Invoicing and the Sales Process*, shows you why invoicing is the number-one key to cash flow.

Chapter 8, *Managing Bills and Purchases with Procure-to-Pay in Xero*, discusses how bills and payments are also key to the business cash flow picture.

Chapter 9, *Using Xero on the Go*, talks about using the Xero mobile app on the go and how it is easy and efficient.

Chapter 10, *Managing Fixed Assets in Xero*, talks about managing your assets, from addition to disposal and all that comes in between.

Chapter 11, *All You Need to Know about Manual Journals in Xero*, talks about how Xero makes journal entries easy.

Chapter 12, *Correct Your Mistakes with Find and Recode*, shows how **Find and Recode** was a game-changer and it is a staple for a Xero advisor.

Chapter 13, *Running and Customizing Basic Reports in Xero*, talks about Xero reporting basics and creates a good foundation.

Chapter 14, *Business Analytics with Business Snapshot and Short-Term Cash Flow*, explores the business analytics and cash flow tools every small business owner must use.

Chapter 15, *Creating Custom Reports in Xero Using the Layout Editor*, teaches you about taking Xero reports to the next level with Layout Editor.

Chapter 16, *Running Your Practice with Xero HQ*, shows how Xero HQ is a powerful tool.

Chapter 17, *Exploring Practice-Wide Report Templates*, shows how report templates are powerful firm-wide reporting tools.

Chapter 18, *Exporting Your Data and Reports Out of Xero*, focuses on how getting data out of Xero is as important as getting the data in.

Chapter 19, *Increasing Your Powers with Apps and Xero*, shows how while Xero on its own is great, Xero with apps is amazing.

To get the most out of this book

First, relax; Xero is going to make your life easy. If you are a business owner and you do not already have Xero, start a trial. It is free for 30 days and is fully functional. If you are an accounting professional, you too should have Xero set up, but if you do not, you should start a trial but do sign up to be a partner and gain access to your free firm account. It will give you all of the tools we will explore in the book. Remember that not all feaures will work if you are using a Xero Demo company.

Software/hardware covered in the book	Operating system requirements
Xero	Any web browser; however, Chrome is recommended.

Sign up for a Xero Trial here: `https://www.xero.com/us/signup/`.

Sign up to become a Xero Partner: `https://www.xero.com/us/partner-programme/sign-up/`.

I suggest reading through the book, and then grabbing your laptop, tablet, or phone, and then going chapter by chapter, using the examples, and then seeing how they apply to your business.

Download the color images

We also provide a PDF file that has color images of the screenshots and diagrams used in this book. You can download it here: `https://packt.link/xyXh2`.

Conventions used

There are a number of text conventions used throughout this book.

Bold: Indicates a new term, an important word, or words that you see onscreen. For instance, words in menus or dialog boxes appear in **bold**. Here is an example: "To get to STCF, we click on the **Business** menu, followed by the **Short-term cash flow** option below it."

> Tips or important notes
> Appear like this.

Get in touch

Feedback from our readers is always welcome.

General feedback: If you have questions about any aspect of this book, email us at `customercare@packtpub.com` and mention the book title in the subject of your message.

Errata: Although we have taken every care to ensure the accuracy of our content, mistakes do happen. If you have found a mistake in this book, we would be grateful if you would report this to us. Please visit `www.packtpub.com/support/errata` and fill in the form.

Piracy: If you come across any illegal copies of our works in any form on the internet, we would be grateful if you would provide us with the location address or website name. Please contact us at `copyright@packt.com` with a link to the material.

If you are interested in becoming an author: If there is a topic that you have expertise in and you are interested in either writing or contributing to a book, please visit `authors.packtpub.com`.

Share Your Thoughts

Once you've read, we'd love to hear your thoughts! Scan the QR code below to go straight to the Amazon review page for this book and share your feedback.

https://packt.link/r/1801812209

Your review is important to us and the tech community and will help us make sure we're delivering excellent quality content.

Download a free PDF copy of this book

Thanks for purchasing this book!

Do you like to read on the go but are unable to carry your print books everywhere?

Is your eBook purchase not compatible with the device of your choice?

Don't worry, now with every Packt book you get a DRM-free PDF version of that book at no cost.

Read anywhere, any place, on any device. Search, copy, and paste code from your favorite technical books directly into your application.

The perks don't stop there, you can get exclusive access to discounts, newsletters, and great free content in your inbox daily

Follow these simple steps to get the benefits:

1. Scan the QR code or visit the link below

https://packt.link/free-ebook/9781801812207

2. Submit your proof of purchase
3. That's it! We'll send your free PDF and other benefits to your email directly

Part 1: Hitting the Ground Running

The objective of this section is to familiarize you with the different parts of Xero, as well as the subscription plans that meet your needs the most. Here, we will lay the foundation of using Xero within a business setting so it is set up to succeed when we start posting transactions.

This section comprises the following chapters:

- *Chapter 1, Xero Basics – Subscriptions and When to Use Them*
- *Chapter 2, Exploring Bank Feeds – the Heart of Xero*
- *Chapter 3, Setting Up Your Organization's Financial Settings in Xero*
- *Chapter 4, Restarting with the Fresh Start Method*
- *Chapter 5, Conversion to Xero Made Easy*

1
Xero Basics – Subscriptions and When to Use Them

As we embark on our Xero journey together throughout this book, we are going to review the ways to use Xero on a daily basis in your business. By the time you have finished this book, you will be able to fly through your daily transactions and be an ace at running the reports you need to run your business.

Using the right subscription level is critical to your use of a Xero organization. Here, we will review each of the Xero subscription levels, compare them, and give you an opportunity to find the right plan for your business. You will find the right mix of features and cost to maintain your books while cutting down on expenses.

In this chapter, we're going to cover the following main topics:

- Popular Xero subscription plans
- Xero subscription plans only available as a partner
- Determining the proper subscription for your Xero organization

A bit about Xero

As we embark on our Xero journey together, I think it is important to detail how my Xero journey began. I started the Digital CPA after a breakup with my partner at my former company. That company was built using QuickBooks for the first 5 years of its existence. Later, in 2008, I implemented a full ERP system that was e-commerce-enabled due to the inconsistencies and issues relating to our on-premise use of QuickBooks. No, this system was not cloud-based, but what I learned over the next 2+ years really helped shape me, as I built the Digital CPA a few years later.

I was approached by a prospective client about 6 months after starting the Digital CPA, who was looking for help selecting a cloud-based general ledger software that would integrate with FreshBooks, which was used to track contractor hours and perform their billing. They had one stipulation – it could not be QuickBooks. I found two viable candidates, Xero and Kashoo. After digging a little deeper, I found

Xero to be the definitive winner. In my opinion, it had everything to provide my new client with the financial statements and related reports they required.

Within 2 weeks, I found myself Xero-certified and working with my Xero rep and partner consultant to fully immerse myself in the full Xero experience. I was truly excited about this switch to Xero, but I found that most of my prospective clients had never heard of it and were solely focused on using QuickBooks. When I say QuickBooks, I am referring to the desktop version; most of the business owners I encountered were not aware of using the cloud or were nervous to the point of being paralyzed in fear about putting their business data in it. As you are probably aware, this is not an issue today.

Through the years, Xero has received many enhancements, improvements, and additions. We will cover the most up-to-date version we can in this book. Keep in mind Xero releases updates on the fly and the features discussed here may change. For now, let's see the two main subscription plans available in Xero.

Business subscription plans

You may have signed up for a Xero trial or you are currently deciding on which Xero plan fits your business best. The basic plans advertised for Xero fit the general consumer's needs.

There are three plans you can choose from:

- Early
- Growing
- Established

Each plan is set up to meet the needs of your business. We will dive into the differences between each plan in the next section.

Business subscription plan comparisons

Xero is built on a simple platform. Each subscription level unlocks features based on the needs of your business, whether it is in start-up mode, growth or scaling mode, or your business has reached maturity.

The **Early** plan is perfect for start-ups. The cost is low, at $13/month, yet packed with features you need to run your business. The **Early** plan limits the number of sales invoices and quotes to 20 per month and purchase bills (invoices) to 5 per month.

Depending on your business, this might be the perfect fit. Most of the clients I have seen (small start-up businesses) fit this plan perfectly.

Should your business model require more than 20 invoices or 5 bills per month, then the **Growing** plan is the solution for you. The **Growing** plan is Xero's most popular plan, as it is the "complete" package for most businesses based in the US. This is the plan that most clients are on, at least those that require invoicing and purchasing.

If your business operates globally, and in multiple currencies, the **Established** plan is an ideal choice. In addition to multi-currency, the Xero Established plan includes Xero Projects and Xero Expenses:

- **Xero Projects** allows you to track time, costs, and revenue by specific projects. You can see project profitability, send bills by completion percentage, and even track project tasks in Trello.
- **Xero Expenses** gives you the ability to provide your team with an easy-to-use expense tracking and reimbursement system. Utilizing the Expenses mobile app allows a team member to snap a picture and submit expense details. You can approve expenses on the go on the mobile app and reimburse your team in the same way you pay your other bills.

All Xero business plans include **Hubdoc**, Xero's bill and receipt capture tool. Using Hubdoc adds automation to a process, and I personally love automation. The following figure shows a side-by-side comparison of the Xero business plans:

Early	Growing (Most popular)	Established
$11 per month	$32 per month	$62 per month
30% off	30% off	30% off
✓ Send **20** invoices and quotes	✓ Send invoices and quotes	✓ Send invoices and quotes
✓ Enter **5** bills	✓ Enter bills	✓ Enter bills
✓ Reconcile bank transactions	✓ Reconcile bank transactions	✓ Reconcile bank transactions
✓ Hubdoc - data capture	✓ Hubdoc - data capture	✓ Hubdoc - data capture
		✓ Multi currency
		✓ Projects - track project time and costs
		✓ Expenses - capture and manage claims

Figure 1.1: Xero business subscription plans

Now that we have had a chance to review the Xero business plans, let's look at the other options.

Partner subscription plans

If you run or are part of an accounting, bookkeeping, or tax organization, Xero has an awesome partner program. A main benefit of being a Xero partner firm is having access to its partner subscription plans.

There are two Xero partner plans you can choose from:

- Ledger
- Cashbook

Each plan has its own value and potential benefits for your firm. We will dive into the differences between each plan in the next section.

Partner subscription plan comparisons

The Xero **Ledger** plan is just that – a ledger. It has the most basic features, a reporting function, and the ability to post manual journals, which we will dive into later in *Chapter 11*.

Firms that use the **Ledger** plan are usually early in their Xero adoption, capture client financial details in order to use the Xero reporting function, or use the extensive app marketplace to add value or efficiency to their workflow.

Cashbook, the remaining partner plan, is one of my favorites and the other plan most of my clients use. This plan is similar to the **Growing** plan with the invoicing and purchasing functions removed. In the following figure, we can see the Xero partner plans side by side:

Ledger $1 per month	**Cashbook** $3.50 per month
✓ Annual accounts preparation for fully managed clients ✓ Clients can only view reports	✓ For managed clients who do not require invoicing ✓ Clients can only view reports ✓ Bank feeds ✓ Tax reporting

Figure 1.2: Xero partner-only plans

Xero has a subscription plan for you and your business, whether you work with a Xero advisor or not.

Summary

As we have seen in this chapter, Xero has several subscription plans, including partner plans (**Ledger** and **Cashbook**) and business plans (**Early**, **Growing**, and **Established**). Each of these plans meets the unique needs of diverse business owners, regardless of where they are in the business life cycle.

In the next chapter, we will jump right into the heart of Xero – bank feeds. This is where the fun begins.

2
Exploring Bank Feeds – the Heart of Xero

In this chapter, we will look at the bank feed, a list of the cleared transactions from your bank that are imported to Xero for you to easily record and reconcile. Xero puts a tremendous emphasis on the bank feed, even enforcing a *no manual journal to a bank account* policy. You will see how to set up your bank feed, reconcile your transactions, and your bank statement at the end of the period, keeping your accounts tied out and your business in the know.

In this chapter, we're going to cover the following main topics:

- Why bank feeds?
- Setting up your bank feeds
- Balancing your bank feed to the bank

By the end of this chapter, you will know why bank feeds are at the heart of Xero and why they are so important in using it. You will also know how to set up your own bank feeds and, finally, have them balanced to a bank account before you start your business's books in Xero.

Why bank feeds?

Xero connects to your bank and imports your bank account transactions directly into your company or organization, beginning the efficiency that I love in Xero. By using the bank feed, a Xero user gets the details of their banking transactions made available directly in the accounting platform, allowing them to reconcile their transactions quickly and easily. We will get into how to process daily bank transactions when we get to *Chapter 6* where we will show you the process of what Xero calls reconciliation.

Your bank transactions are the key to recording your revenues and expenses in your books. By having these details available in the accounting platform, you are assured that you have captured your financial transactions in your books. All that is left is to properly categorize the transactions.

The Xero bank feed automatically updates daily as transactions clear your bank account. This allows you to use the Xero Reconciliation screen to record the transactions into the general ledger while marking each one as reconciled, making the bank reconciliation process a breeze. We will get to bank reconciliation in *Chapter 6* as well, but first, we must set up the bank feed, which we will accomplish together in the next section.

Setting up your bank feeds

There are two main types of bank feeds in Xero, **Direct feeds** and **Yodlee feeds**. There are a few main differences that we will address here.

Direct feeds are the result of an agreement between Xero and a financial institution, which gives Xero access to their API endpoints in their banking system.

> **Note**
>
> **API** stands for **application programming interface**. An API is code that allows two systems to connect to each other.

This allows Xero direct access to the bank account to give you the most accurate and secure access to your banking data. This is evident when connecting to a direct feed, as you are authenticating your access to your bank and its web portal. A token is used to secure your access and create the bank feed.

Yodlee feeds are supplied by a third-party company, Yodlee. Yodlee is what is known as a data aggregator and has remained a staple of the Xero bank feed, going back to before my first experience with Xero in June 2012. Yodlee stores the banking credentials for the bank feed you are creating. It uses these credentials to allow its platform to perform *screen scraping* of the banking data, which is then sent to your Xero organization.

Xero does not store passwords in either case.

In addition to direct and yodlee feeds, Xero also has PayPal and Stripe feeds, which act very much the same as regular feeds.

Setting up your bank feeds 11

So, now that we have discussed the different types of bank feeds available in Xero, let's walk through setting up a direct feed and a yodlee feed:

1. There are multiple ways to access the Xero banking pages or set up a new bank account – for example, as shown here, you can add the first bank account directly from the Xero dashboard:

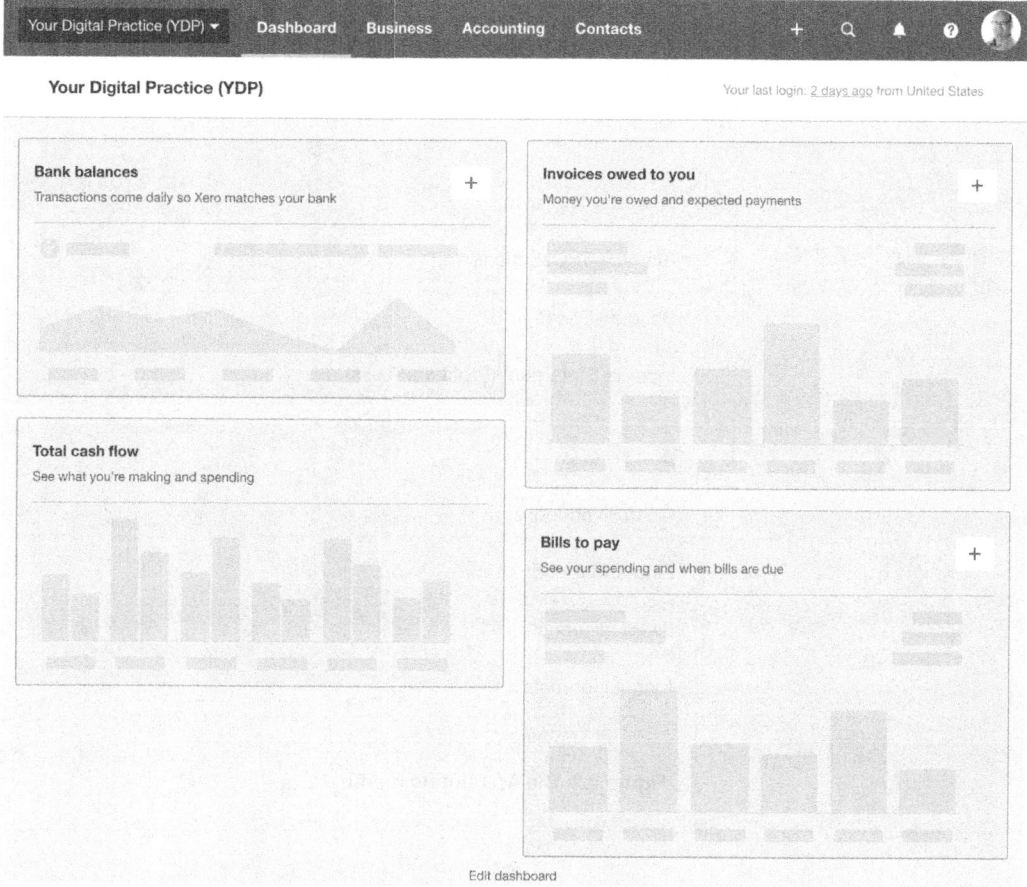

Figure 2.1: The Xero dashboard from a brand-new organization

Alternatively, you can do so via the **Accounting** menu, as shown here:

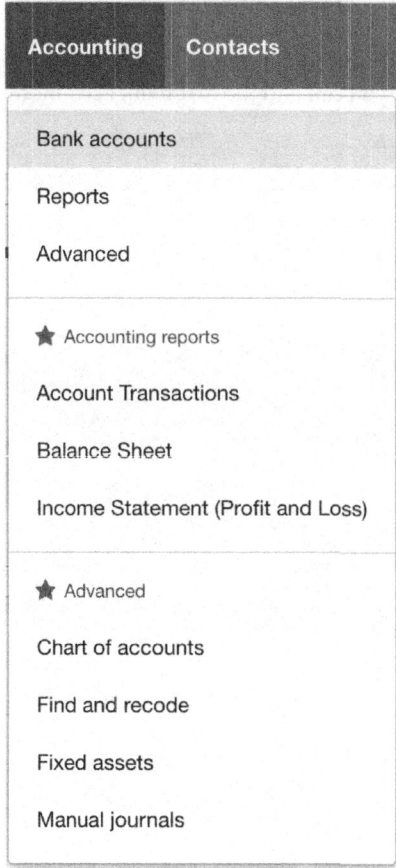

Figure 2.2: The Accounting menu

2. Either way will navigate you to the **Find your bank** screen:

Find your bank

🔍 Search for your bank...

Popular banks in United States

American Express (US)

Bank of America (US)

Capital One (US)

Chase (US)

Citibank (US)

City National Bank (US)

Farm Credit Services of America (US)

Frontier Farm Credit (US)

PayPal

Silicon Valley Bank (US)

Stripe

SVB Financial Group

Wells Fargo (US)

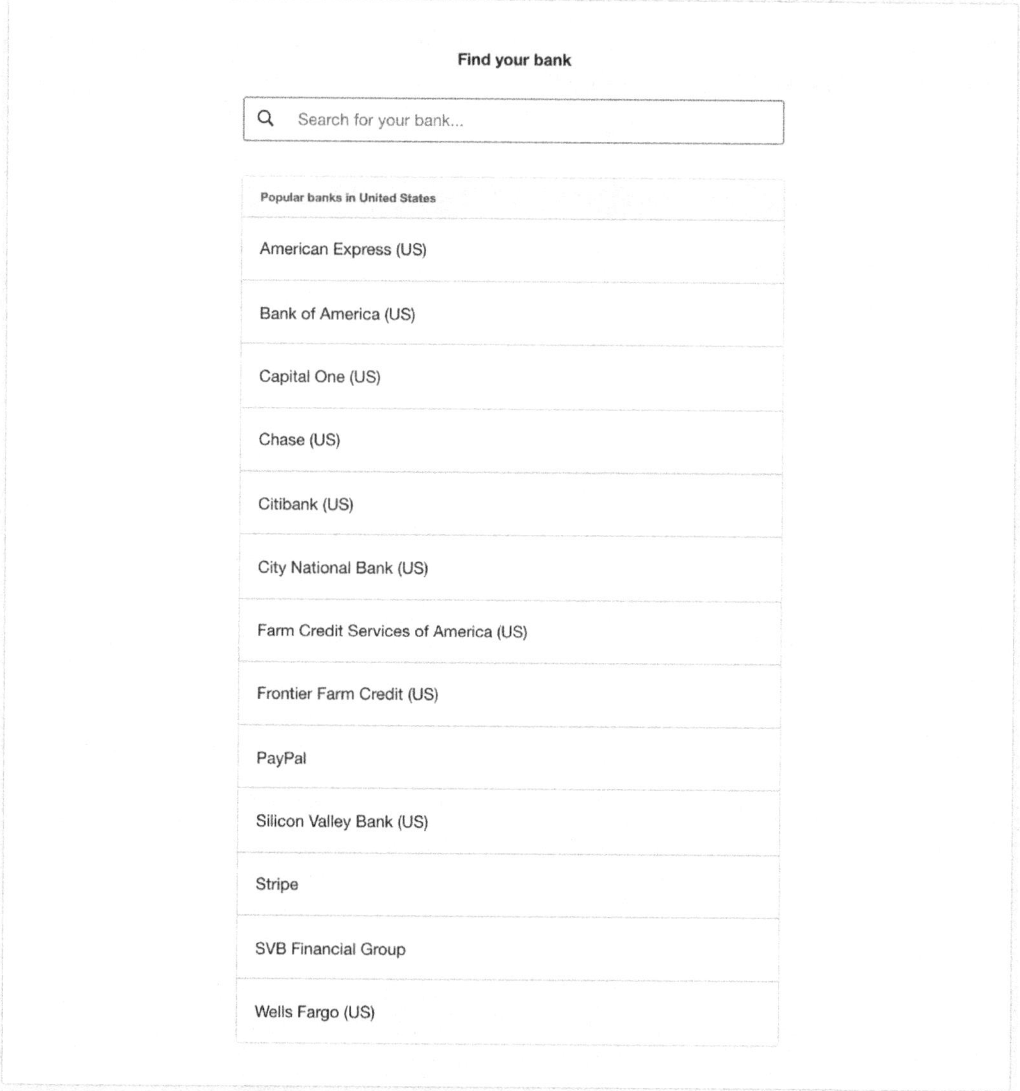

Figure 2.3: The Find your bank screen

As you can see from the preceding screenshot, the banks listed on the **Find your bank** screen are the current direct feeds.

3. Let's start the process of setting up a direct feed. I have chosen an account for Wells Fargo. The next screen asks for some account details:

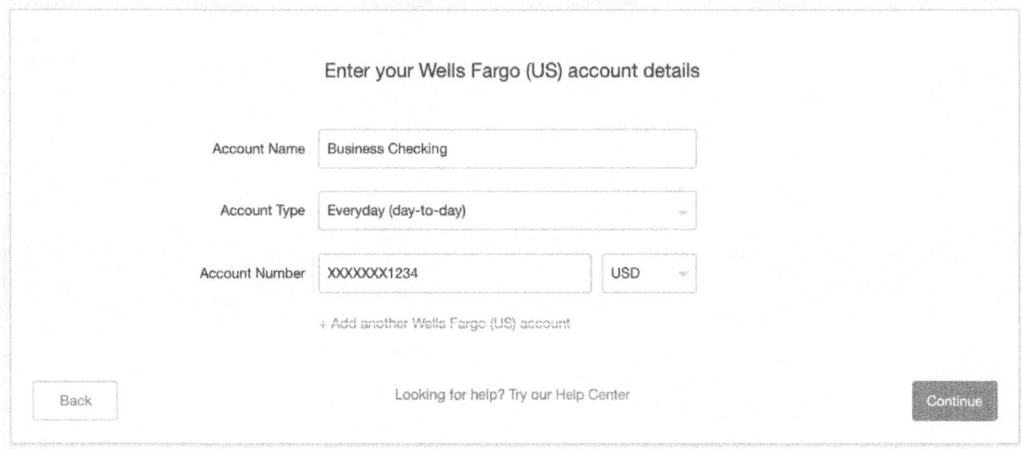

Figure 2.4: Filling in your account details

4. When we click **Continue**, we will navigate to the pre-login screen, as shown here:

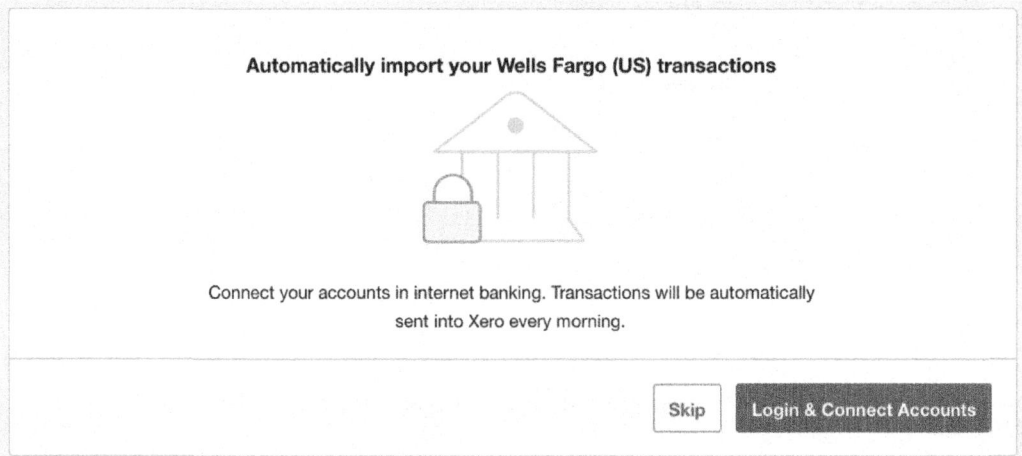

Figure 2.5: The pre-login screen

Setting up your bank feeds   15

5. Next, we click on the **Login & Connect Accounts** button, and we are taken directly to the Wells Fargo website to authenticate and continue with the next steps, starting with verification, as shown here:

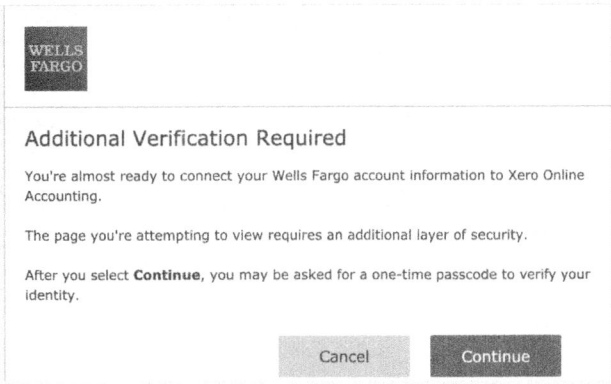

Figure 2.6: Additional verification to log in to the Wells Fargo website

6. This sends you a text message with a verification code. Enter that code, which takes you to your list of accounts:

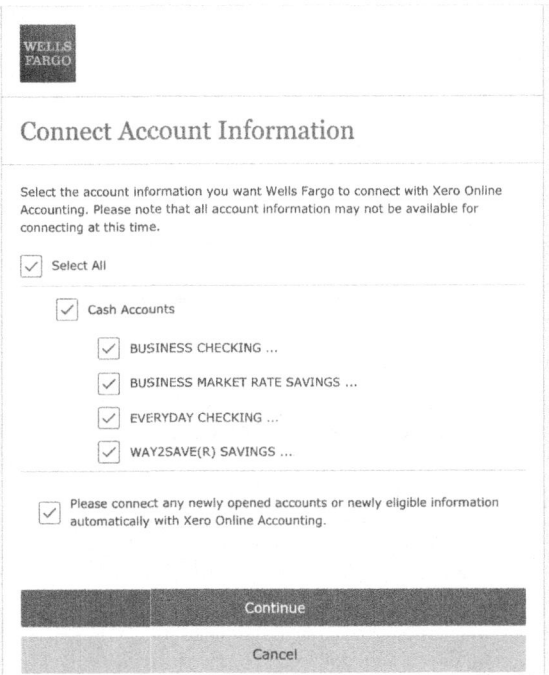

Figure 2.7: Account information

16   Exploring Bank Feeds – the Heart of Xero

That is the screen where you choose exactly which accounts you intend to add to Xero. Make sure to check the boxes of the accounts you want to add to Xero, and remove checks from the accounts you are not planning to add.

> **Note**
>
> Note the message at the bottom of the preceding screen. If you want any new account added to this banking user profile, make sure to check the box next to the last message on the page.

7. The next screen asks you to agree to the terms and conditions, and then click **Connect Account Information**:

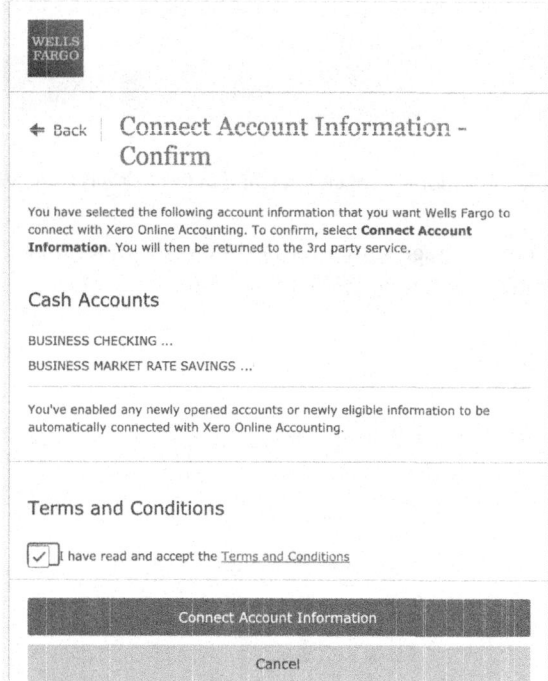

Figure 2.8: Adding the direct feed terms and conditions

8. Next, let's start adding our Wells Fargo accounts:

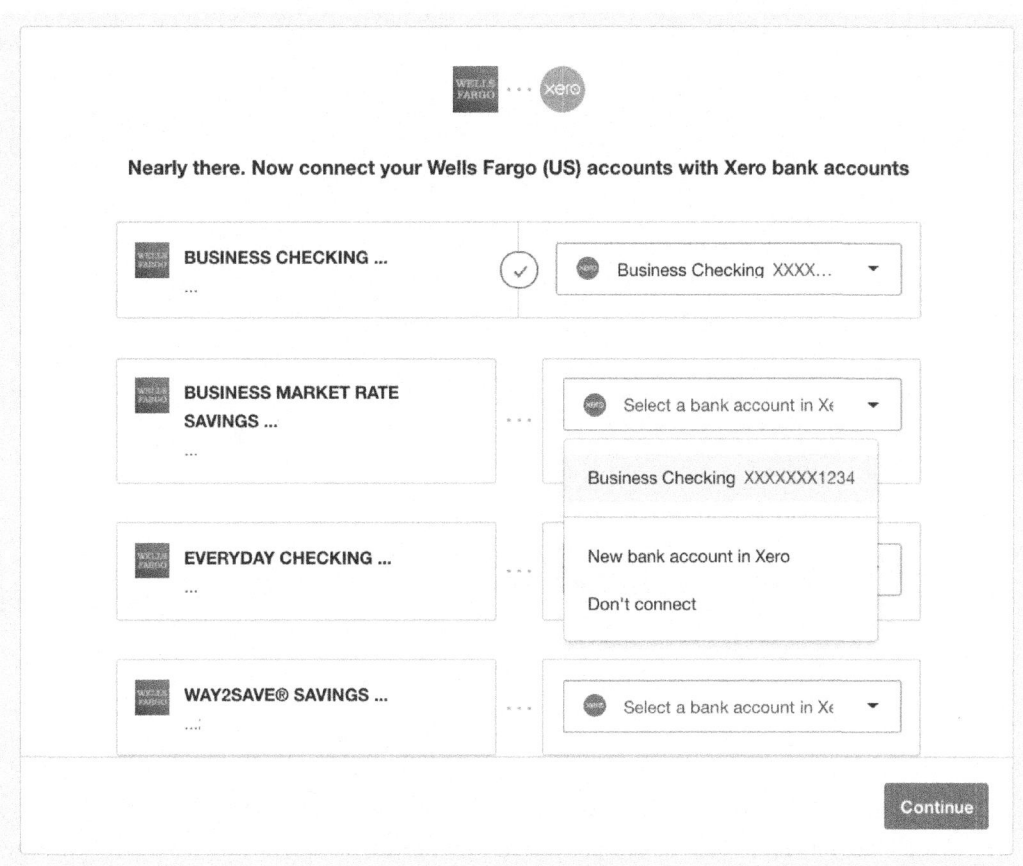

Figure 2.9: The account selection page

9. Now, we select the Xero account that matches the bank account. As you can see in the preceding screenshot, the account we added a few moments ago is showing and is now selected by us. The second option is a savings account we were not aware of, so we opt for the **New bank account in Xero** option. We select the **Don't connect** option for the other accounts. Then, we click **Continue**.

18 Exploring Bank Feeds – the Heart of Xero

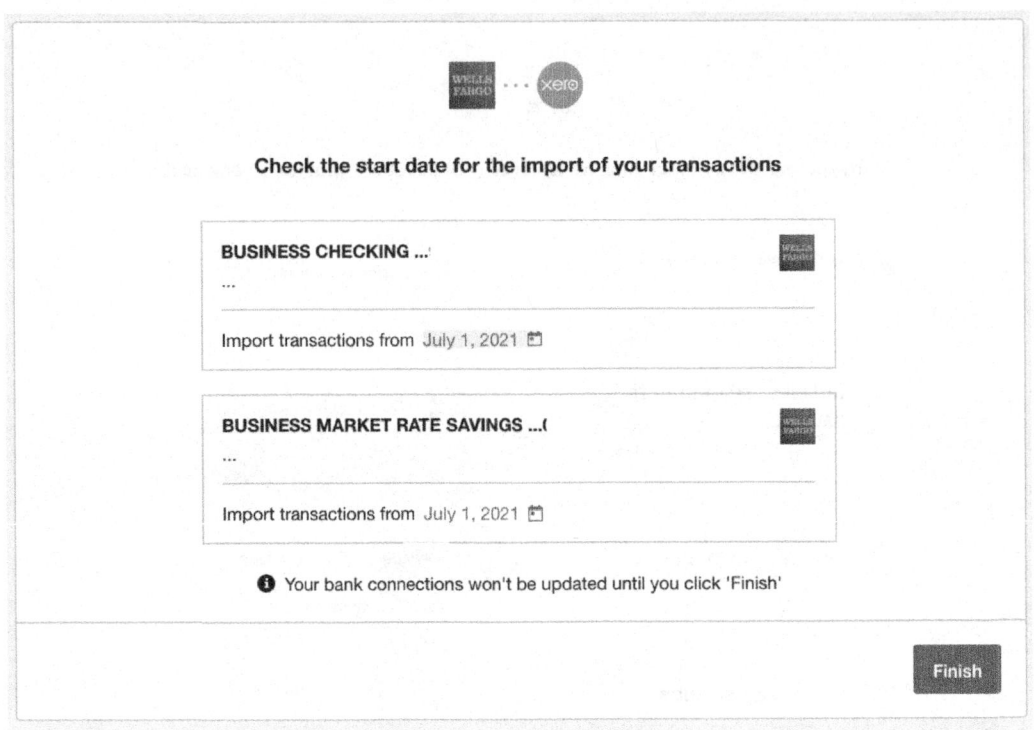

Figure 2.10: The account start date selector

10. We choose **July 1, 2021** as the date to begin importing transactions. We will address that further in the next section. You must click **Finish** here, and when you do, your accounts are created, as shown on the Xero dashboard here:

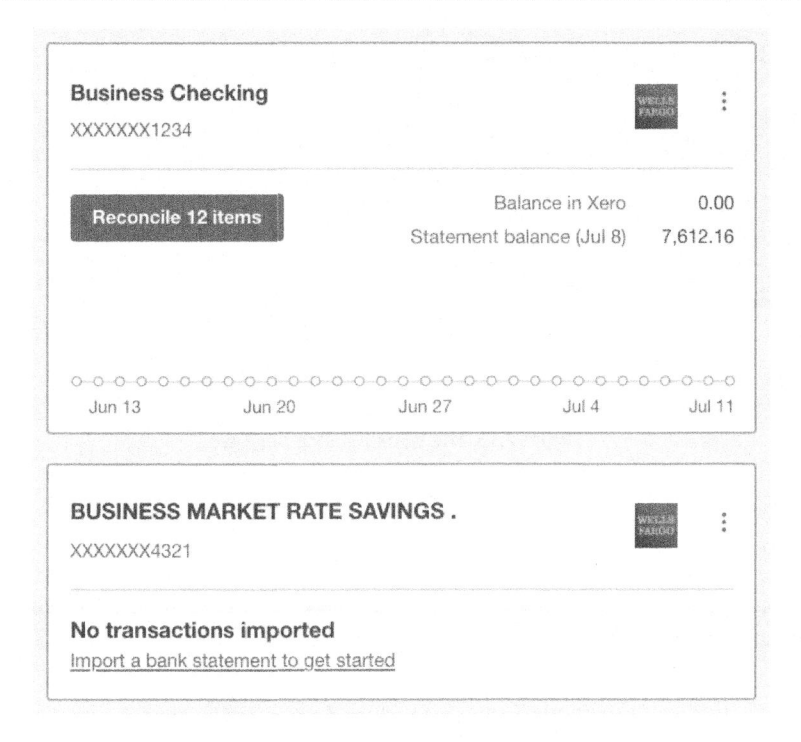

Figure 2.11: The dashboard bank account view

At the time of writing, there are almost no differences between adding a direct feed and a Yodlee feed.

Now that we have the bank feed set up, we will show you how to balance it in the next step. This will ensure that you are set up for success.

Balancing the bank feed

We started the bank feed on July 1, 2001, as we stated earlier. Let's assume we are going to use the Fresh Start conversion method (which we will dive deeper into in *Chapter 4*). For now, let's just reconcile the bank feed to the bank balance as of today:

1. We need to compare the bank balance per the bank website:

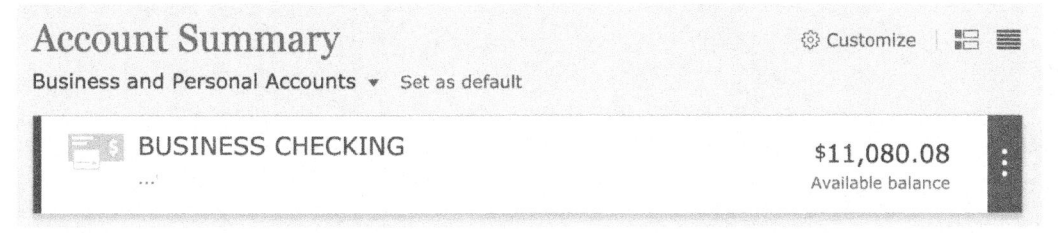

Figure 2.12: The bank balance per the bank website

We go to the bank website, and access the data we need.

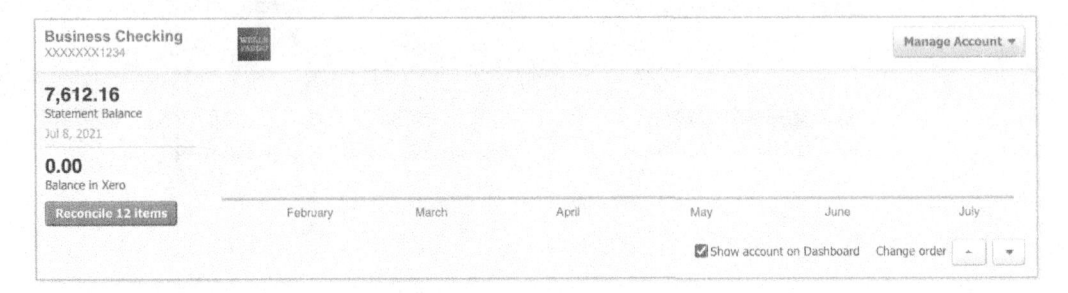

Figure 2.13: The bank balance per Xero

2. Since we started the feed transactions on July 1, we need the bank balance as of June 30. We have that, as shown here:

Ending balance on 6/30   **$3,467.92**

Figure 2.14: The prior month-end statement balance

3. So, as stated previously, we will cover the Fresh Start conversion in *Chapter 4*, but here, we need to add the June 30 balance of $3,467.92 to the conversion balance for the checking account.

> **Note**
> The conversion balance can be found on the **Advanced settings** page.

Enter your account balances as at Jun 30, 2021

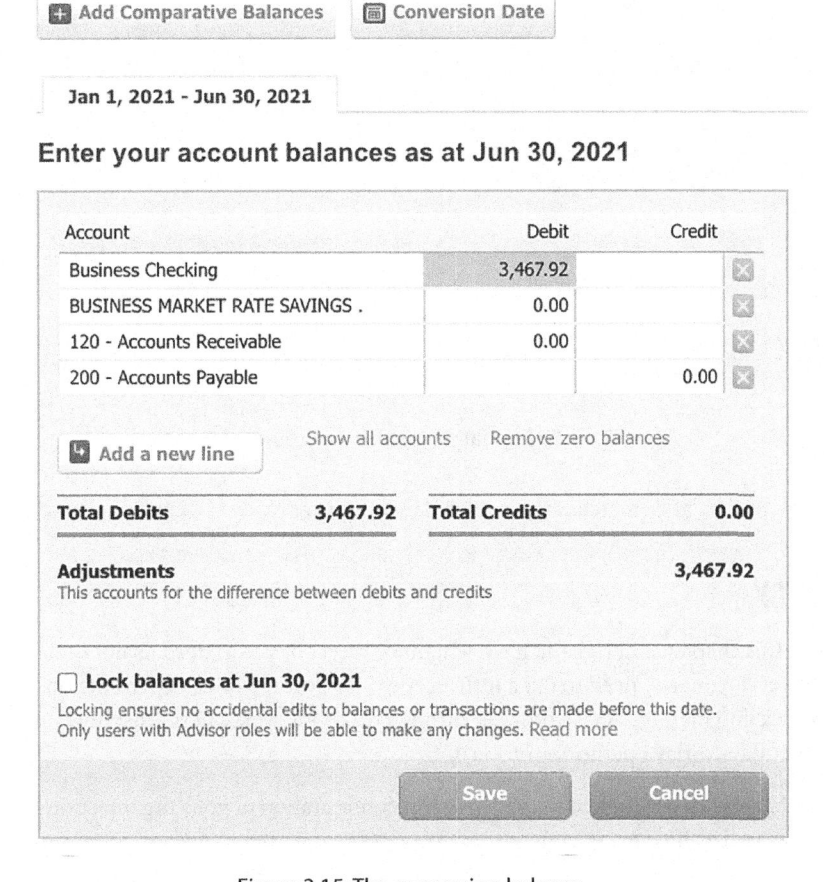

Account	Debit	Credit
Business Checking	3,467.92	
BUSINESS MARKET RATE SAVINGS .	0.00	
120 - Accounts Receivable	0.00	
200 - Accounts Payable		0.00

Total Debits 3,467.92   **Total Credits** 0.00

Adjustments 3,467.92
This accounts for the difference between debits and credits

☐ **Lock balances at Jun 30, 2021**
Locking ensures no accidental edits to balances or transactions are made before this date. Only users with Advisor roles will be able to make any changes. Read more

Figure 2.15: The conversion balance

4. After clicking **Save** on the conversion balance, go back to the dashboard or the bank account page and review the statement balance on the account. As you can see here, the statement balance is now $11,080.08 and matches the bank's details.

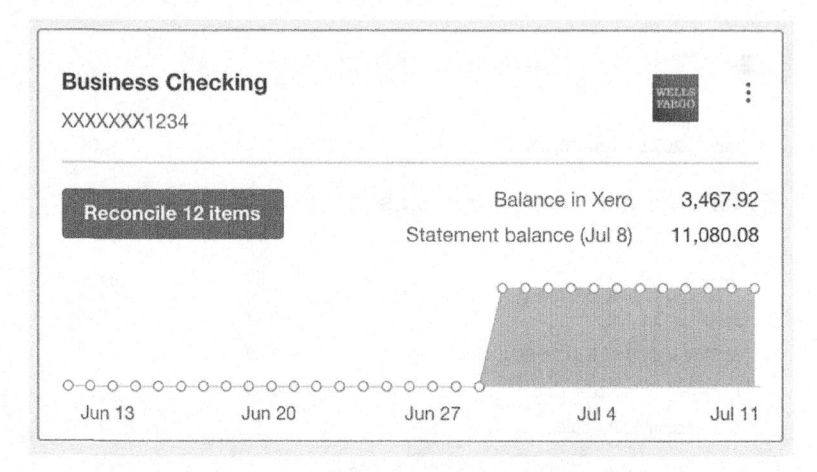

Figure 2.16: The updated Xero bank account information

Now the bank feed balance matches the bank balance, you are ready to begin processing transactions.

Summary

As we saw in this chapter, a Xero bank feed, whether a direct or yodlee feed, is not difficult to set up or balance. However, you may need to dig a little deeper into how it works, depending on the conversion date and conversion method. As we proceed through this book, you will see just how integral the bank feed is in your day-to-day operations of Xero.

In our next chapter, we will look at the settings and configuration of your organization to get the most out of Xero, as well as how to set yourself and your company up for success.

3
Setting Up Your Organization's Financial Settings in Xero

In this chapter, we will look at the settings used by Xero, making sure your Xero organization has the optimal setup for your business. Having the proper setup ensures your Xero organization will operate as you need and will provide the required financial results and data for your business to allow you to make timely and accurate business decisions.

In this chapter, we're going to cover the following main topics:

- Why are settings so important?
- **Chart of accounts (COA)**
- Tracking categories
- Organization settings

By the end of this chapter, you will know how to set up a new Xero organization for your company, including setting up a new **COA**, using tracking categories to make better use of your accounting data, and how to add users to your account. You will also know how to secure your data in closed periods, ensuring everything stays in balance. Lastly, you will know what questions to ask to drive how you set up your next Xero company.

Why are settings in Xero so important?

Xero is the financial hub of your business. In most cases, it is the system of record for all your business's financial transactions. This is the point where you set your business up for success. You will want to address the major settings we will detail in this chapter early on in your Xero journey. Some of these settings are needed at the transactional level, some at the report level, and some at the security level. As we progress through this chapter, we will see how each of these types of settings is important and how they impact your business.

Before jumping into the settings, we need to address the most important setting in Xero. In the next section, we begin discussing the COA settings.

Your first major Xero decision – the COA

The COA for your business is like a table of contents. It has major sections (assets, liabilities, equity, revenue, and expenses). It also has sub-sections (current assets, non-current assets, and more) and line items. Your COA is involved in everything you do in Xero moving forward. The choices here lay out how you record your transactions and how they will be reported later.

How do you plan on laying out your COA? Are you going with a flat structure or a broad structure? What I mean by flat is using as few accounts as necessary, such as a single sales account, let's say *Revenue*. A broad structure involves using multiple accounts in an area. Let's say we want to track sales by channel; we might have *Revenue – Retail*, *Revenue – Online*, and *Revenue – Wholesale*. This should be driven by what the data and reporting needs are of your company and its management. We will cover tracking categories later in this chapter, which could help you develop your COA ad reporting needs.

As with everything, there are multiple ways of accomplishing tasks in Xero. As shown in the following screenshot, you can click the name of any account to modify the account data, or if you have multiple changes to make, you can export the COA, make changes in MS Excel, and then import those changes back; we will cover this later in this chapter:

Chart of accounts

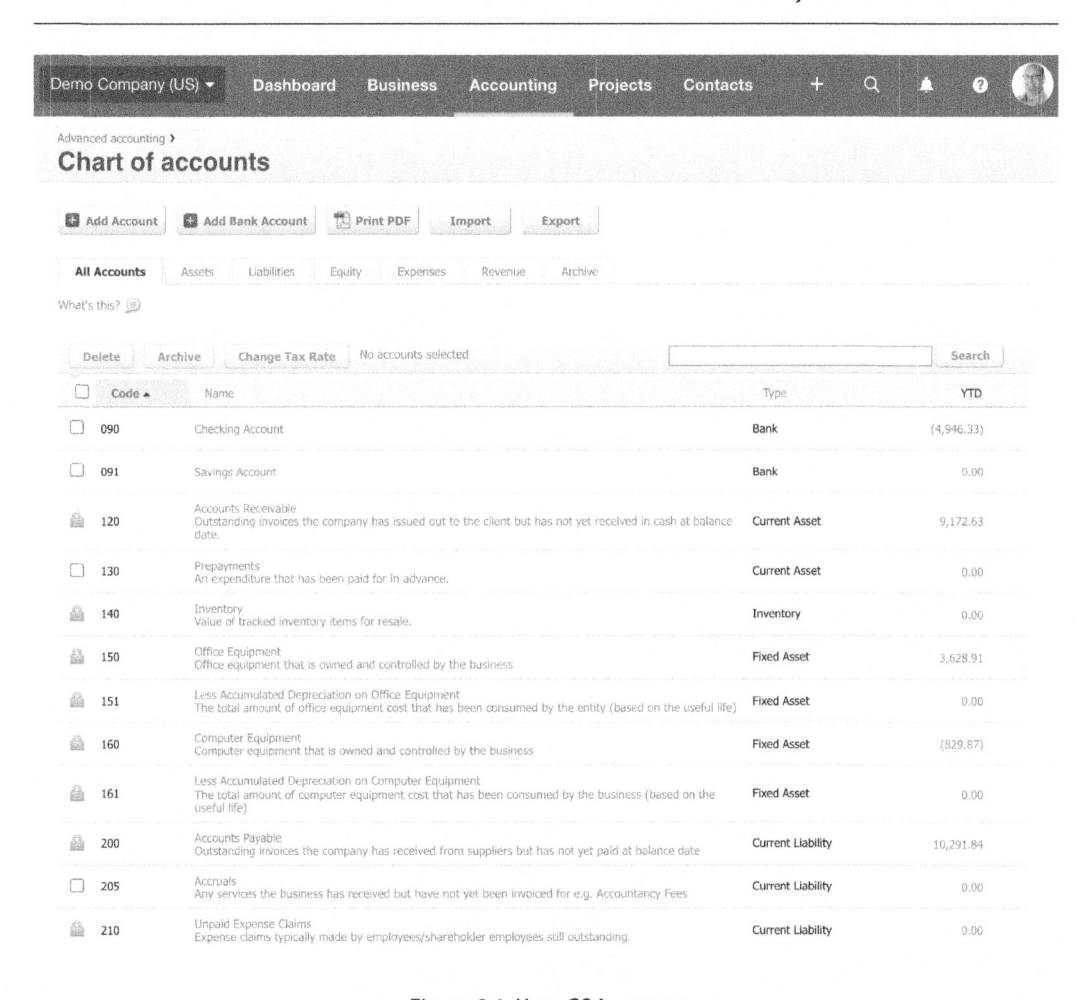

	Code ▲	Name	Type	YTD
☐	090	Checking Account	Bank	(4,946.33)
☐	091	Savings Account	Bank	0.00
🔒	120	Accounts Receivable Outstanding invoices the company has issued out to the client but has not yet received in cash at balance date.	Current Asset	9,172.63
☐	130	Prepayments An expenditure that has been paid for in advance.	Current Asset	0.00
🔒	140	Inventory Value of tracked inventory items for resale.	Inventory	0.00
🔒	150	Office Equipment Office equipment that is owned and controlled by the business	Fixed Asset	3,628.91
🔒	151	Less Accumulated Depreciation on Office Equipment The total amount of office equipment cost that has been consumed by the entity (based on the useful life)	Fixed Asset	0.00
🔒	160	Computer Equipment Computer equipment that is owned and controlled by the business	Fixed Asset	(829.87)
🔒	161	Less Accumulated Depreciation on Computer Equipment The total amount of computer equipment cost that has been consumed by the business (based on the useful life)	Fixed Asset	0.00
🔒	200	Accounts Payable Outstanding invoices the company has received from suppliers but has not yet paid at balance date	Current Liability	10,291.84
☐	205	Accruals Any services the business has received but have not yet been invoiced for e.g. Accountancy Fees	Current Liability	0.00
🔒	210	Unpaid Expense Claims Expense claims typically made by employees/shareholder employees still outstanding.	Current Liability	0.00

Figure 3.1: Xero COA excerpt

26 Setting Up Your Organization's Financial Settings in Xero

You can find the COA in the **Advanced accounting** menu, as shown here:

Advanced accounting

Advanced features

- ★ **Find and recode**
  Fix incorrect categorisation across multiple transactions at once

- ★ **Manual journals**
  Work directly with the general ledger

- ★ **Fixed assets**
  Create and manage assets

- ☆ **Assurance dashboard**
  Monitor the accuracy of financial data within your organisation

- ☆ **Export accounting data**
  Export data from Xero for importing into other systems

- ☆ **History and notes**
  View a summary of the actions made by all users to your transactions

Advanced settings

- ☆ **Financial settings**
  Edit financial settings like tax periods and lock dates

- ★ **Chart of accounts**
  Add, edit, archive, delete, import or export your accounts

- ☆ **Tax rates**
  Add, edit or delete tax rates

- ☆ **Fixed assets settings**
  Manage asset types and account defaults

- ☆ **Tracking categories**
  Manage tracking items for more powerful reporting

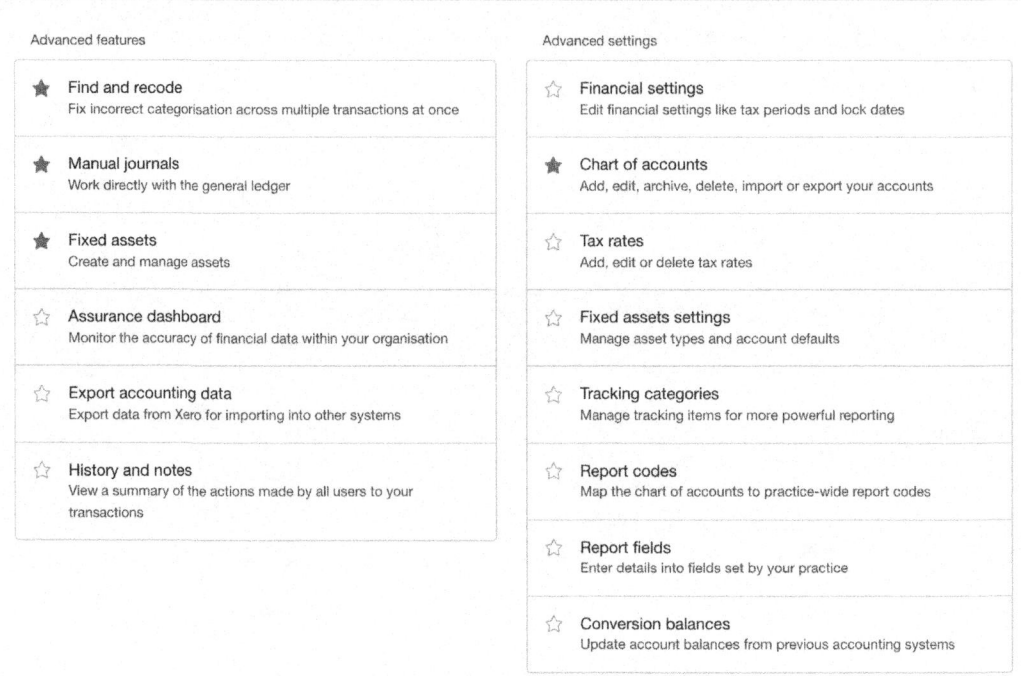

- ☆ **Report codes**
  Map the chart of accounts to practice-wide report codes

- ☆ **Report fields**
  Enter details into fields set by your practice

- ☆ **Conversion balances**
  Update account balances from previous accounting systems

Figure 3.2: Xero's Advanced accounting menu

> **Note**
> Like other menu items, if you select and mark the star next to the menu option, you can mark it as a favorite.

As shown here, you can see that **Chart of accounts** is also under the **Accounting** menu. This is because I starred this menu option in the **Advanced accounting** menu:

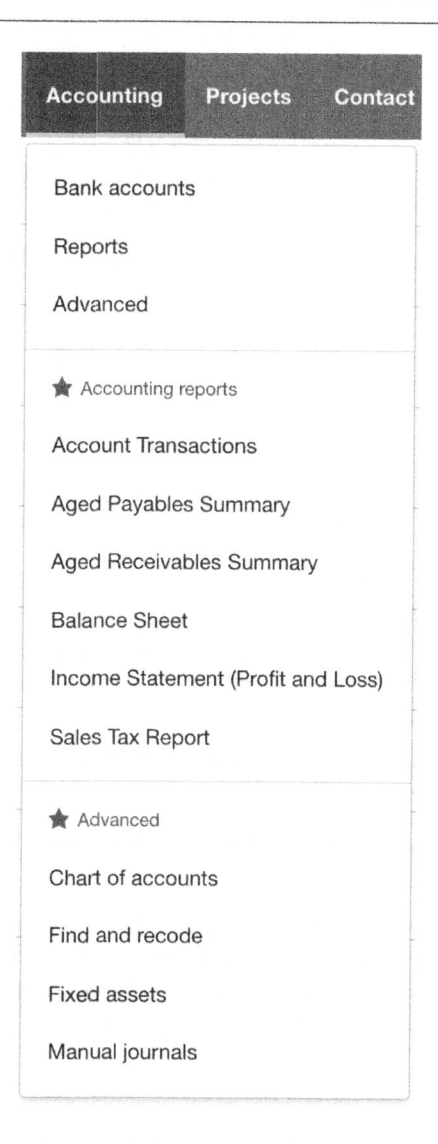

Figure 3.3: Xero's Accounting menu

As you can see from the following screenshot, it is easy to create or update a COA account:

1. Using the dropdown, select the correct account type.

> **Note**
> The choices for account type are shown on the right-hand side of the **Edit Account Details** window for your reference.

2. Enter the account code you wish to assign to this account. Xero will let you know whether it is available once you move to the next field.
3. Enter a name for this account; it should be descriptive yet concise. It, too, should be unique from other accounts already used.
4. Xero will allow you to use a different name on reports should you need to. You can click the + **add Reporting Name** link to activate that field.
5. Add an optional **Description**.
6. Select the proper **Tax** (sales tax) option for your account type by using the drop-down menu.
7. Select the proper **Options** for your account:
   - **Show on Dashboard Watchlist** will add the account to a card on your dashboard so that you can easily see the account's activity.
   - **Show in Expense Claims** allows the expense to be used by **Xero Expenses** (for expense reporting).
   - **Enable payments to this account** allows you to include this account when applying payments to invoices or bills, each of which will be shown in later chapters. This is most useful for clearing accounts used with payments and merchant accounts.
8. Just click **Save** and you are set!

Your first major Xero decision – the COA 29

Edit Account Details

Account Type
Current Asset

Code
A unique code/number for this account (limited to 10 characters)
130

Name
A short title for this account (limited to 150 characters)
Prepayments
+ add Reporting Name

Description (optional)
A description of how this account should be used
An expenditure that has been paid for in advance.

Tax
The default tax setting for this account
Tax Exempt (0%)

☐ Show on Dashboard Watchlist
☐ Show in Expense Claims
☐ Enable payments to this account

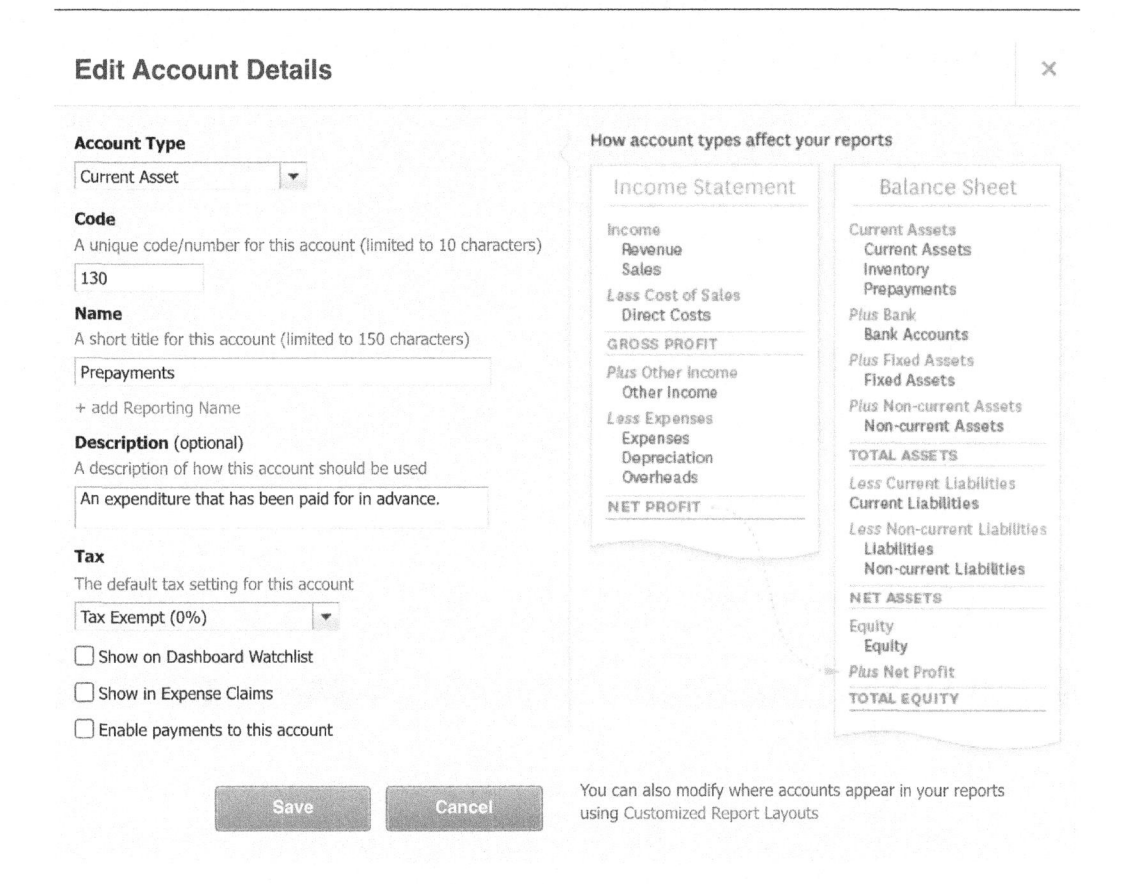

Save   Cancel

How account types affect your reports

Income Statement
Income
  Revenue
  Sales
Less Cost of Sales
  Direct Costs
GROSS PROFIT
Plus Other Income
  Other Income
Less Expenses
  Expenses
  Depreciation
  Overheads
NET PROFIT

Balance Sheet
Current Assets
  Current Assets
  Inventory
  Prepayments
Plus Bank
  Bank Accounts
Plus Fixed Assets
  Fixed Assets
Plus Non-current Assets
  Non-current Assets
TOTAL ASSETS
Less Current Liabilities
  Current Liabilities
Less Non-current Liabilities
  Liabilities
  Non-current Liabilities
NET ASSETS
Equity
  Equity
Plus Net Profit
TOTAL EQUITY

You can also modify where accounts appear in your reports using Customized Report Layouts

Figure 3.4: Xero's COA Edit Account Details window

Now that we have explored the chart of accounts, let's look at alternatives to manually entering or editing your chart of accounts in the app, one account at a time.

Setting Up Your Organization's Financial Settings in Xero

Importing your chart of accounts

Many of us have a COA template we use with our clients, and we just import that specific COA into Xero and move on. You can do this very easily as well.

Do you recall the earlier screenshot, *Figure 3.4*, of the COA window? There were buttons for **Import** and **Export**. We can use these buttons to accomplish just that:

Figure 3.5: Xero COA's Import and Export buttons

1. Upon clicking the **Export** button, you get an immediate CSV file export of the current COA in Xero:

*Code	Report Code	*Name	Reporting Na	*Type	*Tax Code	Description	Dashboard	Expense Clai	Enable Paym	Balance
90	ASS	Checking Account		Bank	Tax Exempt (0%)		No	No	No	
91	ASS	Savings Account		Bank	Tax Exempt (0%)		No	No	No	
120		Accounts Receivable		Accounts Re	Tax Exempt (	Outstanding	No	No	No	
130	ASS	Prepayments		Current Asse	Tax Exempt (	An expenditu	No	No	No	
140	ASS.CUR.INV	Inventory		Inventory	Tax Exempt (	Value of trac	Yes	No	No	
150	ASS	Office Equipment		Fixed Asset	Tax on Purch	Office equipi	No	Yes	No	
151	ASS	Less Accumulated Depreci		Fixed Asset	Tax Exempt (	The total am	No	No	No	
160	ASS	Computer Equipment		Fixed Asset	Tax on Purch	Computer eq	No	Yes	No	
161	ASS	Less Accumulated Depreci		Fixed Asset	Tax Exempt (	The total am	No	No	No	
200		Accounts Payable		Accounts Pay	Tax Exempt (	Outstanding	No	No	No	
205	LIA	Accruals		Current Liabi	Tax Exempt (	Any services	No	No	No	
210		Unpaid Expense Claims		Unpaid Expe	Tax Exempt (	Expense clai	No	No	No	
215		Wages Payable		Wages Payal	Tax Exempt (	Xero automa	No	No	No	
216	LIA	Wages Payable ñ Payroll		Current Liabi	Tax Exempt (0%)		No	No	No	
220		Sales Tax		Sales Tax	Tax Exempt (	The balance	No	No	No	
230	LIA	Employee Tax Payable		Current Liabi	Tax Exempt (	The amount	No	No	No	
231	LIA	Federal Tax withholding		Current Liabi	Tax Exempt (0%)		No	No	No	
232	LIA	State Tax withholding		Current Liabi	Tax Exempt (0%)		No	No	No	
233	LIA	Employee Benefits payabl		Current Liabi	Tax Exempt (0%)		No	No	No	
234	LIA	Employee Deductions pay:		Current Liabi	Tax Exempt (0%)		No	No	No	
235	LIA	PTO payable		Current Liabi	Tax Exempt (0%)		No	No	No	

Figure 3.6: Excerpt of the COA exported in CSV format

> **Note**
> If you chose the import method, never change both the account code and account name. If you do, Xero will not modify the existing account; instead, it will add a new account, leaving the old existing account as it was originally.

The column headings should look familiar, although we have not covered **Report Code**. Report codes are used by Xero partners to assign accounts to report templates; we will cover this in *Chapter 17*.

2. Once your COA has been updated and is ready to be imported, save the CSV file. Then, click the **Import** button:

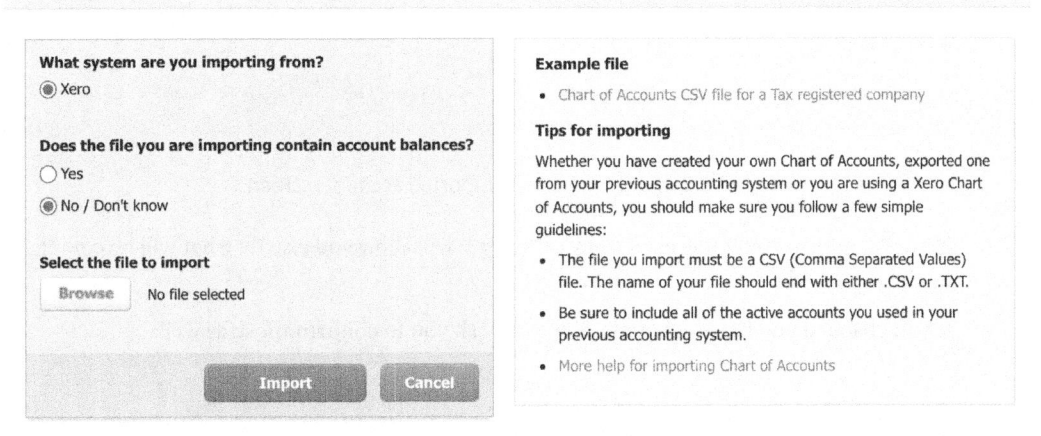

Figure 3.7: The Import your Chart of Accounts screen

This is where you will choose your COA CSV file by clicking **Browse** and selecting the correct file.

If you are updating your COA, you can click **Import**. If you are doing a setup or migration, there are some other details to consider.

Does the file you are importing contain account balances? We will cover conversion and migration in more detail in the next chapter, but if you want the balances imported, select **Yes**. If not, select **No**.

3. Click **Import**. Xero will ask you to **Confirm** your import:

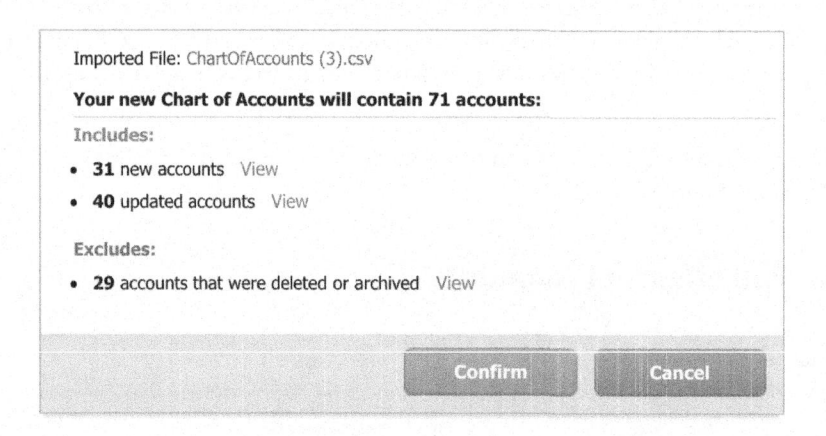

> **Confirm your imported accounts**
>
> Imported File: ChartOfAccounts (3).csv
>
> **Your new Chart of Accounts will contain 71 accounts:**
>
> Includes:
> - **31** new accounts   View
> - **40** updated accounts   View
>
> Excludes:
> - **29** accounts that were deleted or archived   View
>
> [Confirm] [Cancel]

Figure 3.8: The Confirm your imported accounts screen

Xero will inform you if there were any errors and will show you exactly what will be completed by the export when you click **Confirm**.

4. If you changed any **Bank** accounts, Xero will ask you to confirm those as well:

Confirm your bank & credit card accounts

Code	Name	Account Type	Country	Currency	Account Number
90	1st Checking Account	Bank	United States	USD United States Dolla	0000000000000000
91A	1st Savings Account	[Bank / Credit Card / Paypal / Current Asset]			

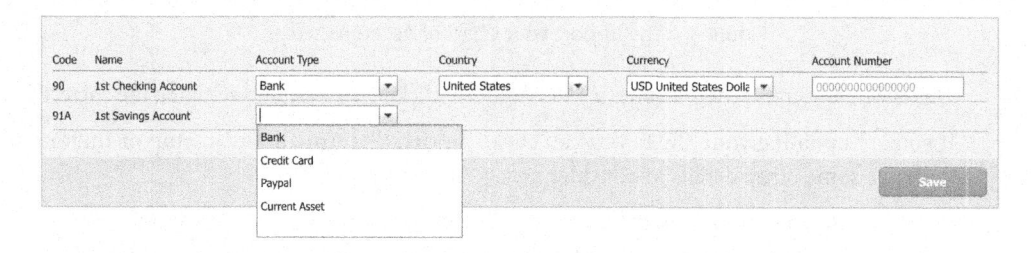

Figure 3.9: The Confirm your bank & credit card accounts screen

5. Select the appropriate choice for **Account Type**, confirm your **Country** and **Currency** **information**, and add your **Account Number** if you have one. Click **Save**.

Maneuvering through the Chart of accounts screen

When you select **Chart of accounts** from the menu, your view will include all the accounts in the COA. As shown in the following screenshot, there are tabs at the top of the window. These tabs will filter your COA to the accounts in that major category. This makes it easy for you to look at your COA, use **Delete** or **Archive** for accounts, or select **Change Tax Rate**:

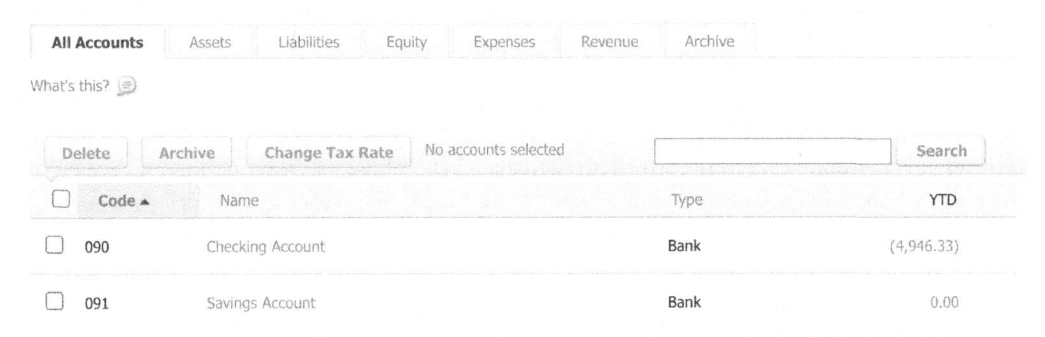

	Code ▲	Name	Type	YTD
☐	090	Checking Account	Bank	(4,946.33)
☐	091	Savings Account	Bank	0.00

Figure 3.10: Chart of accounts tabs

Just select the accounts you want to change by clicking the box to the left of the account.

To remove the account, choose **Delete** or **Archive**. If the account was previously used, it will need to be archived, allowing it to appear in reports, but it will not be able to be used in any future transaction.

> **Note**
> If you must edit a transaction that contains an archived account, you must restore that account before proceeding. You can archive the account again once you have made the change.

There's one last thing to mention about COA in Xero:

🔒	120	Accounts Receivable Outstanding invoices the company has issued out to the client but has not yet received in cash at balance date.	Current Asset	9,172.63
☐	130	Prepayments An expenditure that has been paid for in advance.	Current Asset	0.00

Figure 3.11: Chart of accounts system or locked accounts

You may have noticed a padlock in the left column where the checkbox is on some accounts. These are either system accounts, such as **Accounts Receivable**, or a locked account, which is used in a repeating transaction, a bank rule, as part of the fixed assets setup, or an account used by a payment service. You can change some components of these accounts, but you cannot delete or archive them.

With that, we have covered the basics of the COA. In the next section, we will look at how to add depth to our COA without adding multiple accounts.

Tracking categories

As we covered earlier in this chapter, you can have a flat or a broad COA. By using tracking categories, you can have both. Tracking categories allow you to keep your COA flat while adding the multi-dimensional aspect of the broader COA. This allows you to track different areas of your business and see how they are performing.

Xero gives you two tracking categories with an unlimited number of tracking options within each category. *To be honest, I would not keep adding tracking options past 100.*

Let's go back to our earlier discussion on revenue accounts. We talked about having multiple revenue accounts for the sales channel. If we went that route, let's face it – we would want to track more than just the revenue. We would want to track the costs associated with those sales so that we can get a picture of the performance of each of those sales channels. We might even want to allocate other operating expenses as well as overhead to those sales channels. To do this in the COA, we would have to add three to four additional accounts to the COA for each account we want to track. That would make setting up and managing the COA more difficult, and as for reading the financial results, it would require a lot more attention as there are many more accounts to focus on. We will look at reports that use tracking categories in *Chapter 15*.

Setting up tracking categories

You will find **Tracking categories** in the **Advanced settings** area of the **Advanced accounting** menu, see *Figure 3.2*. Click on the **Tracking categories** menu option to go to the **Tracking categories** page:

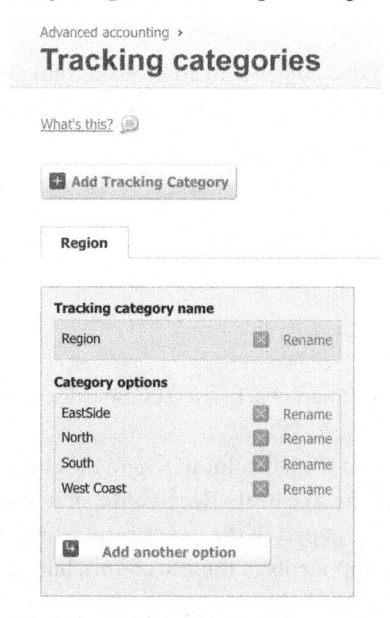

Figure 3.12: The Tracking categories page

As you can see, there is an existing tracking category named **Region**, with the options **EastSide**, **North**, **South**, and **West Coast**. In this case, the company tracks sales from its sales regions.

Let's add another tracking category:

1. We will start by clicking + **Add Tracking Category** near the top of the page:

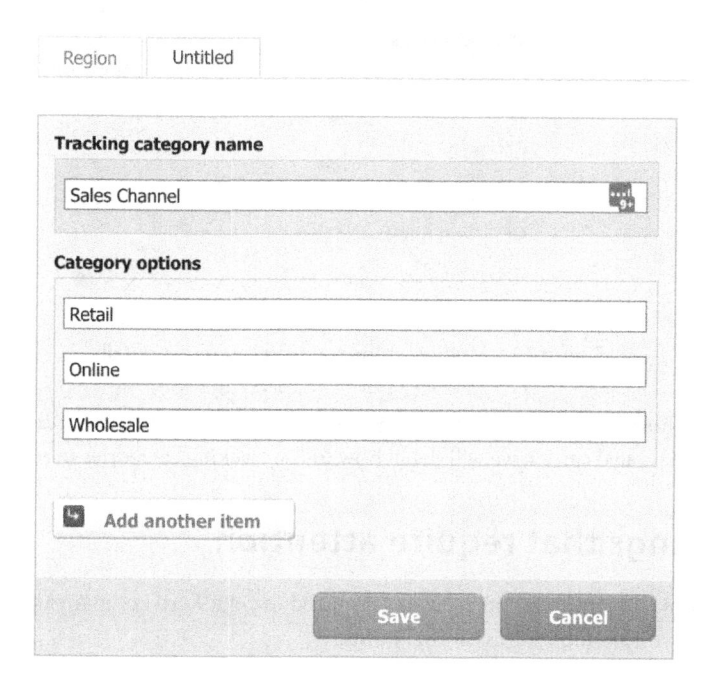

Figure 3.13: Adding a tracking category input

2. Here, you will add the name of your tracking category. Below, you can add your tracking options for this category. I specified `Sales Channel` under **Tracking category name** and `Retail`, `Online`, and `Wholesale` under **Category options**.
3. To finish adding the `Sales Channel` category, click **Save**.

Now, to modify your tracking categories, click on the name of the category you want to change and click **Rename**. Then, make your change and click **Save**. Alternatively, you can add additional options:

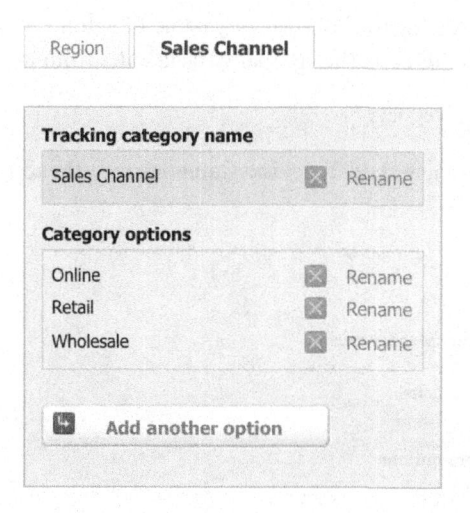

Figure 3.14: Modifying the tracking category's details

We will show you how to use the tracking categories in transactions as we address those transactions later in the book. As stated earlier, we will detail how to use tracking categories in reports in *Chapter 15*.

Other settings that require attention

So far, we have looked at the two main settings required to get a Xero company up and running. Let's look at the others you should address at this point.

Organizational details

Organizational details allow you to add things such as your business name, logo, social media, and website details to your Xero company. If you are going to be sending invoices, quotes, and even purchase orders, this is a must-do.

In that case, you should include these details in your online documents. At the top of the screen is a box asking whether you want to share these details on your online invoices. Of course, you do. Go ahead and click **On** if that is what you wish:

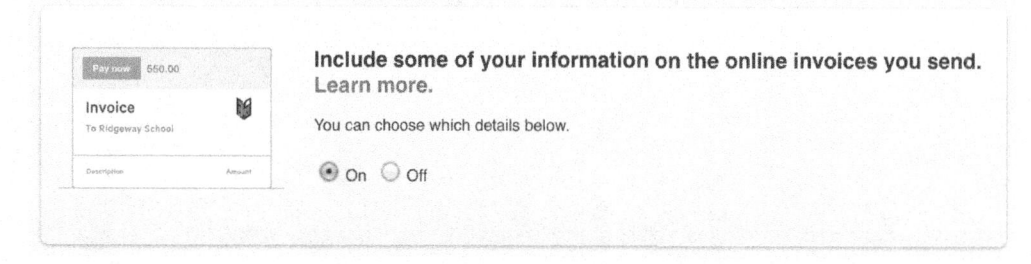

Figure 3.15: Online invoice information selector

This will add a checkbox to the right of each item to allow you to choose what is included in those invoices:

Figure 3.16: The Contact Details input page

On this page, you will add each of the basic details of your business:

- Display name (the name Xero shows in the system)
- Your legal or trade name (this name will appear on invoices, reports, and so on)
- Your logo
- Your line of business (enter what you do and Xero will search its built-in categories for a match)
- Your organization type (this is the tax entry type for your business – for example, **Corporation**, **S Corporation**, **Partnership**, **Sole proprietor**, and so on)
- **Employer Identification Number (EIN)**
- A description of your company (let the world know what you do)

From there, you will want to add your contact details, such as your postal and physical addresses. Xero uses a Google lookup, so start typing in your address and look for a match. When you see a match, click it. If your physical address is the same as your postal address, click the **Same as postal address** box and your physical address will be populated.

Enter your telephone, email, and website details:

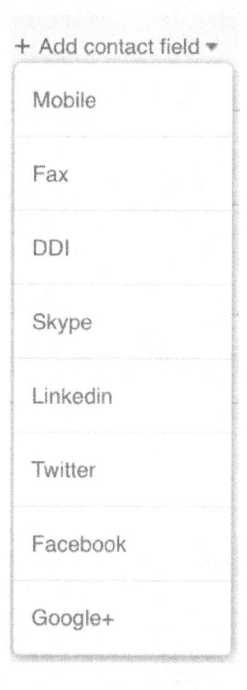

Figure 3.17: The + Add contact field selector

By clicking the + **Add contact field** link, you can add additional fields such as a **Mobile** or **Fax** number, along with your social media accounts. I highly recommend this, as it provides social proof to your new customers.

Lastly, make sure you click the box to accept the terms at the bottom of the screen before clicking **Save**.

Let's add a user

Nobody wants to be the only user on their accounting platform. Let's make some friends. On the **Current users** screen, you can see the current users of the company, their login history, as well as the **Add Xero Support** and **Invite a user** buttons:

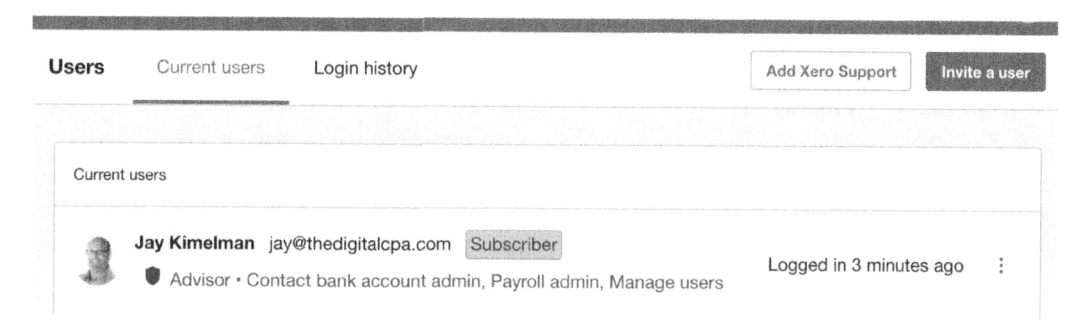

Figure 3.18: The Current users page

Should you need Xero support, you can provide them access from this point, or you can do the same thing when you are submitting a support ticket via Xero Central.

Let's add a new user:

1. Start by clicking **Invite a user**:

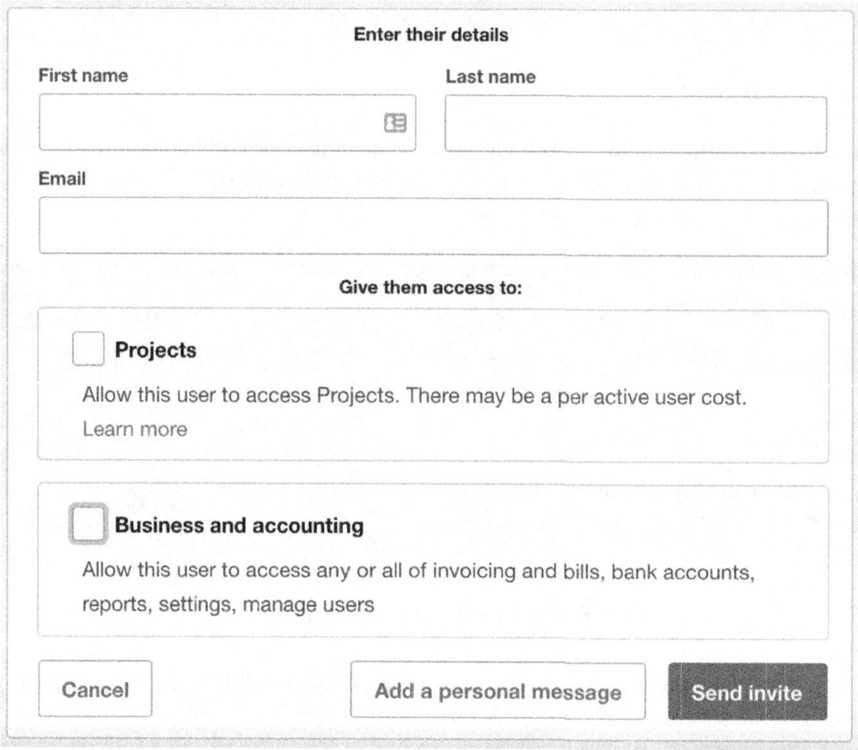

Figure 3.19: The Invite a user dialog box

2. Add the user by typing in their name and email details. Then, you need to decide what access are you going to provide.
3. As shown in the following screenshot, when you select **Business and accounting**, several options are unlocked:

Other settings that require attention 41

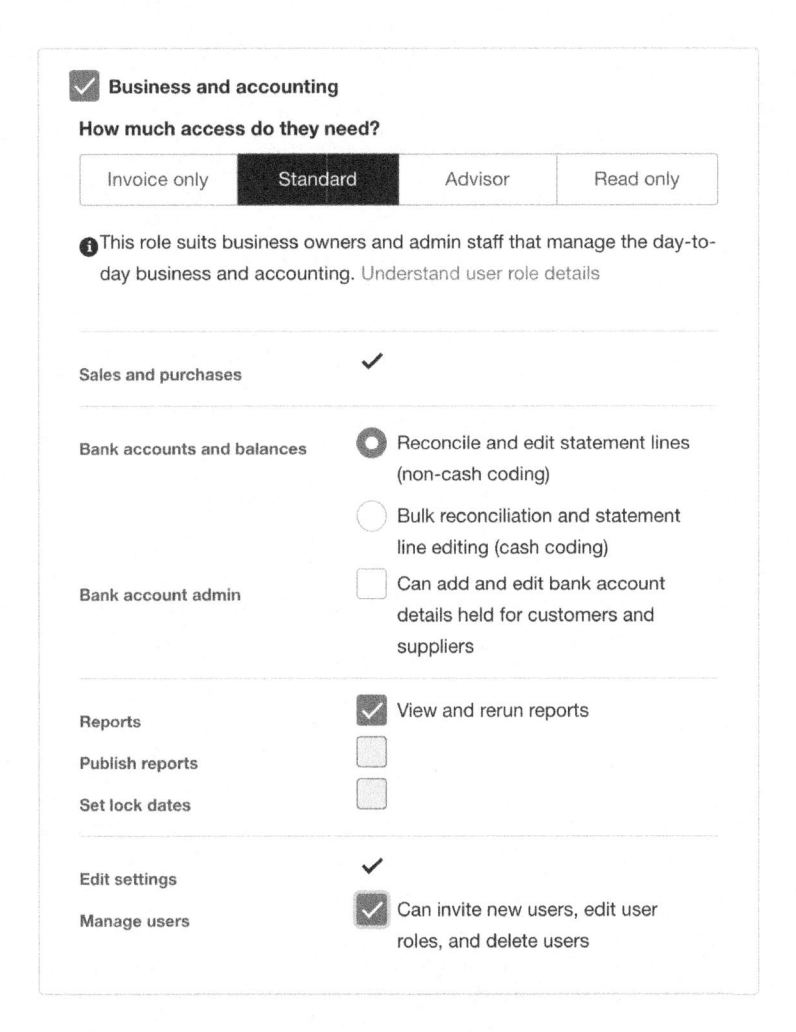

Figure 3.20: The Business and accounting role options

In most cases, this depends on the user. If you are a business owner and you want to give your partner the same access, you will give them **Advisor** access.

> **Note**
> You should be careful with **Advisor** access as this user can do everything in Xero, including post manual journals. I highly recommend that you do not post manual journals and leave that to your bookkeepers and accountants.

Standard is the most used role, and I recommend using the options I selected in the preceding screenshot:

	Advisor	Standard	IO + draft	IO + approve & pay	IO + sales	IO + purchases	Read only
Checks, bank accounts, transactions and statements	✔	✔	-	-	-	-	✔
Contacts	✔	✔	✔	✔	✔	✔	✔
Classic expense claims	✔	✔	✔	✔	✔	✔	✔
Files	✔	✔	✔	✔	✔	✔	✔
Fixed Assets	✔	✔	-	-	-	-	✔
Inventory	✔	✔	-	✔	✔	✔	-
Multicurrency	✔	✔	✔	✔	✔	✔	-
Purchases	✔	✔	✔	✔	-	✔	✔
Reports, budgets and manual journals	✔	-	-	-	-	-	✔
Sales	✔	✔	✔	✔	✔	-	✔
Settings	✔	✔	-	-	-	-	-

Figure 3.21: The Xero roles access chart, as provided by Xero Central

4. From here, you can add a personalized message to the new user and click **Send invite**. The new user will receive an email and can accept the invite, create a Xero login, if they do not already have one, and start using Xero right away.

Subscription and billing

If you are managing your Xero subscription and decide you need to upgrade for one reason or another, this is the place to do it. Just click the appropriate box to select the new subscription level and click **Save**.

This also is where you will update your payment method.

Financial settings

This is where you can edit your tax settings and lock your dates:

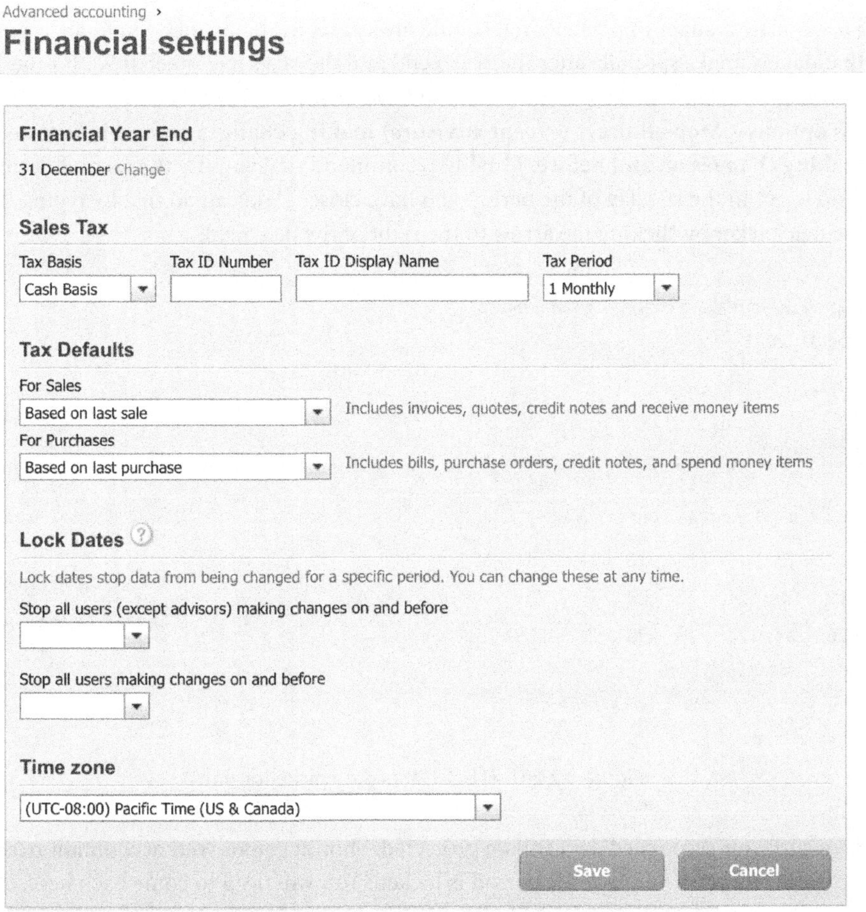

Figure 3.22: The Financial settings dialog box

If you collect **Sales Tax**, this is the first place you will want to start. We will get into sales tax later in this book. Under **Tax Basis**, select **None** if you are not required to collect and remit sales tax. If you are required, select **Cash Basis** or **Accrual** based on your state's rules, and add your **Tax ID Number** and **Tax ID Display Name** if you have these. Also, add your **Tax Period** – that is, whether it is 1, 2, 3, or 6 months or annually.

For the **Tax Defaults** area, if you have no sales tax requirement, and selected **None**, this is filtered out. If you do have a requirement, indicate whether the tax is inclusive or exclusive of the price you are charging on an invoice or paying on a bill.

For example, if you are selling a T-shirt for $16.00, including tax, you would choose **Tax inclusive**, and Xero will calculate the tax based on that. If it was $16.00 before tax, choose **Tax exclusive** and Xero will calculate the tax on top of the $16.00.

Setting a lock date is super important. You should always set the dates after you finalize a period and know that data is final, especially after the year's end and the taxes have been filed. It is never a good thing to change data for a previous year after you have filed your taxes. Setting the date is easy; you have two options – **Stop all users (except advisors) making changes on and before** and **Stop all users making changes on and before**. I highly recommend that you use the second option; all you need to do is put in the last day of the period you have closed. You can do that by typing the date or using the date picker by clicking the arrow to the right of the date field:

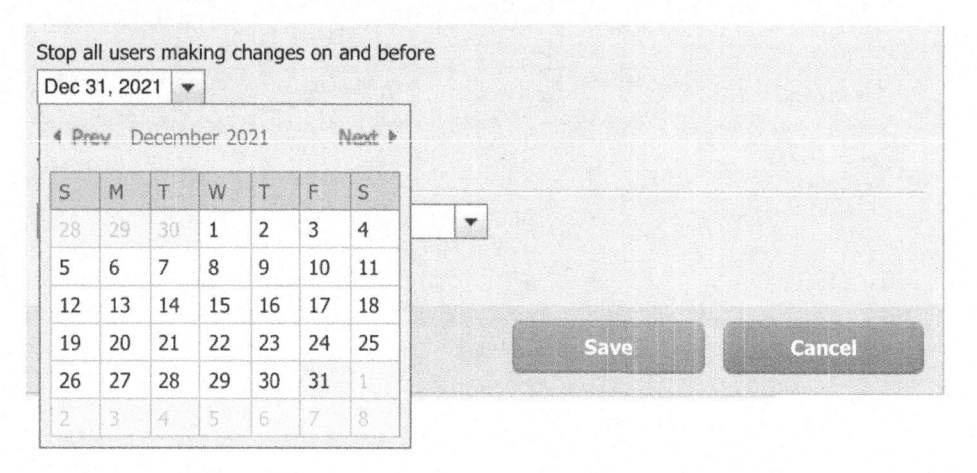

Figure 3.23: The Lock Dates date picker options

Click **Save** and your reconciled data will be protected. Should you or your accountant need to make a change, Xero will warn you that the period is locked. You will need to come back here, change the date, make your change, and add the lock date back.

Summary

We covered a lot of material in this chapter. The required settings we covered include setting up your COA, tracking categories, financial settings, and even adding a user. Completing this setup gives you the foundation for your new Xero company so that you are ready to start processing transactions. We will cover the remaining settings that you can see in the menu in detail as we address the subjects they specifically affect later in this book.

In the next chapter, we will look at the settings and configurations you must complete for your organization to get the most out of Xero and set yourself and your company up for success.

4
Restarting with the Fresh Start Method

In this chapter, we cover getting started with Xero by using the **Fresh Start** (**FS**) method. This is the cleanest, quickest way to get Xero up and running and get you back to running your business.

By the end of this chapter, you will know how to prepare your new Xero organization for use by your company, including determining your conversion balances and importing your COA with those balances. Lastly, you will know exactly when to use the FS method.

In this chapter, we're going to cover the following main topics:

- When to use Fresh Start
- Where do the starting balances come from?
- Importing your balances
- Setting up the bank feeds

When to use Fresh Start

Before we get into when to use the FS method, let's discuss what it is. FS is the easiest, cleanest, and quickest way to set up Xero. You load the balances from the last known good period and roll with it from there. You set up your bank feeds and balance them. We will get into the details of exactly how we accomplish this later in this chapter.

You have your Xero company set up for use. Now, you have the decision of how you want to get the data from your old system into Xero. You should go into this process with this decision before you sign up and set the software's settings, as we did in the previous chapter.

Looking back, you either have a brand-new business and are ready to proceed from this point, or you have an existing business, and you kept your books on something other than Xero, such as QuickBooks, used a spreadsheet, or you didn't keep books at all and worked from bank statements.

Using a spreadsheet or bank statements to track your business's financial results and moving to Xero is a no-brainer – FS all the way. Coming from QuickBooks to Xero? There are two options. You can perform a conversion, which we will cover in the next chapter, or you can perform an FS.

There are many factors in the decision of when to convert or perform an FS, one of which is whether you need your Xero company to bill or invoice right away. Conversion takes a few days, and you cannot use your QuickBooks during that time. Some businesses cannot wait during that time to invoice their clients and should proceed with an FS to get up and running quickly.

Here is my take on this. You are starting your business's financial journey; you want to start with a clean slate and a good firm foundation. Many of the QuickBooks files I have seen over the years, whether they were via desktop or online, were a complete mess. They required cleanup before conversion, which could take considerable time. In addition, most automated conversions will create more transactions than necessary since bank transactions are posted through clearing accounts. In my opinion, your time is best spent using FS and utilizing the bank feeds to catch up with Xero. Let's jump in and show you where to get started.

Where do we find our beginning balances?

As Xero is a full double-entry accounting system, it maintains both income statement and balance sheet accounts. Many small businesses have come to my firm only to track sales and expenses. That is OK if you are on the cash basis of accounting and your US federal business tax return does not require you to complete Schedule L (Balance Sheet).

> **Note**
>
> If the business has total receipts and total assets at the close of the tax year lower than $250,000, then you do not need to complete the Schedule L section of the form that includes a detailed summary of everything on the balance sheet.
>
> Keep in mind that we recommend that you always complete Schedules L and M (1, 2, 3) if applicable.

You want to ensure the beginning balances you enter into Xero are correct to avoid issues over time as you perform your bookkeeping and reporting in Xero.

In most cases, the best-known balances come from your tax return. That means you will use the prior year's ending balances as your beginning balance. In most cases, that would be December 31, making the conversion date in Xero January 1. The conversion date, January 1, is the date you will begin using Xero, while the conversion balances come from the day or period before, December 31.

If you are keeping up with your QuickBooks data and are sure the data is correct, you can go back to the most recent reconciled period and use the Trial Balance report for that period as your conversion/beginning balances. Doing this eliminates any catch-up you may need to perform to bring your Xero company up to date.

Here's what you need to start using the FS method:

- Prior year tax return (with balance sheet completed)
- Trial Balance from your current accounting system (as of the last reconciled period)
- Bank statements for all accounts (as of the day before the conversion date)
- Access to bank accounts (bank transaction details that may be needed)

Now that we know what we need to start the FS method, let's jump right in and begin the setup of Xero using the FS method.

Importing your beginning balances

Once you have your balances, you are ready to import your beginning balances into Xero. This can be done in two ways – by importing the COA or by direct entry using the Conversion Balance function.

Importing using the COA

The first way you can import your beginning balances is via the COA import, which we discussed in *Chapter 3*:

1. The difference is that you will load the account balances in the COA import template in the **Balance** column and indicate that the import file does contain account balances. Then, you must enter the conversion date on the **Import your Chart of Accounts** screen, as shown here:

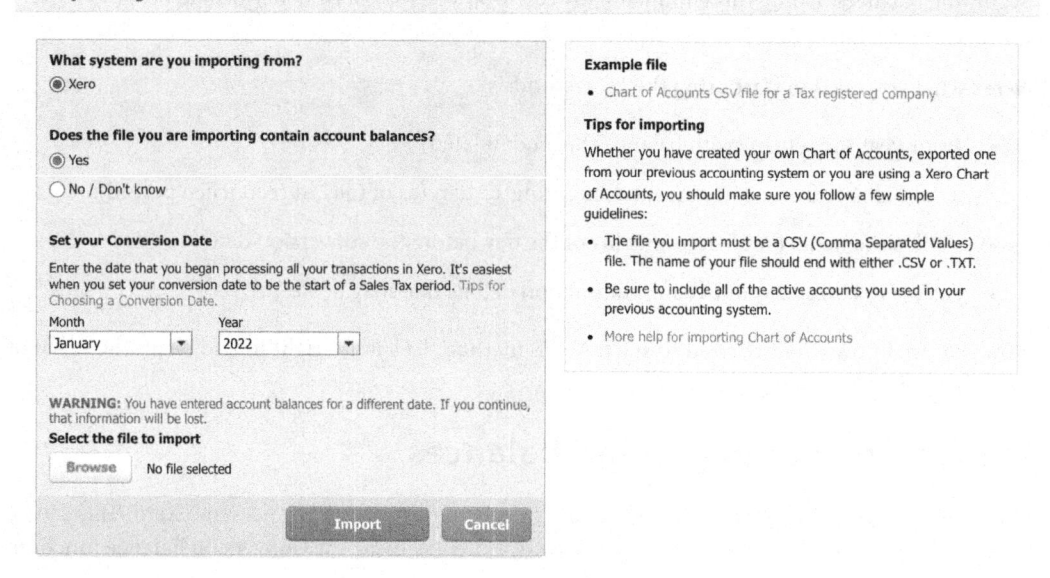

Figure 4.1: The Import your Chart of Accounts screen

2. Once you have processed your import, Xero requires you to confirm your import, including the balance information. Notice that the **Debits** and **Credits** properties match, in the following screenshot, leaving no **Adjustments**:

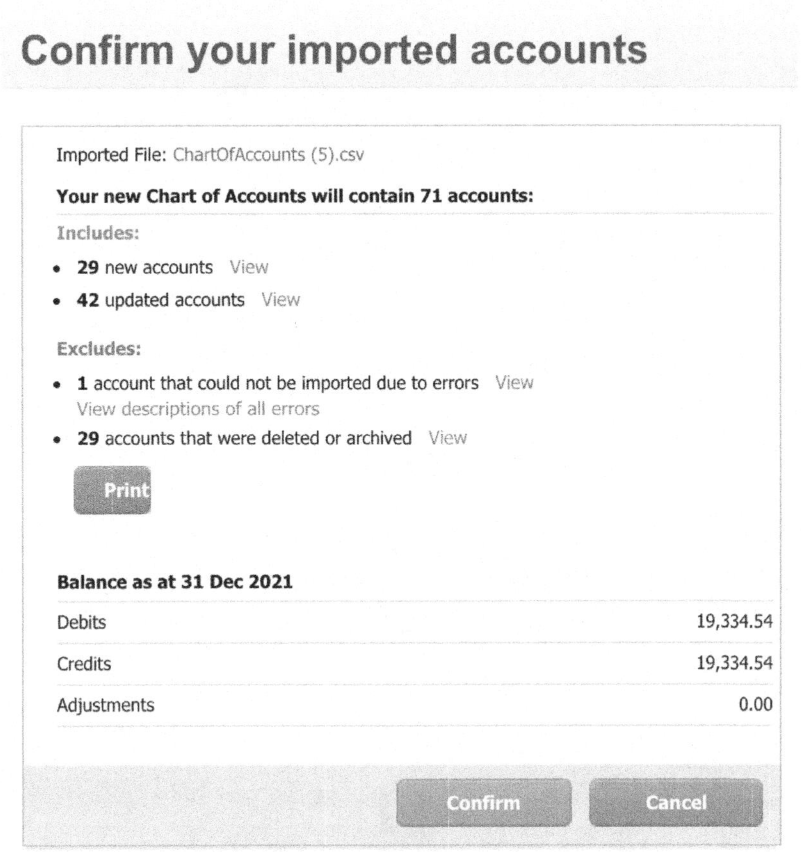

Confirm your imported accounts

Imported File: ChartOfAccounts (5).csv

Your new Chart of Accounts will contain 71 accounts:

Includes:
- **29** new accounts   View
- **42** updated accounts   View

Excludes:
- **1** account that could not be imported due to errors   View
View descriptions of all errors
- **29** accounts that were deleted or archived   View

Print

Balance as at 31 Dec 2021

Debits	19,334.54
Credits	19,334.54
Adjustments	0.00

Confirm   Cancel

Figure 4.2: The Confirm your imported accounts screen

3. You must then go to the **Conversion balances** menu option in the **Advanced accounting** settings menu:

50   Restarting with the Fresh Start Method

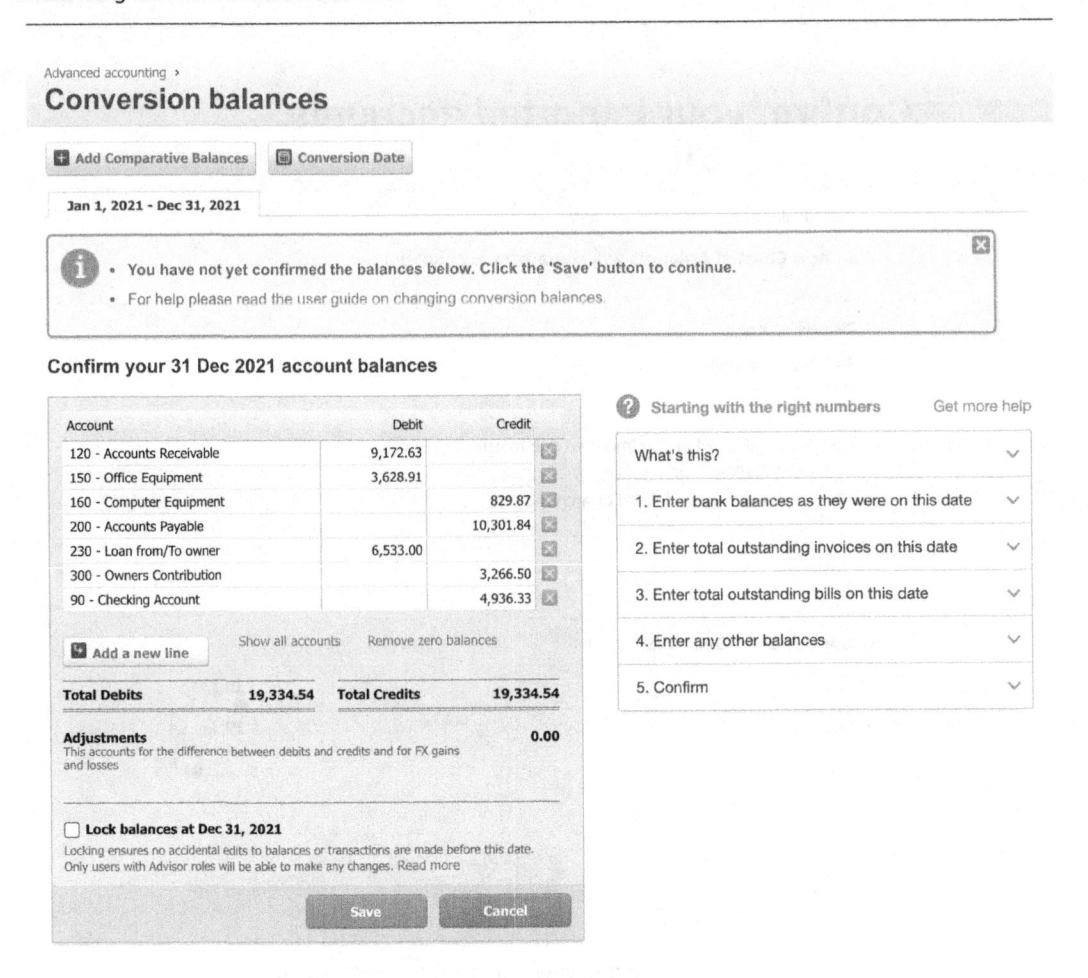

Figure 4.3: The Conversion balances screen

4. From here, you might see warnings indicating that you haven't confirmed your balances. If everything looks correct, click **Save**.

   If you have an **Accounts Receivable** or **Accounts Payable** balance, you must ensure the subledger agrees with the balance you entered:

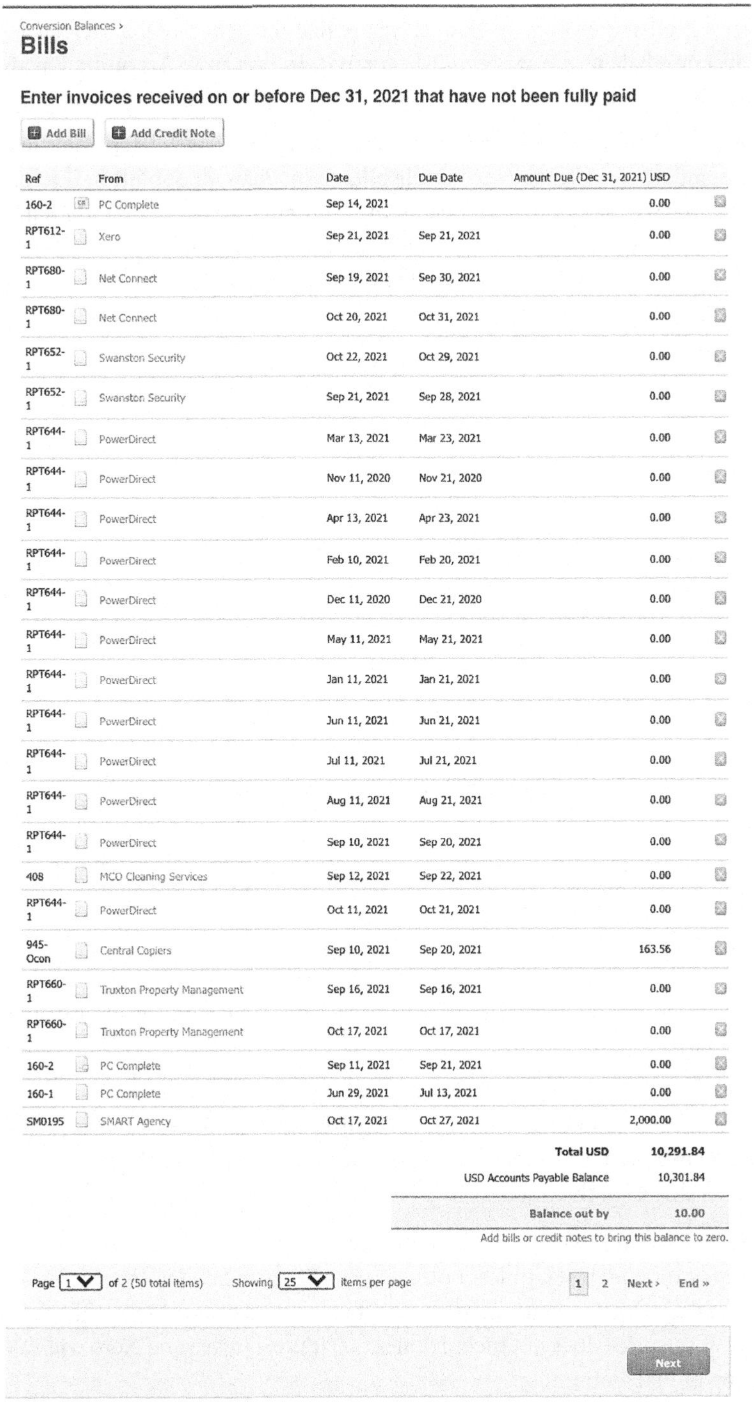

Conversion Balances >
Bills

Enter invoices received on or before Dec 31, 2021 that have not been fully paid

Add Bill   Add Credit Note

Ref	From	Date	Due Date	Amount Due (Dec 31, 2021) USD
160-2	PC Complete	Sep 14, 2021		0.00
RPT612-1	Xero	Sep 21, 2021	Sep 21, 2021	0.00
RPT680-1	Net Connect	Sep 19, 2021	Sep 30, 2021	0.00
RPT680-1	Net Connect	Oct 20, 2021	Oct 31, 2021	0.00
RPT652-1	Swanston Security	Oct 22, 2021	Oct 29, 2021	0.00
RPT652-1	Swanston Security	Sep 21, 2021	Sep 28, 2021	0.00
RPT644-1	PowerDirect	Mar 13, 2021	Mar 23, 2021	0.00
RPT644-1	PowerDirect	Nov 11, 2020	Nov 21, 2020	0.00
RPT644-1	PowerDirect	Apr 13, 2021	Apr 23, 2021	0.00
RPT644-1	PowerDirect	Feb 10, 2021	Feb 20, 2021	0.00
RPT644-1	PowerDirect	Dec 11, 2020	Dec 21, 2020	0.00
RPT644-1	PowerDirect	May 11, 2021	May 21, 2021	0.00
RPT644-1	PowerDirect	Jan 11, 2021	Jan 21, 2021	0.00
RPT644-1	PowerDirect	Jun 11, 2021	Jun 21, 2021	0.00
RPT644-1	PowerDirect	Jul 11, 2021	Jul 21, 2021	0.00
RPT644-1	PowerDirect	Aug 11, 2021	Aug 21, 2021	0.00
RPT644-1	PowerDirect	Sep 10, 2021	Sep 20, 2021	0.00
408	MCO Cleaning Services	Sep 12, 2021	Sep 22, 2021	0.00
RPT644-1	PowerDirect	Oct 11, 2021	Oct 21, 2021	0.00
945-Ocon	Central Copiers	Sep 10, 2021	Sep 20, 2021	163.56
RPT660-1	Truxton Property Management	Sep 16, 2021	Sep 16, 2021	0.00
RPT660-1	Truxton Property Management	Oct 17, 2021	Oct 17, 2021	0.00
160-2	PC Complete	Sep 11, 2021	Sep 21, 2021	0.00
160-1	PC Complete	Jun 29, 2021	Jul 13, 2021	0.00
SM0195	SMART Agency	Oct 17, 2021	Oct 27, 2021	2,000.00

Total USD	**10,291.84**
USD Accounts Payable Balance	10,301.84
Balance out by	10.00

Add bills or credit notes to bring this balance to zero.

Page 1 of 2 (50 total items)   Showing 25 items per page   1 2 Next > End »

Next

Figure 4.4: The Bills/Accounts Payable balance screen

Whether it is bills or invoices, you must ensure that the details of the subledgers match up with the conversion balances you previously entered. In this case, **Accounts Payable** is $10 more than the subledger and the bills or credit need to be adjusted.

You can leave this **Conversion balances** screen and come back later. You can add a bill or an invoice manually, or if you have multiple bills or invoices, one solution is to pull the listing of AR or AP from the previous system and import them into Xero using the supplied templates. The process of importing invoices and bills is similar. Here, we will focus on the bills and AP; invoices and AR are completed similarly in the **Invoice** section of Xero.

5. From the **Bills** screen, choose **Import**:

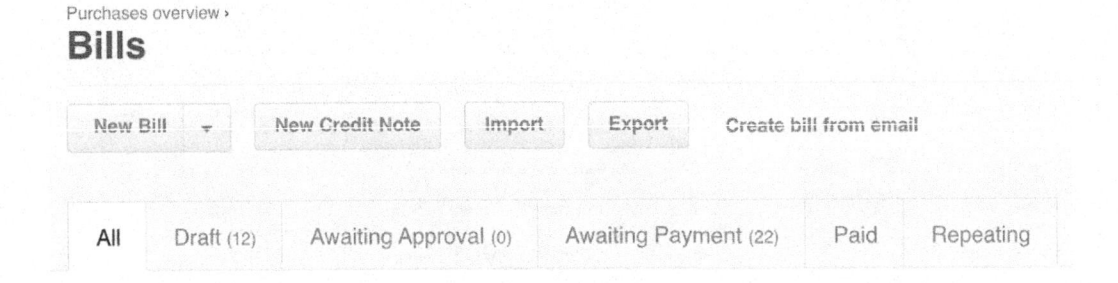

Figure 4.5: The Bills screen

You will be taken to the **Import bills to Xero** screen, as shown in *Figure 4.6*.

From there, you can download the template to use to perform the import. Once you have added the details to the template, you can attach it below by dropping and dragging or selecting the file from your computer.

> **Note**
> As with all Xero import templates, make sure you do not change the headings; otherwise, your import will fail.

6. You must choose to update the contact records' address details. In most cases, I select **No, ignore all address details** here unless I am adding contacts for the first time, and have all of the contact details in the import file.

The other selection indicates if amounts are tax inclusive or exclusive. In most cases, you do not have tax on purchases, unless you are recording use tax. On the sales side, if the product price includes sales tax, you would choose **Tax inclusive**, and Xero will calculate the correct sales tax. If the price does not include sales tax, it is exclusive and Xero will calculate the sales tax on top of that amount:

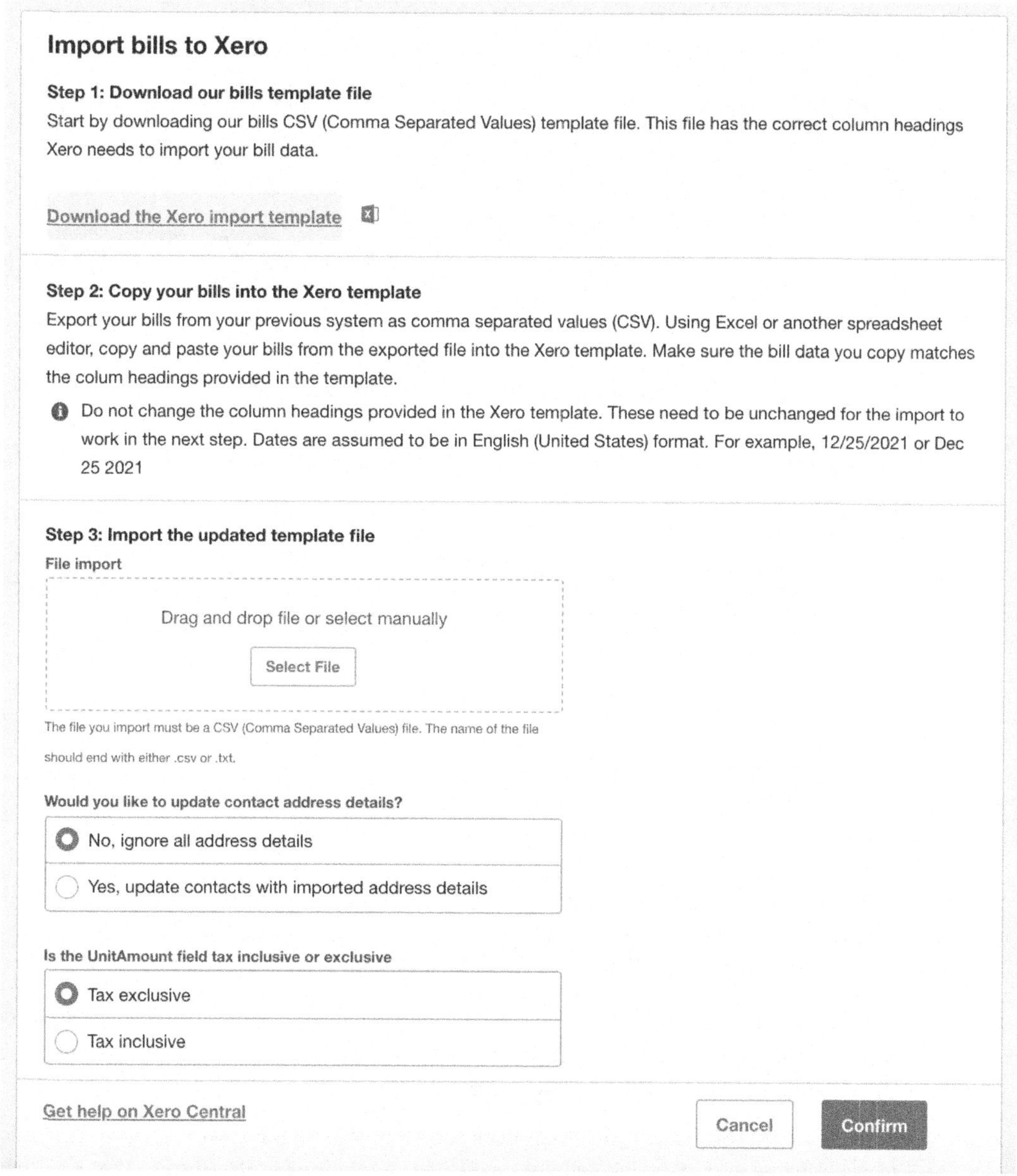

Import bills to Xero

Step 1: Download our bills template file
Start by downloading our bills CSV (Comma Separated Values) template file. This file has the correct column headings Xero needs to import your bill data.

Download the Xero import template

Step 2: Copy your bills into the Xero template
Export your bills from your previous system as comma separated values (CSV). Using Excel or another spreadsheet editor, copy and paste your bills from the exported file into the Xero template. Make sure the bill data you copy matches the colum headings provided in the template.

> Do not change the column headings provided in the Xero template. These need to be unchanged for the import to work in the next step. Dates are assumed to be in English (United States) format. For example, 12/25/2021 or Dec 25 2021

Step 3: Import the updated template file
File import

    Drag and drop file or select manually
    [Select File]

The file you import must be a CSV (Comma Separated Values) file. The name of the file should end with either .csv or .txt.

Would you like to update contact address details?
- ● No, ignore all address details
- ○ Yes, update contacts with imported address details

Is the UnitAmount field tax inclusive or exclusive
- ● Tax exclusive
- ○ Tax inclusive

Get help on Xero Central   [Cancel] [**Confirm**]

Figure 4.6: The Import bills to Xero screen

7. Once you have all of that settled, click **Confirm**.

   This will bring you to the import confirmation screen. In this case, we are specifying that one bill will be imported as a draft, as shown here:

54 Restarting with the Fresh Start Method

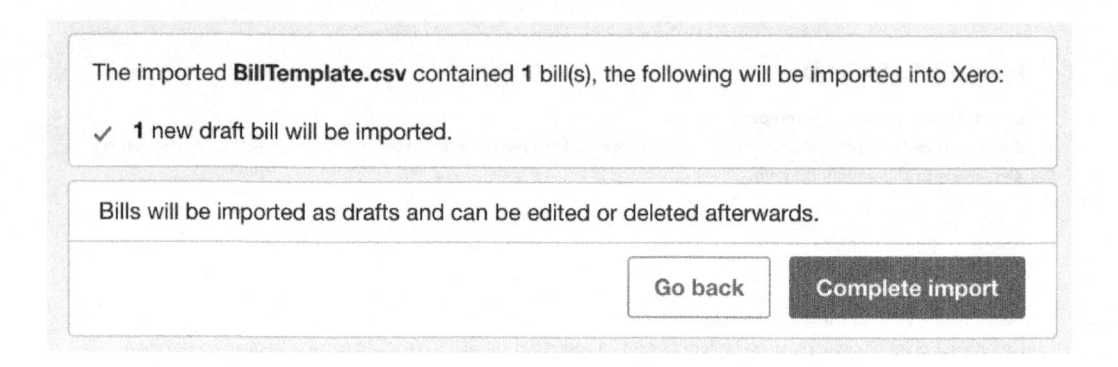

Figure 4.7: The bill import confirmation screen

8. Click **Complete import**; you will be taken to the **Draft** tab of the **Bills** screen to review and approve the imported bills:

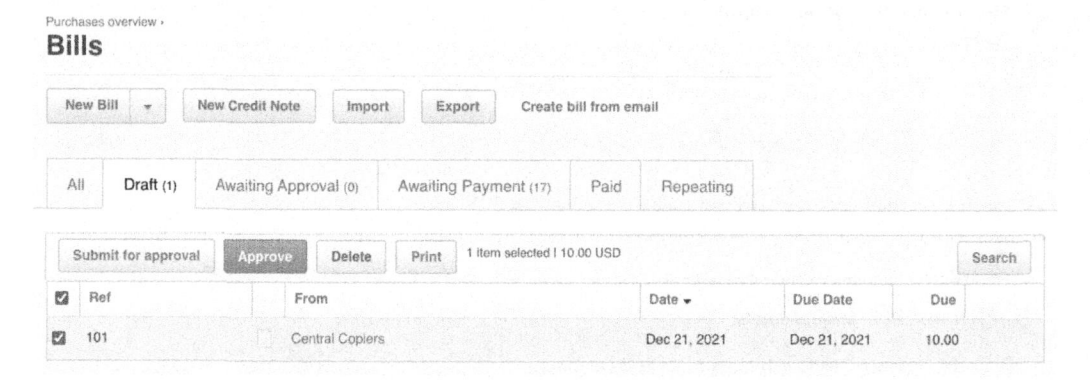

Figure 4.8: The Bills Draft tab

You can review the draft bills manually by clicking **Approve** for each one or you can do so in bulk, as shown in the preceding screenshot. Click the box to the left of the draft bills you wish to approve and click **Approve**. Click **OK** to confirm.

9. Now, head back to the **Conversion balances** screen and click **Save**. At this point, I would also lock the balance at the conversion date by clicking the box at the bottom that specifies **Lock balances**:

Jan 1, 2021 - Dec 31, 2021

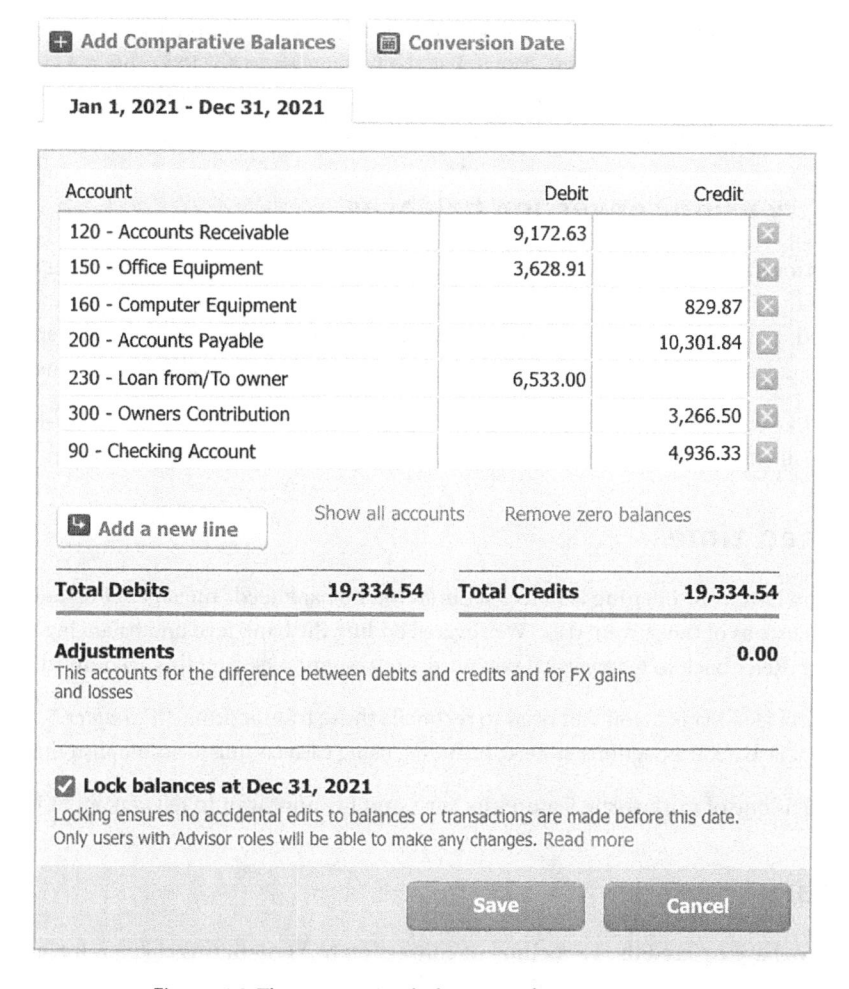

Account	Debit	Credit
120 - Accounts Receivable	9,172.63	
150 - Office Equipment	3,628.91	
160 - Computer Equipment		829.87
200 - Accounts Payable		10,301.84
230 - Loan from/To owner	6,533.00	
300 - Owners Contribution		3,266.50
90 - Checking Account		4,936.33
Total Debits	**19,334.54**	
Total Credits		**19,334.54**
Adjustments		**0.00**

This accounts for the difference between debits and credits and for FX gains and losses

☑ **Lock balances at Dec 31, 2021**
Locking ensures no accidental edits to balances or transactions are made before this date. Only users with Advisor roles will be able to make any changes. Read more

Figure 4.9: The conversion balance confirmation screen

If your **Accounts Payable** and **Accounts Receivable** balances are in agreement, your confirmation screen will post a confirmation your balances have been saved:

✓ Balances saved for period **Jan 1, 2021 - Dec 31, 2021.**

Figure 4.10: Conversion balance saved confirmation

This indicates that your opening balances have been posted and saved in Xero. I recommend running a balance sheet in Xero and ensuring it matches the balance sheet for the same period in your old system. If all looks good, you are ready to add your bank accounts and the related feeds, which we will look at in the next section.

Data entry using conversion balances

The process for this method is the same as it is for the import method, with one main exception: you will go directly to the **Conversion balances** screen and enter your trial balance details. Once entered and balanced, you will follow the same steps mentioned previously, entering your conversion date and subledger details such as your **Accounts Payable** and **Accounts Receivable** open items.

Again, just like when importing the conversion balances, I recommend running a balance sheet in Xero and ensuring it matches the balance sheet for the same period in your old system.

Bank feed time

Now that you have your opening balances set in Xero, the bank feeds must be set up and balanced to the bank balance as of the current date. We covered adding the bank feed and balancing the bank feed in *Chapter 2*. Refer back to *Chapter 2* if you need a refresher on getting this accomplished.

With the bank feed loaded, you will need to reconcile those transactions. In *Chapter 6*, we will cover how to reconcile bank transactions in Xero, including using cash coding to accomplish this task in bulk.

Cash coding is one of my favorite features in Xero, and I cannot wait to tell you about it.

Summary

With that, we have covered the FS method of conversion to Xero. In this chapter, we learned how to import our COA with balances. Then, we imported our subledger details for AR and AP and confirmed our balances. At this point, you are ready to try the FS method on your own.

In the next chapter, we will perform a conversion using Jet Convert, a Xero-approved provider.

5
Conversion to Xero Made Easy

Knowing when to convert your business from QuickBooks or another accounting software is an important detail. Just as important is knowing what the current platform needs in order to qualify it for conversion and ensuring a successful conversion thereafter.

In the previous chapter, we discussed the FS method for getting up and running quickly. In reality, you may need historical transactions in your new Xero file. By the end of this chapter, you will know what makes a good conversion candidate, exactly what is needed in the source data for a successful conversion, and what tasks are needed to complete the conversion.

In this chapter, we will cover the following main topics:

- What is a good candidate for conversion
- What are the conversion prerequisites
- How to convert your file
- Post-conversion tasks

When to convert versus using The Fresh Start method

In the last chapter, we detailed The FS method, which means taking the balance at a point in time, dropping all the earlier balances, and moving forward with your accounting. Well, you may need more – you may need access to your transaction detail for one reason or another, maybe for warranty purposes, or you have a long return time allowed in your return policy, and so on. In that case, having the transactions in Xero would be of more benefit than having two systems to operate. You may want to have the details in Xero for comparison purposes or to have that information handy. In any of those cases, you will be covered. There are many ways to convert your data. We are going to cover the Xero-supported method, the automated conversion, here. The longer manual conversion is an advanced topic and is not covered in this book.

Next, we will begin the automated conversion process.

Automating your Xero conversion with Jet Convert

There are multiple conversion apps in the Xero App Store, but there is one that is endorsed and financially supported. **Jet Convert** is the best choice for converting your **QuickBooks Online (QBO)** or **QuickBooks Desktop (QBDT)** accounting to Xero. You prepare your file, upload it, and choose the conversion package you wish to purchase. Jet Convert takes it from there.

Preparing for conversion by looking into the prerequisites

The first thing you need to consider is what you can convert and what the limitations are. QBO and most versions of QBDT are supported by Jet Convert. This includes Pro, Premier, Accountants, and Enterprise. Yes, even the macOS version can be converted using Jet Convert. But what are the limitations? You can not convert payroll, multi-currency files, or tracked inventory utilizing Jet Convert.

Now let's look at some important factors that you must consider while preparing to convert your QBDT and QBO files into Xero with Jet Convert.

Preparing your QBDT file

The following are the steps you should take to prepare your QBDT file:

1. Remove all users except the admin user.
2. Ensure the admin user's username is **Admin**.
3. Ensure there are no duplicate descriptions in your chart of accounts and add an account number to make the entry unique.
4. Ensure your file is set to your correct accounting basis (cash versus accrual).
5. Ensure the Accounts Payable detail is reconciled to the general ledger.
6. Ensure the Accounts Receivable detail is reconciled to the general ledger.
7. Ensure all invoices/bills and credit notes are still outstanding.
8. Ensure Accounts Payable, Accounts Receivable, and Sales tax do not have the account type of **Bank Account**.
9. If you used Undeposited Funds for sales, ensure the account is set up as Bank Account to link to the contact history.
10. Reconcile the bank and credit cards on the conversion date; this will ease the post-conversion process.
11. Ensure all clearing accounts are reconciled.
12. Make any final changes to the chart of accounts if needed.
13. Run, verify, and rebuild the file.
14. Create a backup of the QBDT file.

Preparing your QBO file

Follow these steps to prepare your QBO file:

1. Ensure there are no duplicate descriptions in your chart of accounts.
2. Ensure your file is set to your correct accounting basis (cash versus accrual).
3. Ensure the Accounts Payable detail is reconciled to the general ledger.
4. Ensure the Accounts Receivable detail is reconciled to the general ledger.
5. Ensure all invoices/bills and credit notes are still outstanding and apply all credit notes except the current ones.
6. Ensure Accounts Payable, Accounts Receivable, and Sales tax do not have the account type of Bank Account.
7. If you used Undeposited Funds for sales, ensure the account is set up as Bank Account to link to the contact history.
8. Reconcile the bank and credit cards through the conversion date; this will ease the post-conversion process.
9. Ensure all clearing accounts are reconciled.
10. Make any final changes to the chart of accounts if needed.
11. Turn on account numbers.
12. Set the account numbers to a maximum of 10 digits.
13. The account name should have no more than 200 characters.
14. Turn off the bank fees.
15. Disable any add-ins.
16. Make one last pass through the file and make sure it is clean, reconciled, and ready for export.
17. You must stay out of QBO during the remainder of the conversion process.

Now that we have met the prerequisites, let's start the conversion process

Time to start the conversion

In this section, we will look into how to get started with the conversion with Jet Convert after we have prepared our QBDT and QBO files.

Converting your QBDT file

Once you have prepared your QBDT file for conversion, follow these steps to convert it:

1. Go to Jetconvert.com and click on the button that says **Start Your Xero Conversion By Uploading Your File**:

*Jet*Convert   ✱ Start Your Xero Conversion By Uploading Your File

Figure 5.1: The Jet Convert website

2. Upload your QBDT backup file:

    I. Browse for your backup file.
    II. Indicate your file's country of origin from the drop-down list.
    III. Click on **Upload Your File** to upload your QBDT backup file:

---

1. Prepare file.

Select the correct pre-conversion checklist based on your current accounting software and prepare your file.

2. Upload file.

Use the upload form below to upload your file to our system.

When you upload your file and begin your Xero conversion, it will create a new organisation in Xero. Once the conversion is complete, you will be asked to take over the Xero subscription.

This analysis can take from a few minutes to a few hours, depending on the size of your file.

3. Select conversion package.

Select a conversion package and the number of years of historical data from the options provided.

4. Review data.

Once the conversion is completed, we'll provide an Action Checklist with an analysis of your data and recommended next steps and system differences between your source file and Xero.

◉ **Upload Your File**
○ **QuickBooks Online (AUS)**

[Browse File]

Load

Figure 5.2: The QBDT upload page

3. Enter the remaining requested details:

    - QBDT admin password
    - Contact details
    - Any special instructions
    - Add any Xero promo code should you have one
    - Check the disclaimer boxes

4. Click **Proceed**:

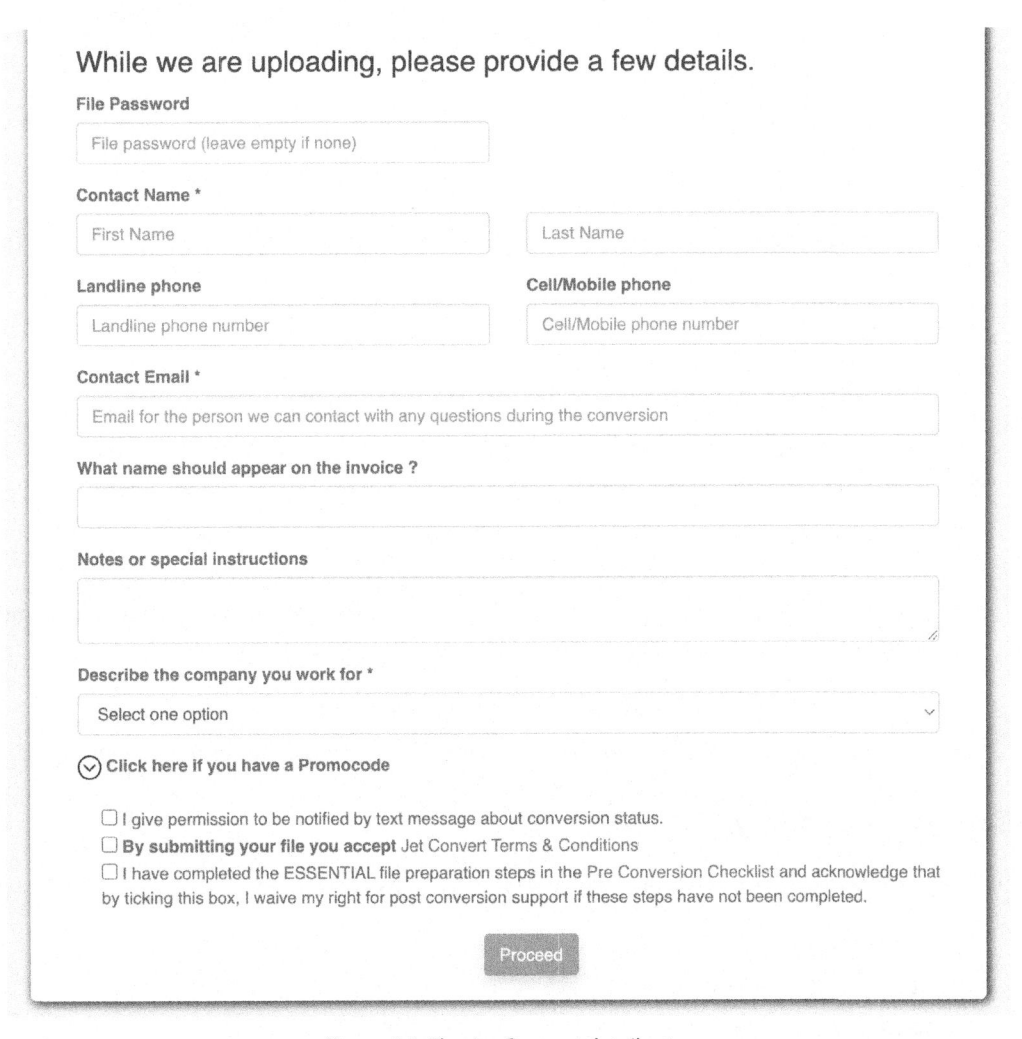

Figure 5.3: The Jet Convert details step

5. Select a package:

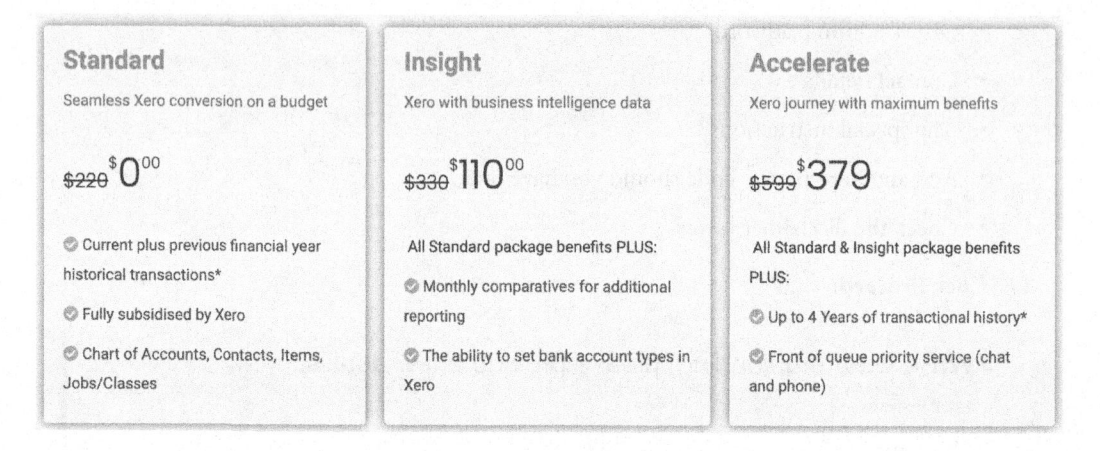

Standard	Insight	Accelerate
Seamless Xero conversion on a budget	Xero with business intelligence data	Xero journey with maximum benefits
~~$220~~ $0.00	~~$330~~ $110.00	~~$599~~ $379
✓ Current plus previous financial year historical transactions*	✓ All Standard package benefits PLUS:	✓ All Standard & Insight package benefits PLUS:
✓ Fully subsidised by Xero	✓ Monthly comparatives for additional reporting	✓ Up to 4 Years of transactional history*
✓ Chart of Accounts, Contacts, Items, Jobs/Classes	✓ The ability to set bank account types in Xero	✓ Front of queue priority service (chat and phone)

Figure 5.4: The Jet Convert service packages

- **Standard**: This is what you will use most of the time. This will load all transactions for the current year and the full (one) prior year.
- **Insight**: This adds the ability to add comparative monthly balances going back past the one year prior in the **Standard** package.
- **Accelerate**: This adds an additional two years of transactions and gives you a priority service.

> **Note**
> Xero subsidizes this service for up to $220. This fully covers the cost of the Standard package.

6. Once the package is selected, you are on the way. Jet Convert will communicate with you until the file is converted. You will receive an email with the instructions to follow from here:

    I. On receiving the subscription transfer request, accept it.
    II. Follow the post-conversion checklist you receive in your email from Jet Convert.

Converting your QBO file

Once your QBO file is ready for conversion, follow these steps to convert it:

1. Go to `Jetconvert.com`.
2. Select **QuickBooks Online (USA)**.
3. Click **Load**:

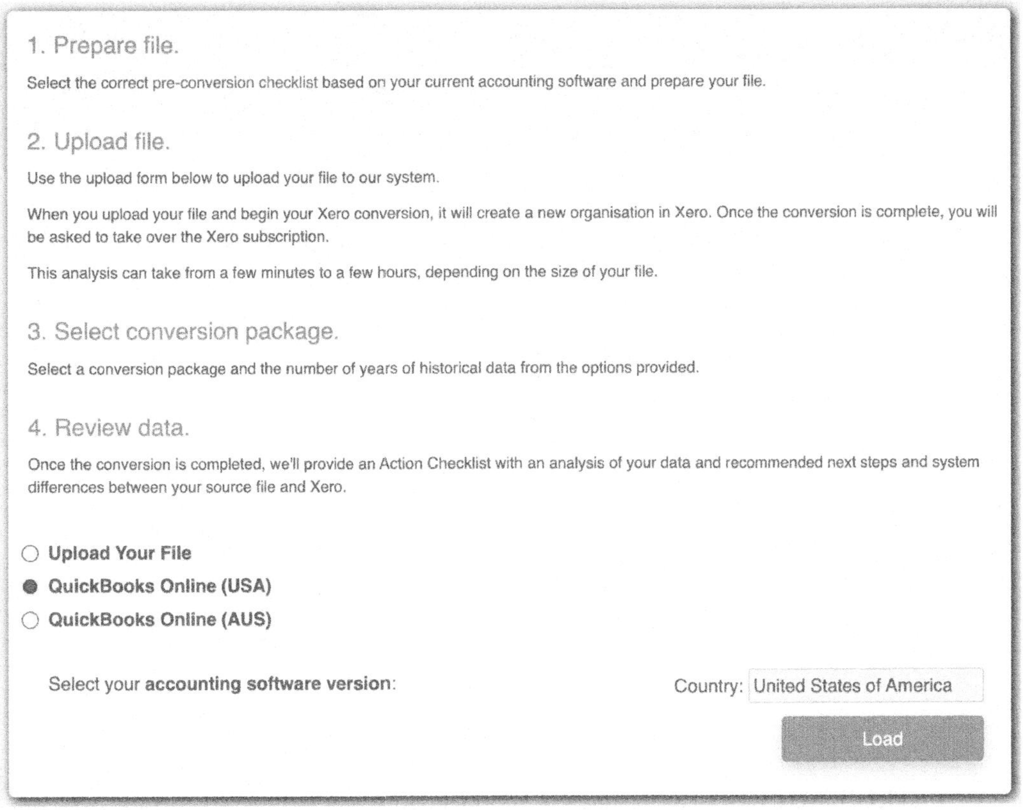

1. Prepare file.
Select the correct pre-conversion checklist based on your current accounting software and prepare your file.

2. Upload file.
Use the upload form below to upload your file to our system.

When you upload your file and begin your Xero conversion, it will create a new organisation in Xero. Once the conversion is complete, you will be asked to take over the Xero subscription.

This analysis can take from a few minutes to a few hours, depending on the size of your file.

3. Select conversion package.
Select a conversion package and the number of years of historical data from the options provided.

4. Review data.
Once the conversion is completed, we'll provide an Action Checklist with an analysis of your data and recommended next steps and system differences between your source file and Xero.

- ○ **Upload Your File**
- ● **QuickBooks Online (USA)**
- ○ **QuickBooks Online (AUS)**

Select your **accounting software version**:   Country: United States of America

[Load]

Figure 5.5: The Jet Convert file selection screen

4. Follow the prompts, just as you did for the QBDT conversion.
5. Retrieve the migration ID from the screen:

64 Conversion to Xero Made Easy

![Jet Convert screenshot showing conversion ID 111486 with instructions to invite them into the QB Online organization]

Figure 5.6: The Jet Convert migration ID

6. Add Jet Convert to QBO as a Company Administrator:

   I. Log in to your QBO account and your organization.

   II. Click on the **Settings** button at the top right of the screen.

   III. Go to **Manage Users | Add a New User**.

   IV. Choose the **Company Administrator** user type.

   V. Enter the qbo@jetconvert.com email.

   VI. Enter Ref into the **First Name** field and provide the six-digit conversion ID that you have been assigned for the **Last Name** value.

7. Select your package, as detailed in the *Converting your QBDT file* section.

Again, now that you have selected your package, your QBO migration is underway. Wait for the email from Jet Convert detailing the next steps and follow along.

Summary

We have covered The Fresh Start method of conversion detailed in the previous chapter, and now the automated conversion via Jet Convert. You should now know what method is best for your client and how to complete the different processes. You should also have an understanding of the different packages, and why you would upgrade from the standard package in Jet Convert. Finally, you should now know the prerequisites for converting from QBO and QBDT, the steps to begin the conversion process, and what is required once Jet Convert hands the file back to you.

This completes the majority of the setup required to get a Xero company file started. In the upcoming chapters, we start looking at transaction handling. We will see you in the next chapter.

Part 2: Handling the Day-to-Day Processes

The objective of this section is to familiarize you with the tools and features you will use daily in the process of creating and managing the transactions of the business. This is the heart of Xero and where you will learn the most.

This section comprises the following chapters:

- *Chapter 6, Recording and Reconciling the Bank*
- *Chapter 7, Invoicing and the Sales Process*
- *Chapter 8, Managing Bills and Purchases with Procure-to-Pay in Xero*
- *Chapter 9, Using Xero on the Go*

6
Recording and Reconciling the Bank

As we have said before, the bank feed is the heart of Xero! This is where the daily transactions start. It does not matter what type of business you have or your industry – you will use the bank feed in Xero. In this chapter, we will show you how to record bank transactions and run through the bank account reconciliation process. Performing these steps right gives you the certainty that you are heading in the right direction.

In this chapter, we're going to cover the following main topics:

- The bank feed basics
- No bank fee? Not a problem – import it
- Rules, rules, rules
- Using Xero to your advantage
- Cash coding
- Reconciling that account

The bank feed basics

In the previous chapters, we detailed setting up the bank feed to import transactions and enter the initial balances. Now, we are going to put that to work. The bank accounts live in the **Bank accounts** section of Xero. You can navigate there by clicking the **Accounting** menu and selecting **Bank accounts**:

Recording and Reconciling the Bank

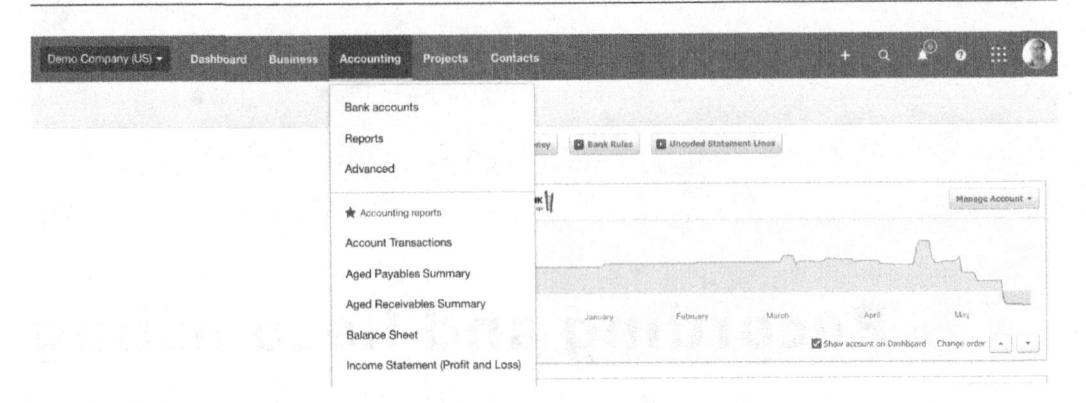

Figure 6.1: The Bank accounts menu option

You have the option to show selected bank accounts on the Xero dashboard. Check the **Show account on Dashboard** check box, as shown in *Figure 6.2*. The arrow buttons on the lower right of the bank account box allow you to move the selected bank account up and down in the display order of all of your bank accounts on the **Bank accounts** screen:

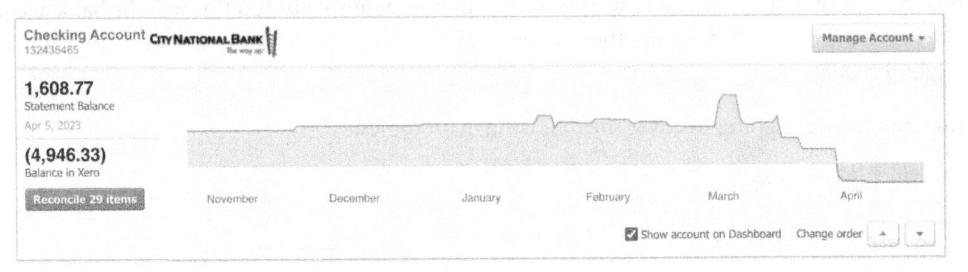

Figure 6.2: Bank account display

The views of the bank account, whether they are from the **Bank accounts** screen or the dashboard, are very similar. They display the number of bank transactions that remain unreconciled from the bank feed, the current Xero transactional balance, as well as the bank balance, and the date of the last import:

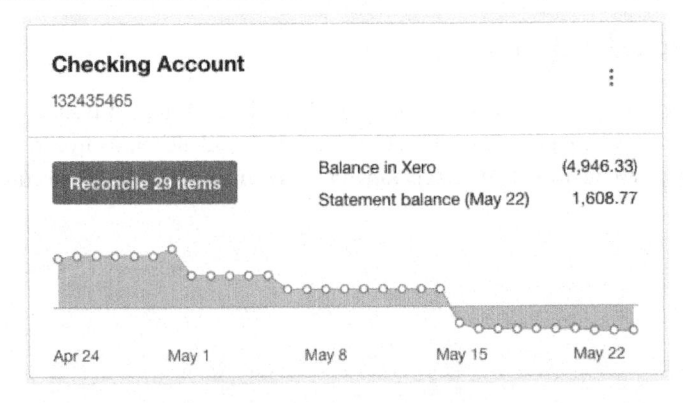

Figure 6.3: Xero dashboard bank account view

You can click on the account name to be directed to the **Account transactions** screen. You can click on the **Reconcile** button and be directed to the **Reconciliation** screen. Lastly, you can click on the **Manage Account** button or the vertical ellipsis and get the banking menu options. We will touch on these menu options as we proceed through this chapter:

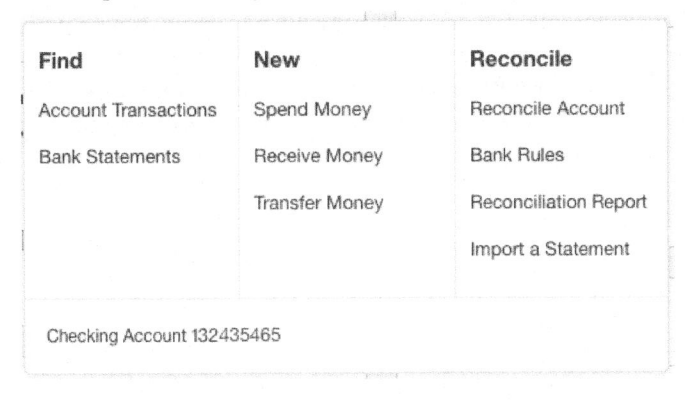

Find	New	Reconcile
Account Transactions	Spend Money	Reconcile Account
Bank Statements	Receive Money	Bank Rules
	Transfer Money	Reconciliation Report
		Import a Statement

Checking Account 132435465

Figure 6.4: Bank account options menu

The main banking screen consists of the same details we saw on the dashboard, but it also includes four tabs: **Reconcile**, **Cash coding**, **Bank statements**, and **Account transactions**:

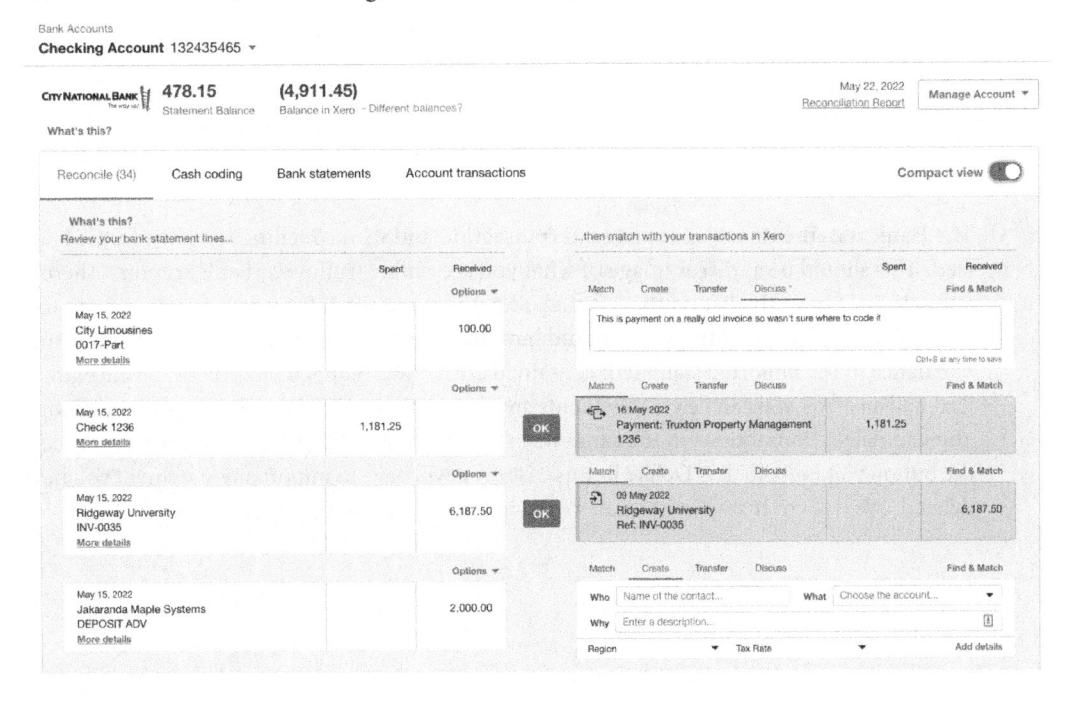

Figure 6.5: Main bank screen

Let's start from the right:

- The **Account transactions** tab contains the banking transactions already recorded in Xero. You can see the date of the transaction, the details of the transaction, the source, and the reconciliation status. You can search by date, amount, and contact to find the transactions you are looking for. You can click through any line to be brought to the transaction to make any edits or change the coding. If you want to remove a specific transaction, you can check the box on the left-hand side of the transaction, which will activate the **Remove & Redo** button. If you click the **Remove & Redo** button, it will delete the transaction as if it never happened, and it will revert the bank feed transaction to an unreconciled status, allowing you to record and reconcile the transaction again:

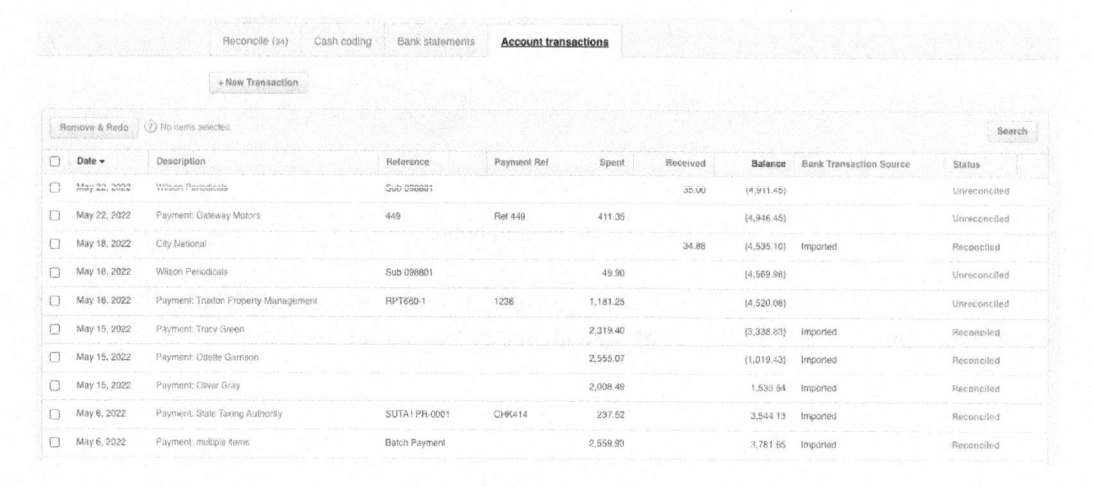

Figure 6.6: Account transactions

- The **Bank statements** tab contains each transaction and its reconciling status from the bank feed. This should be a mirror image of what you see online from your bank account. There is a toggle just above the list on the left that allows you to switch from a transaction view to a statement view. The only time you should have to do anything here is if your bank feed is out of balance. If the imported statement contained errors, was mapped incorrectly, or the banked feed had an error, you can delete statements and transactions; you can only restore transactions. You can delete transactions in the same way that you do for the account transactions, except the button you must click is **Delete** in this case. You will have to import any statement you have deleted. We will cover importing statements in the next section of this chapter:

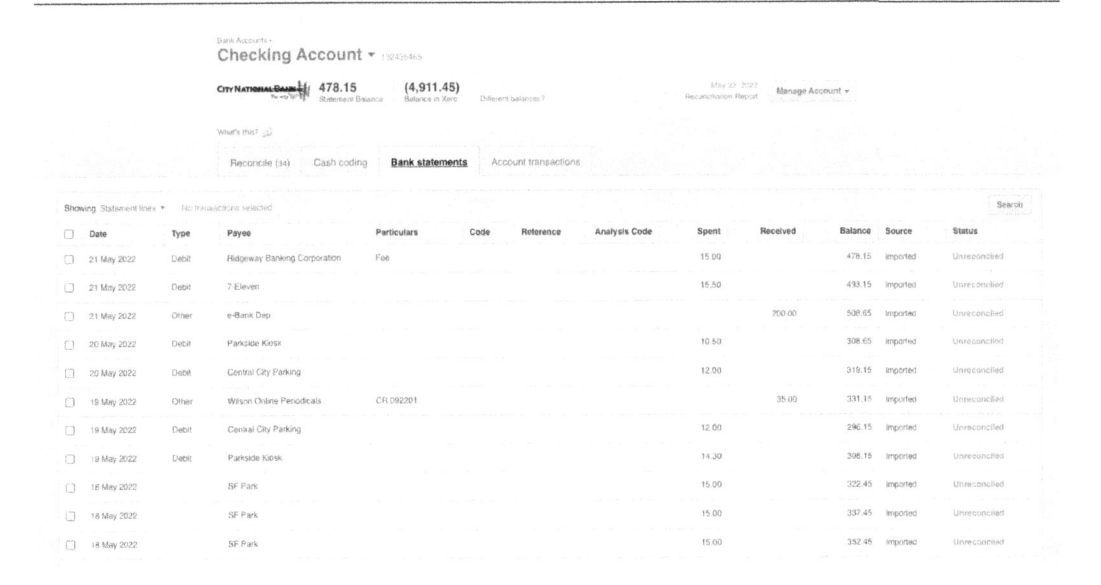

Figure 6.7: Bank statements

We will cover the **Reconcile** and **Cash Coding** tabs later in this chapter, in the *Using Xero to your advantage* and *Cash coding* sections.

Next, we will import a bank statement, just in case your bank does not have a bank feed.

No bank feed? Not a problem – import it

As we have discussed in previous chapters, Xero has bank feeds for most banks, but if you have a bank that does not have a working bank feed, Xero has you covered with an easy-to-use bank statement import process. From the menu options, select **Import a statement**. You will be taken to the **Import Bank Transactions** screen. Here, you will be shown the various file formats that you can use for your bank feed:

Recording and Reconciling the Bank

Bank Accounts › Checking Account ›
Import Bank Transactions

Follow these steps to import your transactions

1. **In a new window, go to your bank web site.**

2. **Download your bank statement.** File type must be OFX, QFX, QBO, QIF or CSV
   The most recent transaction imported was:

	Spent	Received
May 21, 2022 Ridgeway Banking Corporation Fee	15.00	

3. **Upload the bank statement file here...**

   Browse   No file selected

   [Import]   [Cancel]

File formats you can import

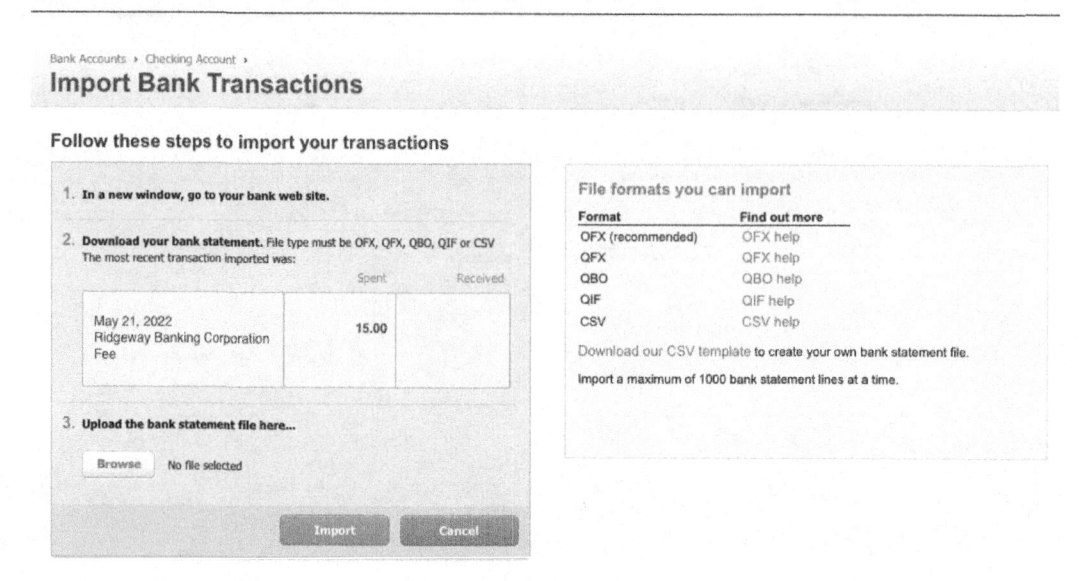

Format	Find out more
OFX (recommended)	OFX help
QFX	QFX help
QBO	QBO help
QIF	QIF help
CSV	CSV help

Download our CSV template to create your own bank statement file.
Import a maximum of 1000 bank statement lines at a time.

Figure 6.8: The Import Bank Transactions screen

The **OFX**, **QFX**, and **QBO** formats contain all of the information needed to import your transactions. The **CSV** format is the most versatile and can be configured for the file that was downloaded from your bank. If the bank offers the **OFX**, **QFX**, or **QBO** formats, I would choose them for simplicity, but if not, the **CSV** format works in every case.

A CSV can contain as much detail as you can download but you must have at least the **Date** and **Amount** columns shown with * in *Figure 6.9*. You can also prepopulate the CSV file with the account data to automatically create a transaction (spend money or receive money), as well as reconcile the transaction line to the statement:

	A	B	C	D	E	F	G
1	*Date	*Amount	Payee	Description	Reference	Check Number	
2	5/22/22	34.88	City National	Interest earned			
3	5/22/22	-100	City National	ATM With			
4	5/22/22	-1020.3	RBS	Loan Payment			
5	5/22/22	-15	SF PARK				
6	5/22/22	-15	SF PARK				
7	5/22/22	-15	SF PARK				
8	5/22/22	-15	SF PARK				
9							
10							
11							
12							

Figure 6.9: Bank transaction CSV file

To start the bank statement import process, click the **Browse** button on the **Import Bank Transactions** screen and select your file. Now, click the green **Import** button. You will be taken to the **Statement Import Options** screen:

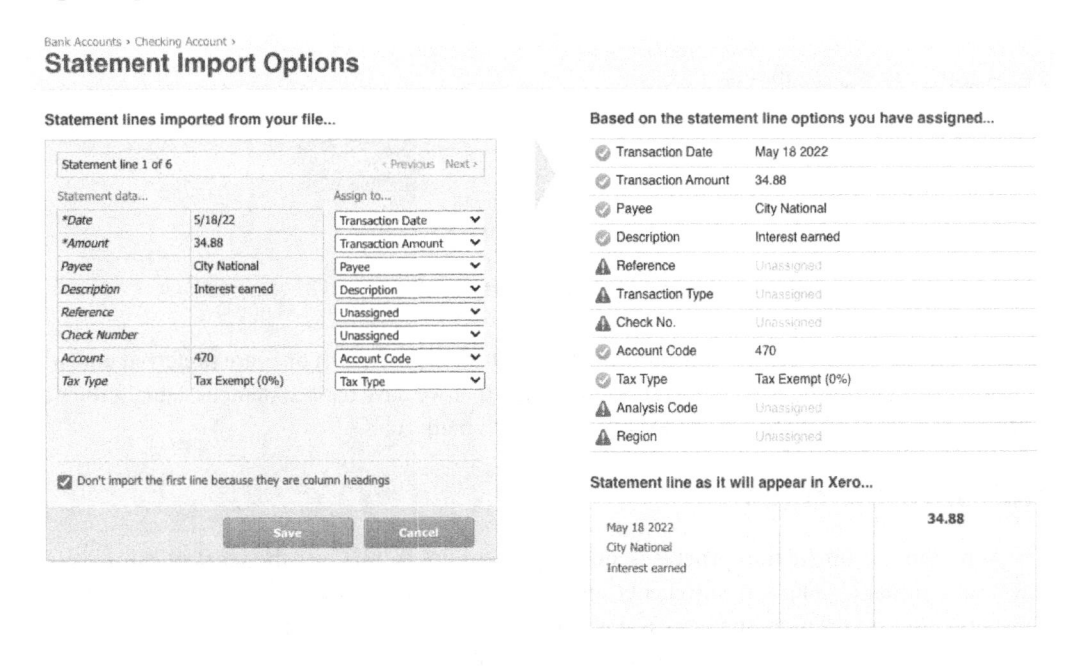

Figure 6.10: The Statement Import Options screen

The **Statement Import Options** screen allows you to map the transactions in the CSV file to the bank transactions in Xero. As you can see in *Figure 6.10*, the transaction details are mapped to the Xero options, including the account with the sample, 470, pulled from the file and mapped to the **Account code** property. You can scroll through the lines by clicking the **Next** button at the center top of the screen. The display on the right will simulate the transaction view in Xero so that you can determine whether the mapping is correct. Once you are satisfied with your mapping, click **Save**; the mapping will be saved for next time and the bank data will be imported into the bank feed. You should get a confirmation of the number of transactions that were imported and an indication of any errors. Click **OK** to continue:

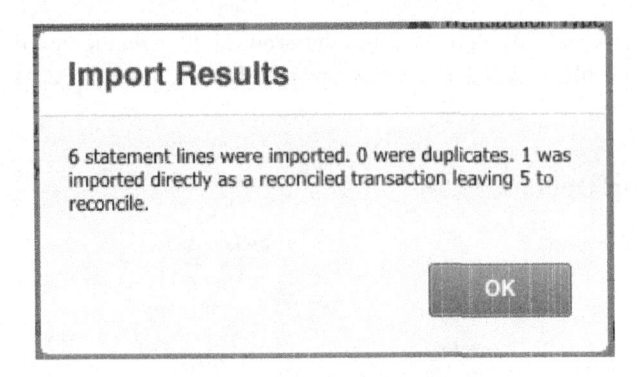

Figure 6.11: Bank import confirmation

In this section, we covered the bank statement import file types, which ones are preferred and why, and how we perform the process for a **CSV** file. Now that we have bank statement data, in the next section, we will show you how to build efficiencies with bank rules.

Rules, rules, rules

The Xero bank reconciliation process is aided by the use of rules. Over the years of using Xero, I have realized that I, along with my clients, am a creature of habit. I use the same vendors time after time – the same gas station, the same restaurants, the same hardware store. This leads to repetitive transactions, and that is exactly where rules come into play. You create a "rule" based on the specific criteria, and based on that information, the bank statement lines are coded, leaving less manual work for you when you're recording your transactions.

Let's take a quick look at how we set up a rule:

1. The following is a bank transaction from the **7-Eleven** company:

Figure 6.12: Bank transaction

2. In this case, let's assume our client is buying gas for their landscaping business. Every day, they stop at the same **7-Eleven** store and top off this tank. This is the perfect case for a bank rule. We will click on the **Option** down arrow and click on **Create bank rule**.

3. As you can see in *Figure 6.13*, there are three tabs on the **Rules** screen: **Spend money rule**, **Receive money rule**, and **Transfer money rule**. They all work the same – add your criteria, add the coding detail, give it a name, and save the details.

4. In this case, you will see that in the first line, I used the dropdown to select **Any** since the **ALL** condition is too restrictive, and it will result in rules running for a fraction of the time.

5. We changed the **Payer** selection to **Any** since the banks have changed their configuration of the feeds many times. This keeps you safe, regardless of which field the detail is in.

6. We have set the **contains** condition since **equal** is too restrictive and the lines may contain descriptive information such as a store number or city that we do not want to include in the criteria. We set the contact to the contact we want to use for this transaction – in this case, **7-Eleven**.

7. In this case, we set the coding to a single line, **Fuel**, and added a description, **Mower gas**. You can split up the coding into multiple lines, so long as the lines total 100% for the distribution.

   Line 3 gives you the option to split out a specific dollar amount, and the remainder will be coded to line 4 automatically. Line 3 is completed similarly to line 4; enter a description, the account, and the amount, and if want you to allocate a specific amount; then, allocate the difference.

> **Note**
> I have used this option minimally over the years I have used Xero.

8. I usually leave line 5, **Set the reference…**, as is. For **Target a bank account…**, on line **6**, I set it to **all bank accounts**, as clients may change banks for credit cards often.

9. That leaves naming the rule. I go with the vendor name – which is the account code here:

Recording and Reconciling the Bank

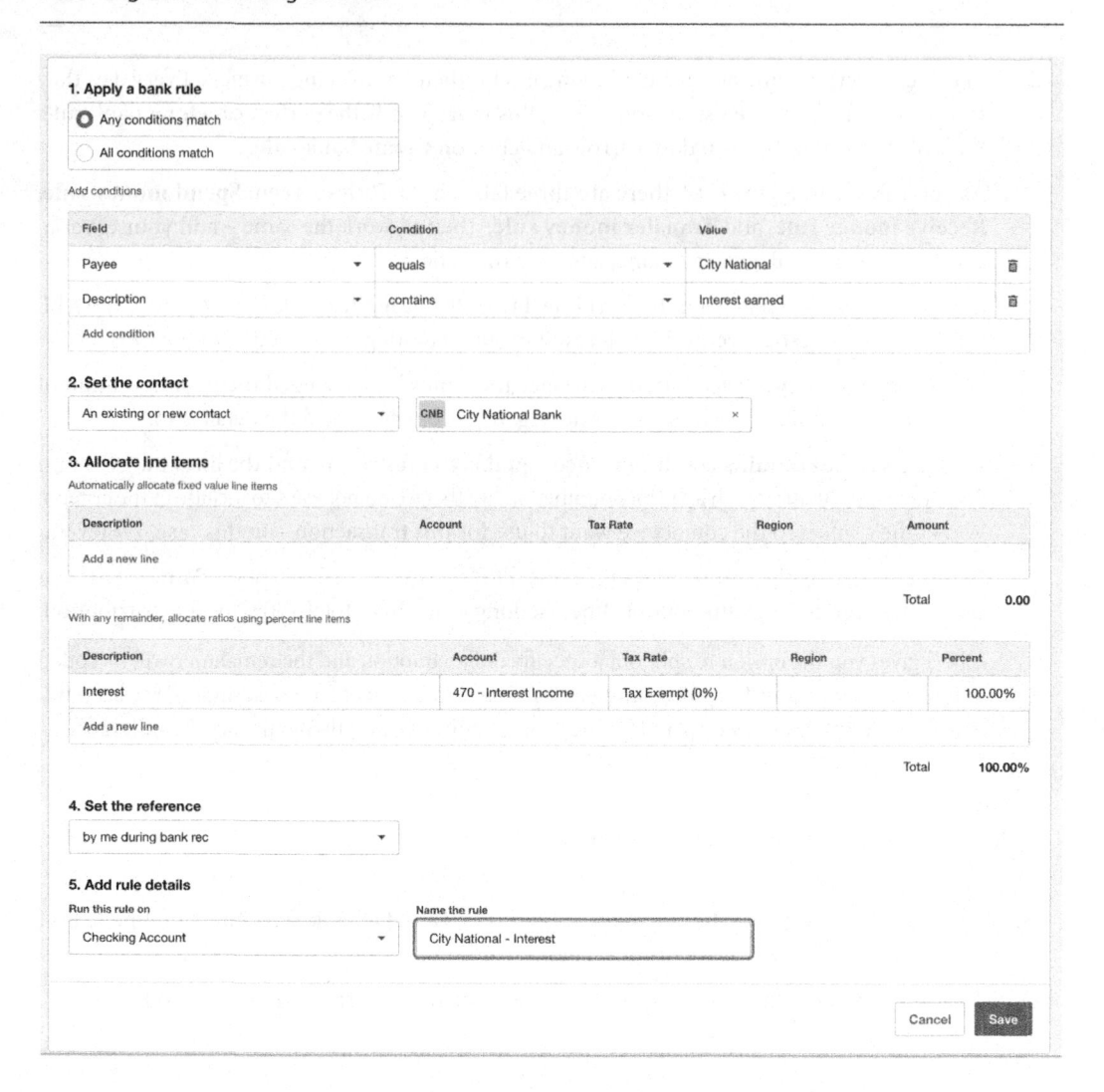

Figure 6.13: Rule creation screen

Once the bank rule has been set up correctly, it will appear in the **Reconcile** tab, as shown in *Figure 6.14*:

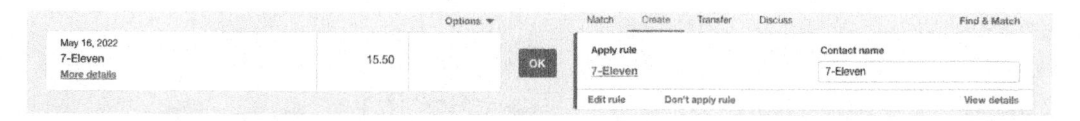

Figure 6.14: Working rule

Now that we have learned how to set up and use bank rules, let's dive deeper into the reconciliation process and see where bank rules fit into that process.

Using Xero to your advantage

Xero has built-in **artificial intelligence** (**AI**) to help you record your bank transactions faster. When you open the **Reconcile** tab, you will see that Xero has used its AI to populate the right column with matches and suggestions based on the machine learning engine that runs within Xero. These transactions will appear in green; I will refer to these as *greenlit* transactions:

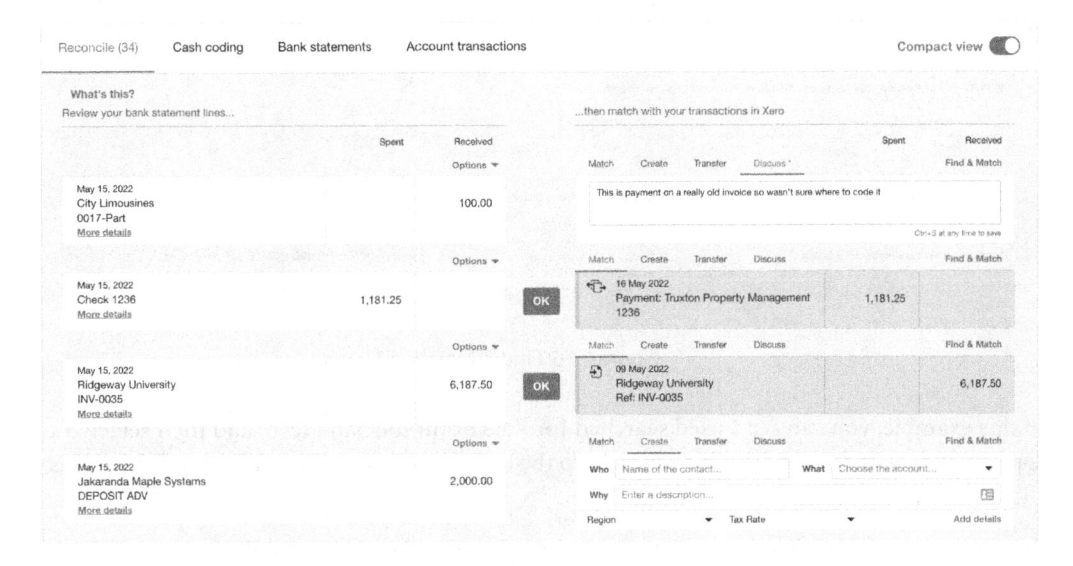

Figure 6.15: The Reconcile tab

Xero will push out transactions that are auto-matched by amount first, then by bank rule, and then auto-suggestions based on previous reconciliations. This helps cut down the time to fully reconcile your bank transactions.

As shown in *Figure 6.15*, you will see two auto-match transactions. My suggestion is to look at the dates, and if the dates are reasonable, they should be a match. Click the **OK** button in the center column to accept each entry. Keep in mind that Xero will be able to match based on the amount, so if there is more than one invoice that was paid, you will need to use the **Find & Match** button at the top right of each transaction to match the appropriate transactions:

Recording and Reconciling the Bank

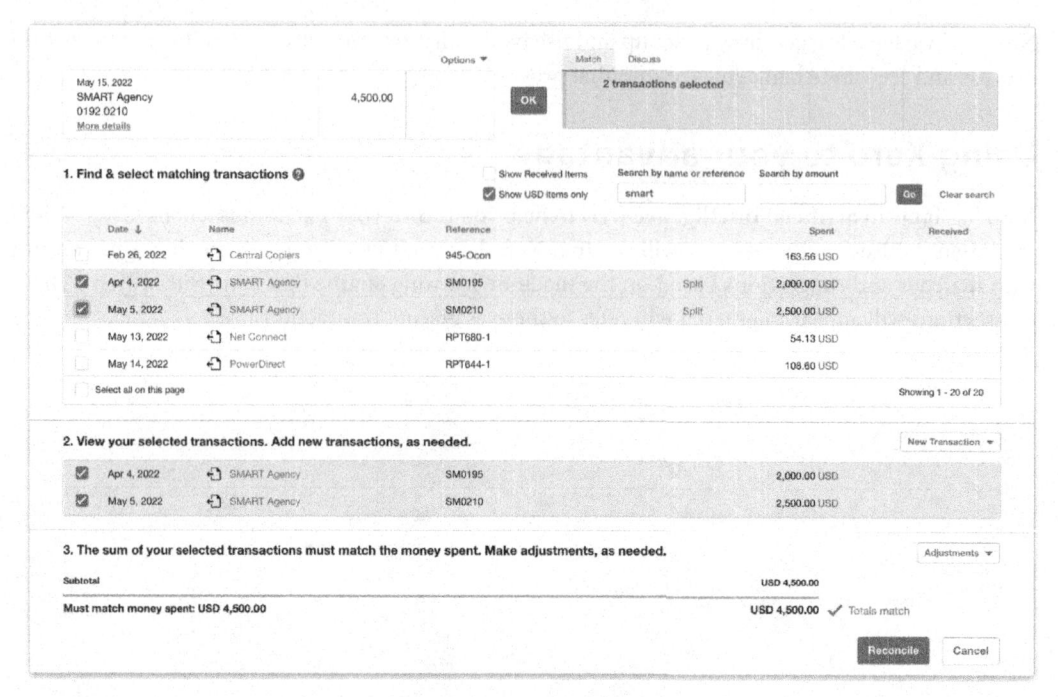

Figure 6.16: Find & Match

In this example, you can see I used searched for `smart` in the bank feed, and then selected the appropriate transactions by checking the box to the left of the transactions. All that is left to do is to click **Reconcile**.

Remember that 7-Eleven transaction we built the rule on earlier? Here it is, ready to be reconciled. Again, review for reasonableness and click **OK**:

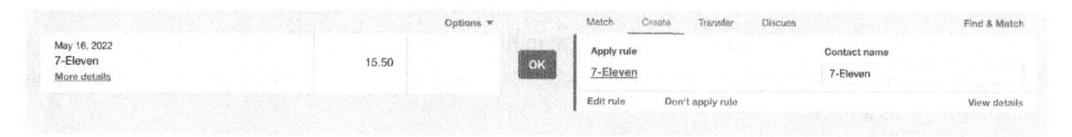

Figure 6.17: Bank rule transaction

Cash coding   81

The last of the assisted transactions is **Auto-Suggestion**. Xero will suggest the proposed transaction based on the history of bank feed transactions previously recorded:

Figure 6.18: Auto-suggested transaction

Ridgeway Bank and **Bank Service Charges** were used in the past for the payer Ridgeway Banking Corporation. Again, apply reasonableness and click **OK** if you think the transaction looks correct.

As you can see, you can manually record spend and receive money transactions by entering the payer's name and entering an accounting code. It is just that easy.

In this section, we learned how to use the **Reconcile** tab using Xero matching and suggestions. In the next section, we will look at cash coding and how we can reconcile bank transactions in bulk, saving us lots of time.

Cash coding

Cash coding allows you to reconcile transactions in bulk by utilizing an Excel-like grid. You can sort the columns that have blue headers by clicking on the header. In the following screenshot, I have sorted it by **Payer**. You can see that **Central City Parking** is highlighted. When you have multiple lines and you want to record the same, you need to check the checkbox to the left of the line. If your transactions are adjacent to each other as **Central City Parking** is, check the checkbox at the top end of the section, hold down *Shift*, and click the last transaction in the section. Xero will select all of the transactions in that range. Now, you can type in any one line and each of the transactions will be changed to reflect the entry you just made. Ensure you have the appropriate payer and add your account code and tax code. Once you have that information, you can click **Save & Reconcile Selected** at the bottom.

Here are some tips: work in small batches. Record the transactions and make additional selections and entries. If you work too fast, you may check a line and make an entry, and change previously checked lines if you inadvertently forget to click **Save & Reconcile Selected**:

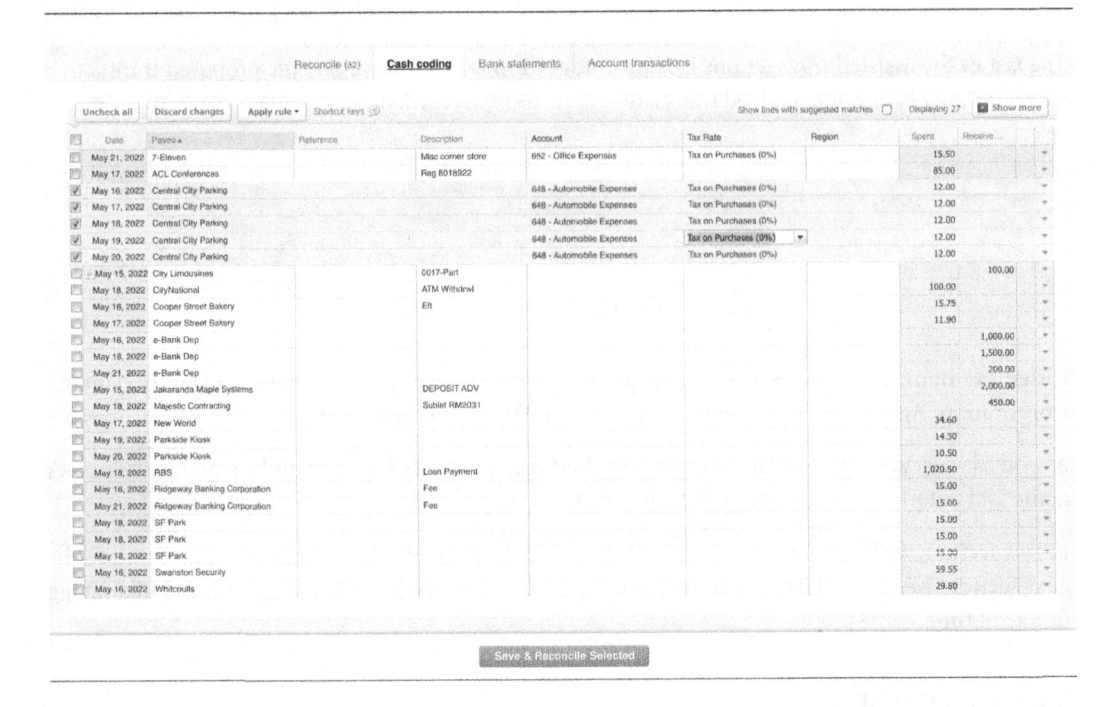

Figure 6.19: Cash coding

To put the power of cash coding into perspective, I had a Xero file that contained over 11,000 transactions. Using cash coding, I was able to record the transactions in hours and not days. This took a lot of concentration, but I used two screens, each with a cash coding screen. One cash coding screen was sorted A-Z by payer, and the other, Z-A, by payer. I reconciled one screen and while Xero was doing its thing, I was working on the other screen, switching back and forth between browser windows until I had reconciled all of the transactions. This was a true game-changer!

Now that we have recorded all of our bank transactions, it is time to reconcile them to the bank statement. We will do just that in the next section.

Reconciling that account

Now that the transactions have been reconciled, it is time to complete the bank reconciliation process. Xero makes this easy:

1. Start by viewing or downloading your most recent bank statement. Note the ending date on the statement, as well as the ending balance:

Reconciling that account   83

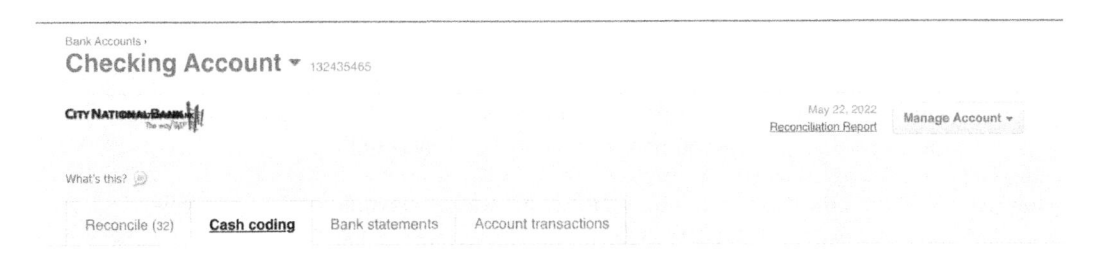

Figure 6.20: Banking header

2. Click on **Reconciliation Report** under the date on the right-hand side near the top of the bank account screen. This will open the **Bank Reconciliation** screen.
3. Enter the date from the bank statement and click **Update**.
4. Review the statement balance from the **Bank Reconciliation** screen against the ending balance of the bank statement. If they match, you are good.
5. Export your reconciliation report and save it to your document management system, along with the statement:

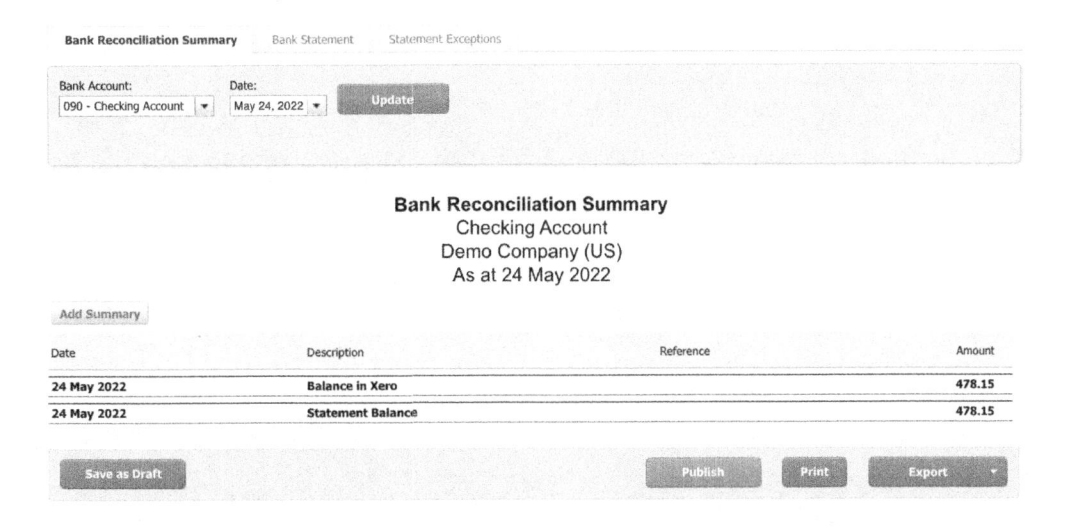

Figure 6.21: The Bank Reconciliation screen

6. If your balance does not match, you need to put in some elbow grease. First, check that the bank statement balance on the feed matches the bank statement. You may need to use the **Bank Statement** tab at the top of the bank reconciliation report. Use the skills you've learned over time as a bookkeeper or accountant and reconcile the account.

Now that we have reconciled our account to the bank, we have completed the cash cycle.

Summary

In this chapter, we covered the cash process, from a bank feed to a transaction and then a reconciled bank account. To get there, we covered a lot, and you should now know all about the **Bank accounts**, **Account transactions**, and **Bank statement** tabs, as well as how to build and use rules, Xero's AI-fed matching and suggestions, and just how fast cash coding is.

This completes the bank feed and reconciliation process. Now, we are ready to look at other transactions. We will see you in the next chapter.

7
Invoicing and the Sales Process

If the bank feed is the heart of Xero, then invoicing and sales are the heart of business! Every business has sales, incoming revenue, and incoming payments. It is how they record the sales and the associated payments, which vary. Here, we will show you how to run through the sales process in Xero for a business that must invoice for its service or product. Once perfected, these steps will bring in revenue, paving the way for a successful business.

In this chapter, we're going to cover the following main topics:

- Products and services
- Quoting your opportunities
- Sending the invoices
- Formatting your sales documents
- Getting paid in Xero

Products and services

Products and services are the building blocks of the sales process and its documents, as well as the procure-to-pay process, which we will discuss in the next chapter. Think of them as the products and services that you sell and possibly buy. Each of the items will contain an item ID, a description, and selling price. If you purchase this item, it will also have the purchase cost. You use the **Products and services** option to standardize your invoicing and establish how the items you sell are coded in Xero. For example, if you are a landscaping company, you may set up your services as follows:

- Mowing – residential
- Mowing – commercial
- Cleanup – residential
- Cleanup – commercial

86　Invoicing and the Sales Process

By setting up your services, you will have a uniform view of your invoice as well as a specific account code to assign to each service, keeping your accounting consistent.

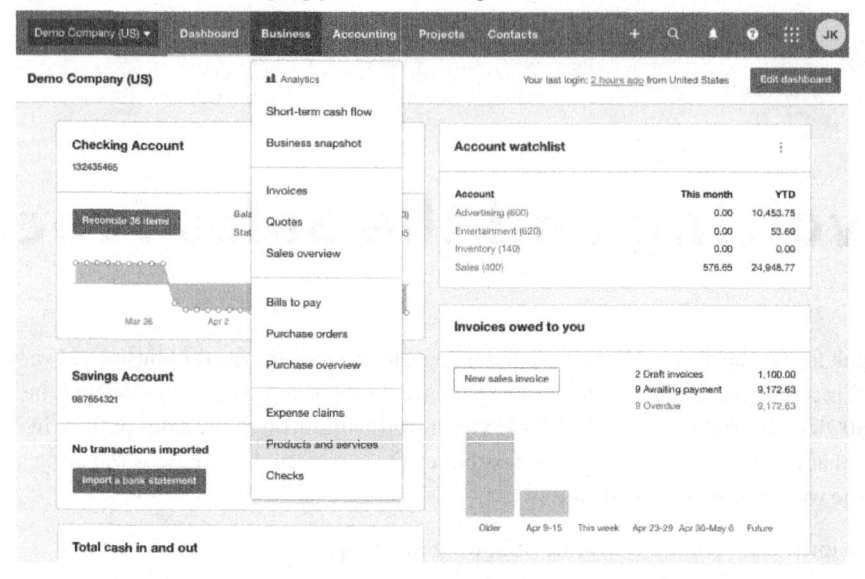

Figure 7.1: The Products and services menu option

Let's look at how we will set up our first service item:

1. Let's start by clicking on **Business** in the main menu and selecting **Products and services** from the dropdown.

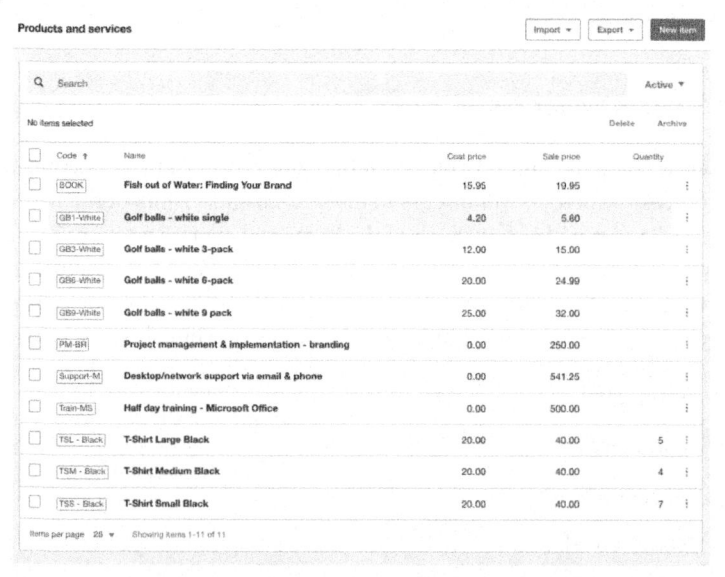

Figure 7.2: Products and services main screen

2. From the **Products and service** main screen, click **New item** in the upper right-hand corner of the screen.
3. There are three checkboxes on the new item setup page (*Figure 7.3*). They are **Track inventory item**, **Purchase**, and **Sell**:

    - **Track inventory item** works with **Tracked inventory** in Xero. By checking this box on an item, it means Xero will track the quantity and value of the item. That means when you process a purchase or bill, it will increase the quantity and value on hand, and when you process a sale, it will reduce the quantity and value on hand. It will also record the cost of goods sold. When this box is checked, an **inventory account** box is activated, and you are allowed to select the account code that all tracked inventory purchases will be coded as.

    - Tracked inventory is not for all organizations that use inventory. The main reason I do not use tracked inventory is that it is not suitable if you use a third-party inventory app. You can ensure you have turned off and deactivated all items that were using tracked inventory by first reducing the inventory down to a quantity and value of zero and then unchecking the **Track inventory item** box.

    - The **Purchase** checkbox indicates to Xero this item is purchased by the company and activates the input fields for **Cost Price**, **Purchase account**, **Tax rate**, and **Description**.

    - The **Sell** checkbox indicates to Xero that this item is sold by the company and activates the input fields for **Sale price**, **Sale account**, **Tax rate**, and **Description**.

Note that adjusting the tracked inventory is an advanced feature and not covered in this book.

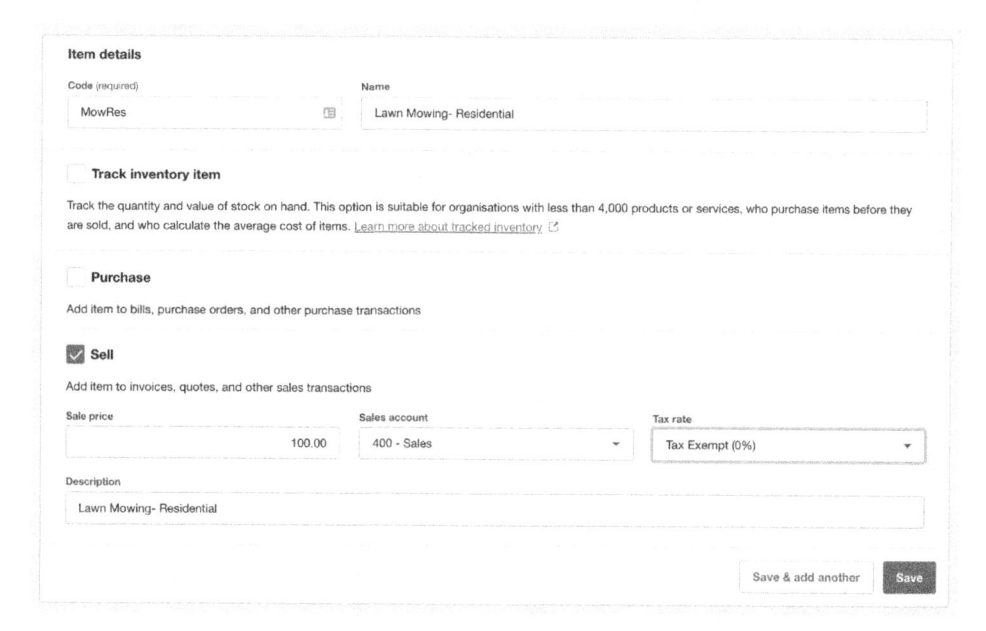

Figure 7.3: The new item entry screen

Invoicing and the Sales Process

The details in *Figure 7.3* are for the residential mowing item we discussed earlier. In this case, it is a service, and the only checkbox we will need to check is **Sell**.

Now that we have created our items, let's see them in action as we move to the next section on setting up the invoices.

Setting up invoices (and other forms)

Just as the main setup of Xero is important, form setup is equally as important to the sales and purchase-to-pay processes. Forms include the onscreen input forms in Xero and the subsequent printed forms, such as purchase orders or the invoices.

Let's take a look at **Invoice settings**:

1. Click on the company name dropdown, select **Settings**, and choose **Invoice settings**.

Figure 7.4: Invoice settings

2. The invoice settings are determined by the **Branding theme** option selected. Xero uses Branding themes to add the specific details you require to your forms and documents. There are two types of Branding themes, **Standard** and **Custom**. We are going to focus on standard themes, as custom themes are based on the DOCX Microsoft Word format, and they involve a complex process that is out of the scope of this book.

   Clicking the **New Branding Theme** button allows you to add a new standard or custom theme. Use the drop-down arrow to choose whether you are setting up a **Standard** or **Custom** theme. Choosing **Custom** allows you to add a theme name and create a new theme. As we said earlier, we will not cover DOCX customizations here. Choosing **Standard** will bring you to the **Edit** theme screen. Enter a theme name and save. We will cover editing the settings next.

3. *Figure 7.4* shows the Branding themes already in my Xero company. We have the **Standard** theme and the custom **Very orange invoice!** theme. Let's begin our look at the **Standard** theme by clicking the **Options** button.

Figure 7.5: The branding theme options

From the **Options** button, you can edit, copy, change the logo of, preview, and delete the current branding theme. You can also have multiple Branding themes. You may want different themes for several reasons; the most common is running multiple brands through one company (that is, multiple brands, not multiple businesses).

We are going to concentrate our efforts here on editing the **Standard** branding theme.

4. Let's go down the fields of the branding theme settings in *Figure 7.6*. We start at the top with the name, page size, and margins. You can edit the font and font size to match your business's branding guide. We will stick to the settings currently entered.

   The next part is the document names. You can adjust these document names to fit your business. For example, if you call your *quotes* an estimate, you can change the **Quote title** field and call it ESTIMATE. This shows the flexibility of Xero.

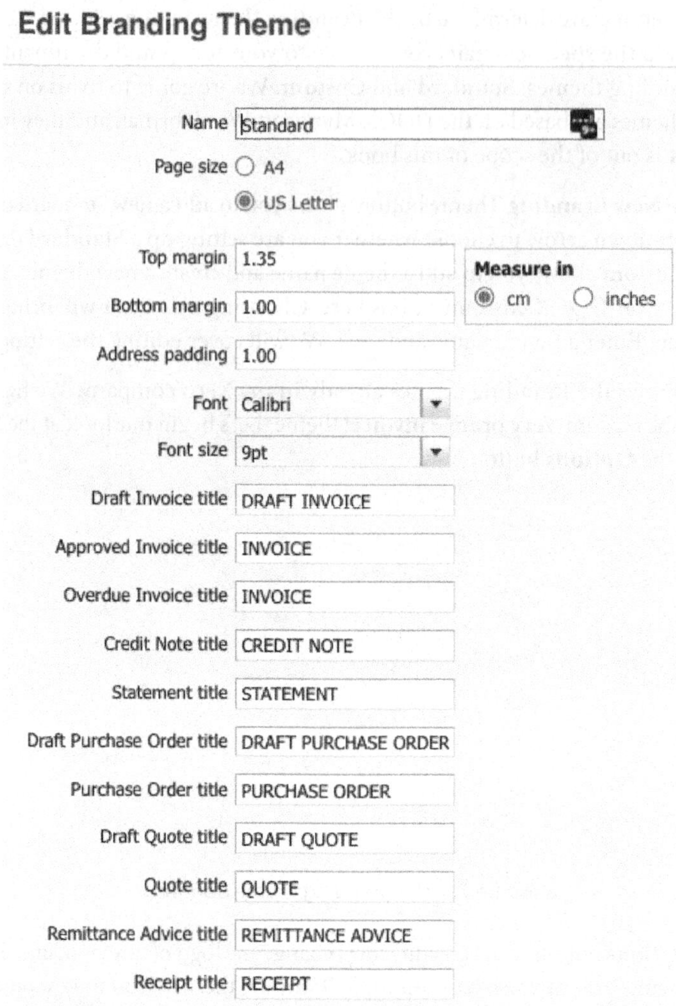

Edit Branding Theme

Name	Standard
Page size	○ A4
	● US Letter
Top margin	1.35
Bottom margin	1.00
Address padding	1.00
Font	Calibri
Font size	9pt
Draft Invoice title	DRAFT INVOICE
Approved Invoice title	INVOICE
Overdue Invoice title	INVOICE
Credit Note title	CREDIT NOTE
Statement title	STATEMENT
Draft Purchase Order title	DRAFT PURCHASE ORDER
Purchase Order title	PURCHASE ORDER
Draft Quote title	DRAFT QUOTE
Quote title	QUOTE
Remittance Advice title	REMITTANCE ADVICE
Receipt title	RECEIPT

Measure in ● cm   ○ inches

Figure 7.6: The branding theme setup screen

5. The next section consists of a number of checkboxes of items that will appear on your forms if you put a checkmark in each box. They will not be displayed if there is no check in each box.

    Directly to the right of this section, you can set the location of your logo, indicate how your taxes are shown, and edit the contact information to be displayed at the top of the company document.

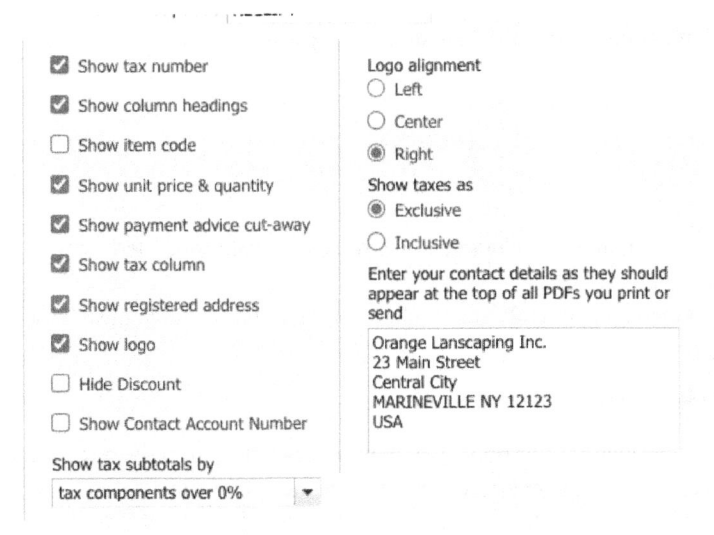

Figure 7.7: The branding theme setup screen continued

The last section of the branding theme setup allows you to choose the payment services you wish to have on this specific branding theme, as well as detail the terms and conditions that will be printed on your invoices and quotes.

Figure 7.8: The branding theme setup screen continued

6. When you have completed your edits, do not forget to click **Save.**

Figure 7.9: The branding theme setup screen continued

Now that we have set up our forms and defaults in action, we will move on to the next section on quotes.

Quoting your opportunities

As we have discussed throughout this book, you may or may not need the next feature we are going to discuss. When engaging with customers, it is best to give them an estimate of the cost of your service. This is accomplished via a quote. Quoting your sales is essential to some businesses and nonexistent to others. The good thing is it is available in Xero if you need it. Quotes give you the ability to send the expected amount to be billed to a customer, allowing them to be fully informed of the cost and approve the purchase.

Let's take a deeper look at the quote feature in Xero:

1. Start by clicking **Business** in the main menu, followed by **Quotes**.

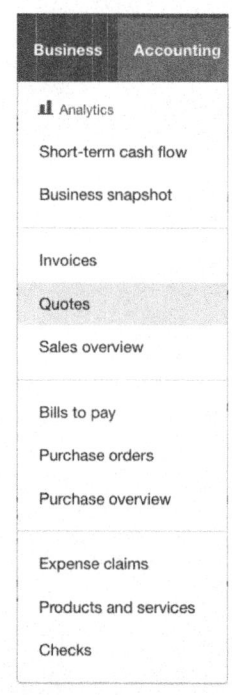

Figure 7.10: The Quotes menu option

2. Once on the **Quotes** main screen, you will see a familiar tab focused on the Xero user experience. On this screen, you can create a new quote and see all existing quotes, which can be filtered by the following statuses, based on the tab you select:

- **Draft**
- **Sent**
- **Declined**
- **Accepted**
- **Invoiced**

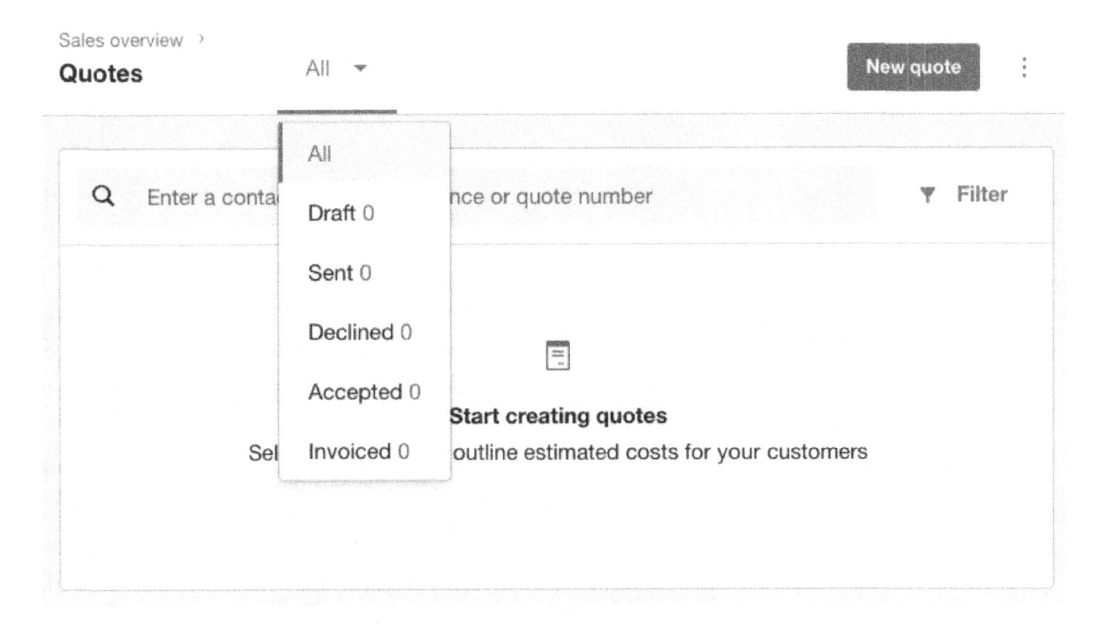

Figure 7.11: The Quotes main screen

94   Invoicing and the Sales Process

3. We will click **+ New Quote** and start the quoting process.

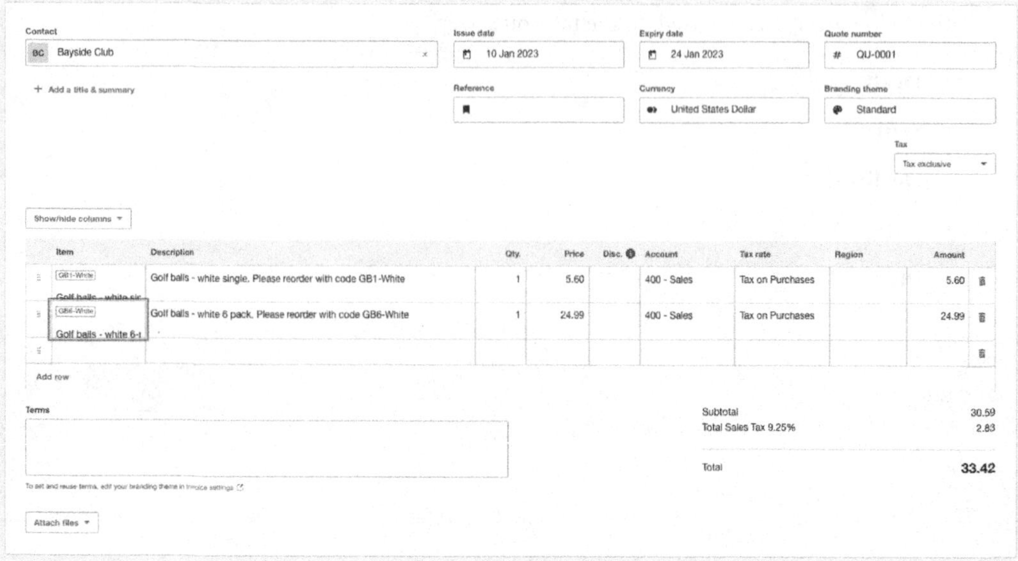

Figure 7.12: The quote creation screen

Just like the tabular status screen, the transaction screen has a familiar look to the invoice, purchase order, and bill screens. Each will have a field or two that is specific to the form, but the look, feel, and functions are very similar.

4. As you can see from *Figure 7.12*, we have entered in the **Contact** window the date of the quote (the expiration is set at 15 days in our settings), the services we plan to offer, and the cost to the customer.

5. The **Terms** box lays out what is required for a quote, and if you want to add any documents or pictures to the quote, you can do so by clicking **Attach files** and choosing the files you want to attach for the customer to see.

6. When you are ready to send the quote, click **Send** at the top of the screen. A **Send quote** box will open, showing the email address and the details of the email going to your customer. All of these details in the email can be customized in **Email settings**. You can access **Email settings** by clicking **Settings** and then **Email settings**, which is in the **Features** column. Click on **Templates** and choose the template you wish to edit. Type your changes and make sure to click **Save** when you are done.

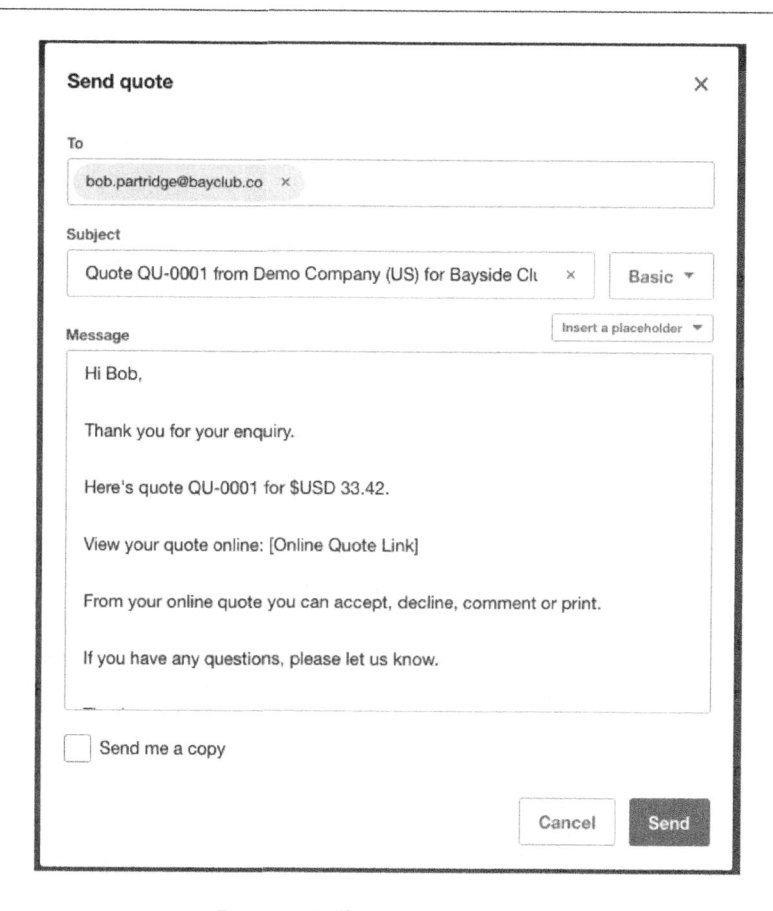

Figure 7.13: The Send quote screen

When the client gets the quote via email, they can review the quote and any attachments sent with it. They then have the opportunity to accept, decline, or comment on the quote. The comment process allows you and your customer to communicate back and forth regarding this quote.

Invoicing and the Sales Process

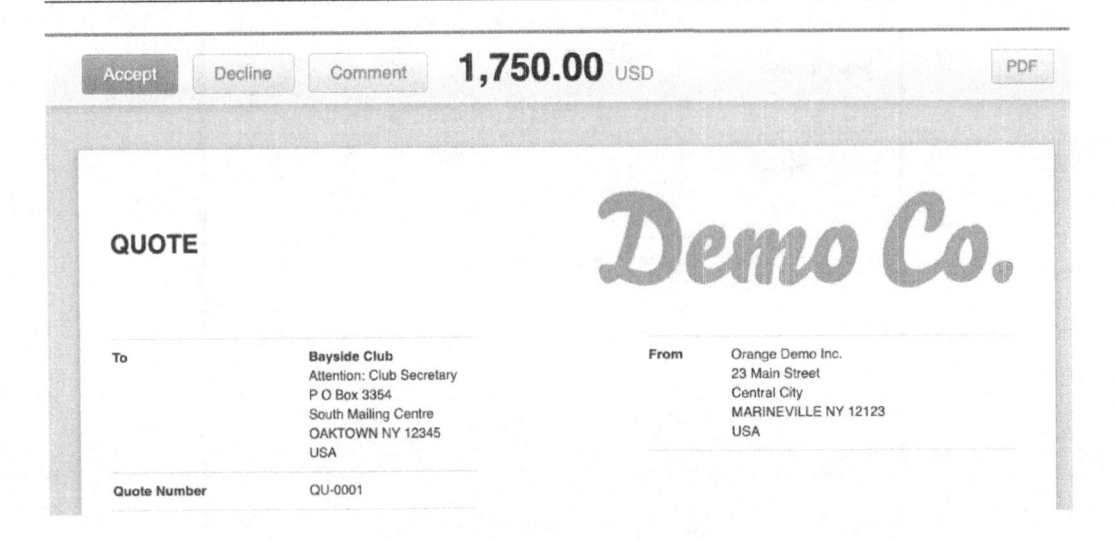

Figure 7.14: The customer quote view

7. You can also accept or decline the quote on the customer's behalf, should they accept the quote using some other method. You have several options when clicking on the ellipse menu on the right.

Figure 7.15: The quote view

8. Once approved, the **Mark as accepted** button changes to **Create invoice**.

    Clicking **Create invoice** will bring up the **Create invoice** window.

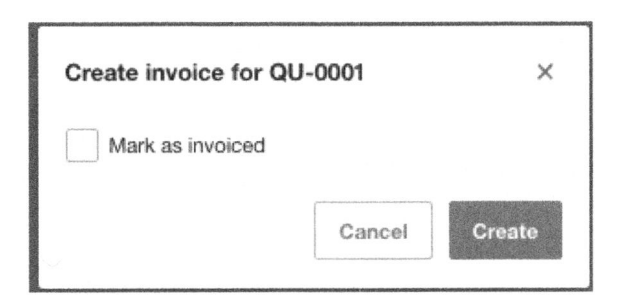

Figure 7.16: Creating an invoice from a quote

9. Check the **Mark as invoiced** box and then click **Create**. This will create the invoice for the customer and include the quote number in the reference field. Once you are happy with the invoice, click **Approve**.

Figure 7.17: An invoice awaiting approval

We have taken a shortcut to create an invoice from a quote. We could easily create the invoice with the exact same method we used to create the quote. We would choose **New Invoice** instead. Now that we have created a quote and received quote approvals, it is time to further discuss invoicing in Xero.

Time to send the invoices

In the last section, we converted an accepted quote into an invoice. In this section, we will take that a bit further.

Let's look at the invoice we just sent in *Figure 7.18*, which is in the **Awaiting Payment** status.

Figure 7.18: Invoice options

By clicking on the **Invoice Options** button, we can do the following:

- Generate a repeating invoice
- Void the current invoice
- Copy the current invoice to a new invoice
- Edit the current invoice
- Add a credit note
- Send the current invoice

Let's dig a little deeper into that list of invoice options. Let's start by making the current invoice a repeating invoice.

Repeat

We will click on the **Repeat** option, which will open the **New Repeating Invoice** window.

There is one major addition to the repeating invoice window, which is the repeating options.

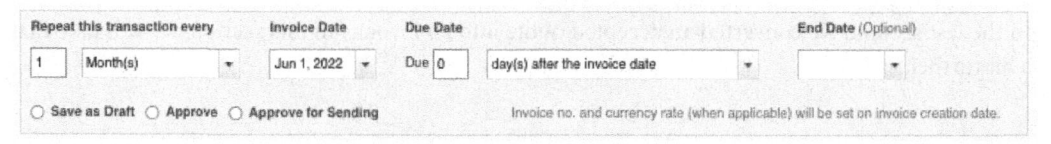

Figure 7.19: Repeating invoice options

The first thing you must identify is the repeating frequency – in this case, the frequency is monthly, starting on June 1. We also set the terms of the invoice, with this one being due upon receipt or on the invoice date. If you have a 12-month contract, you may want to put in an end date, just to have it as 1 or 2 days after the last bill is set to go out. That leads to the most important part of the repeating invoice process – the status. You can set the status as **Save as Draft**, **Approve**, or **Approve for Sending**. The biggest difference here is that if you are billing a set monthly amount, you can skip the draft, and approve the invoice or automatically save it. If you are billing by the job or the hour, you must save the invoice as a draft and update it.

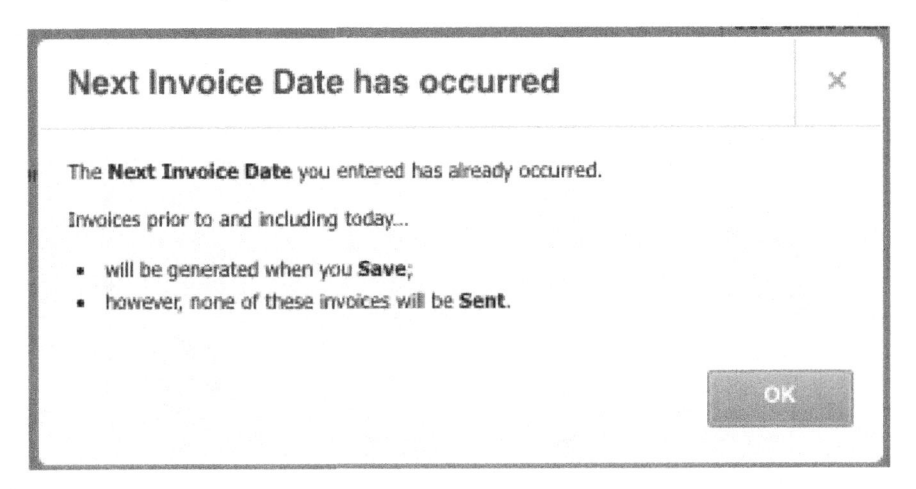

Figure 7.20: The next invoice date warning

If you save your repeating invoice using a date in the past, any invoices that would have been generated are created. However, they are not sent; you must send those to the customer manually. The next scheduled invoice will be sent when it is generated.

Void

When you click **Void** on **Invoice Options**, you can void the current invoice. You will receive a popup to confirm that this is what you actually intend to do. Just click **OK**, and the invoice is then voided.

Copy to

When you click **Copy to…** on **Invoice Options**, you can then create a new invoice, quote, purchase order, or bill with the details of this invoice. All you need to do is choose the contact you want the document created for, and Xero will create a document with the selected contact and the items from the original invoice. You can update anything you may need and save it as a draft or approve it.

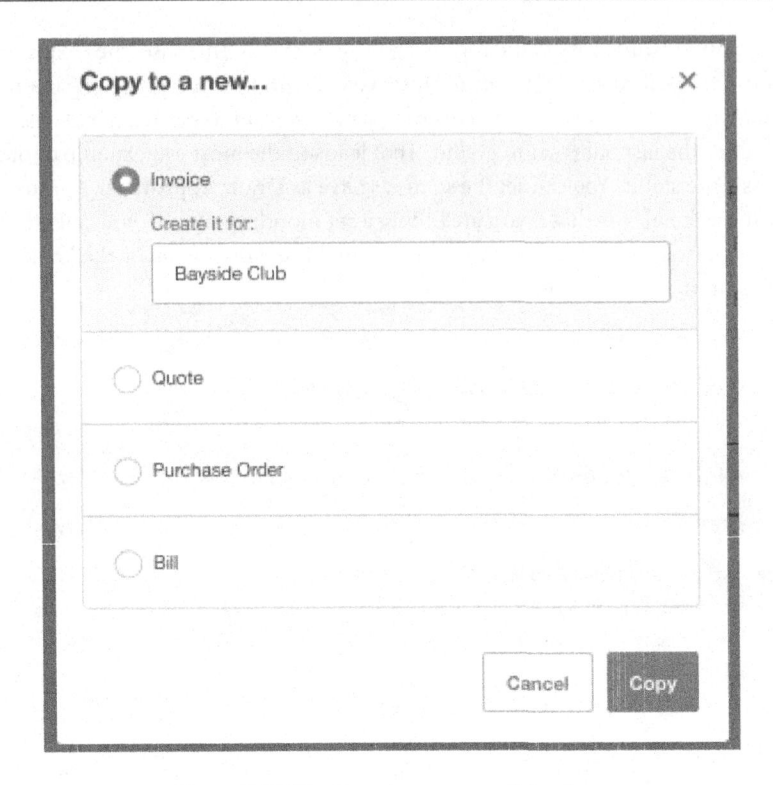

Figure 7.21: The Copy to a new… dialog box

Edit

When you click **Edit** on **Invoice Options**, you can edit the current invoice. You can edit all items on the invoice, except if you have added a payment. That will greatly limit what you can edit. At that point, you can basically change the account the item is being coded to on the general ledger. Should you need to do a deeper edit, you will need to remove the payment from the invoice first, and then edit the invoice. At that point, you can add the payment back in the document.

Add Credit Note

When you click **Add Credit Note** on **Invoice Options**, you can create a new credit note, which will be applied to the current invoice. Xero will fill a document with the details from the invoice you originally started with. It will allocate the balance owed in the invoice to the line items. All you need to do is review this, approve it, and click **Approve**.

Figure 7.22: The new credit note screen

Share invoice

When you click **Invoice** in **Invoice Options**, Xero gives you a link to access the invoice or send it to your customer. You can send it via email, text, or whatever way you communicate. Should the customer open it on an iPhone or an Apple device that supports Apple Pay, they will be able to pay the invoice quickly and easily if you have enabled payment services. We will cover payment services shortly.

We have covered a lot of details regarding the invoice features in Xero. Let's step back and look at the **Invoices** screen. From the main **Invoices** screen, you can see the familiar Xero tabular menu interface. You can see and search for invoices in different statuses, from new to repeating. Clicking on the status will filter the invoices and only show those within those statuses. You can also see whether an invoice has been sent or viewed in the **Sent** column.

Figure 7.23: The Invoices main status screen

You can filter further by clicking the **Search** button, which brings up the search dialog box.

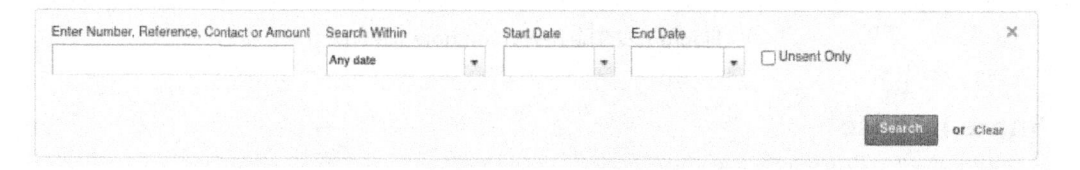

Figure 7.24: The invoice search dialog box

In the search box, you can enter a contact or amount, a date range, or both. Click **Search**, and you will see the results.

The one feature I do want to point out is on the **Awaiting Payment** tab – the **Expected Date** column. You can click the + sign there and the **Notes** dialog will open. This allows you to enter notes about the collection of this invoice and the date on which the customer is expected to pay. This will update the cash flow features in Xero to give a better indication of the positive cash flow from this transaction.

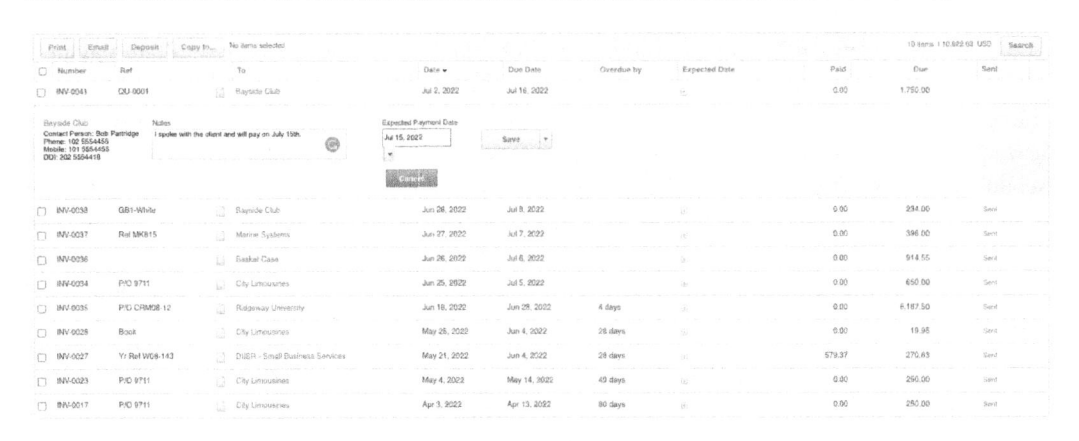

Figure 7.25: The invoice expected date dialog

Now that we have created the invoices, let's get them paid.

Getting paid in Xero

Invoicing is half the battle. Now, you have to get the customer to pay your invoice. Making it easy for the client to pay your invoice will ensure you get paid faster. Xero has payment services that are super easy to set up to aid your cash flow and get paid quicker.

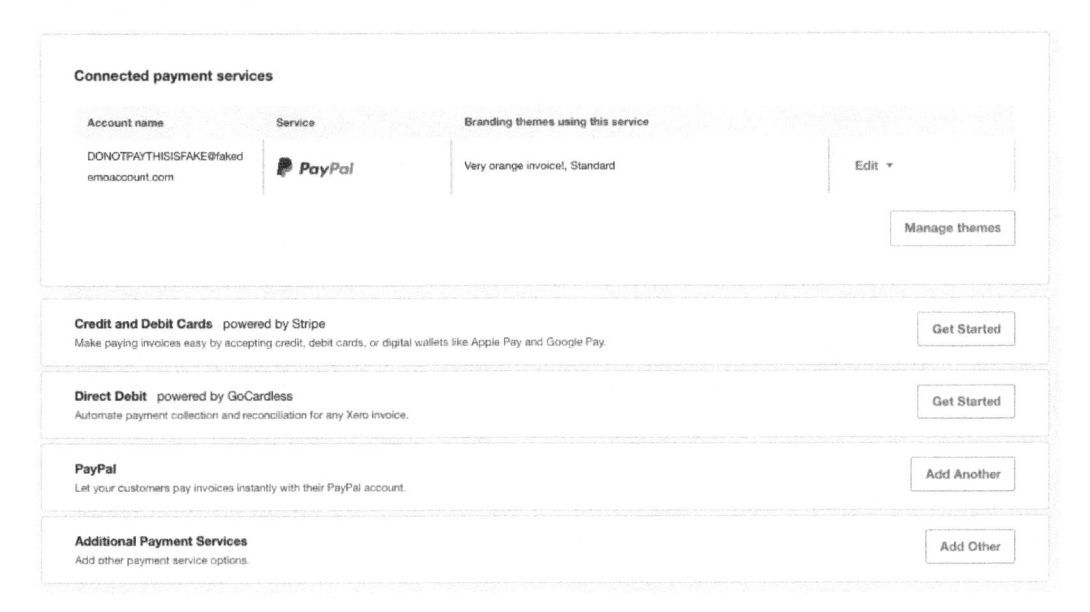

Figure 7.26: Xero payment services

You can select from PayPal, Stripe, and GoCardless, as they are the currently built-in payment solutions. Each of these solutions will allow you to add a **Pay Now** button to your invoice, and once the customer pays the invoice, the built-in automation will apply the payment to the correct place, leaving the deposit to be reconciled to the chosen bank account. These are fairly straightforward to set up. The other option, **Additional Payment Services**, allows you to use your payment gateway, even though it is not directly built into Xero, to accept payment directly from the invoice. I used this extensively when I started using Xero back in 2012, and it is robust, but it takes a little elbow grease to set up. Follow the instructions from Xero Central and the gateway you are using, and you will not have any issues.

When it comes to applying payments received from your customer that were not automated, it is also simple. There are a number of ways to do this, depending on how you create your bank deposits. You could do it directly from the bank feed or invoice by invoice.

Applying payments from the bank feed

Remember when we used the find and match tool back in *Chapter 6*? We are going to use that now:

1. First, we will use the deposit slip, which indicates who paid and how much. In this case, we made a deposit of $6,187.50. It was a single check from Ridgeway University.

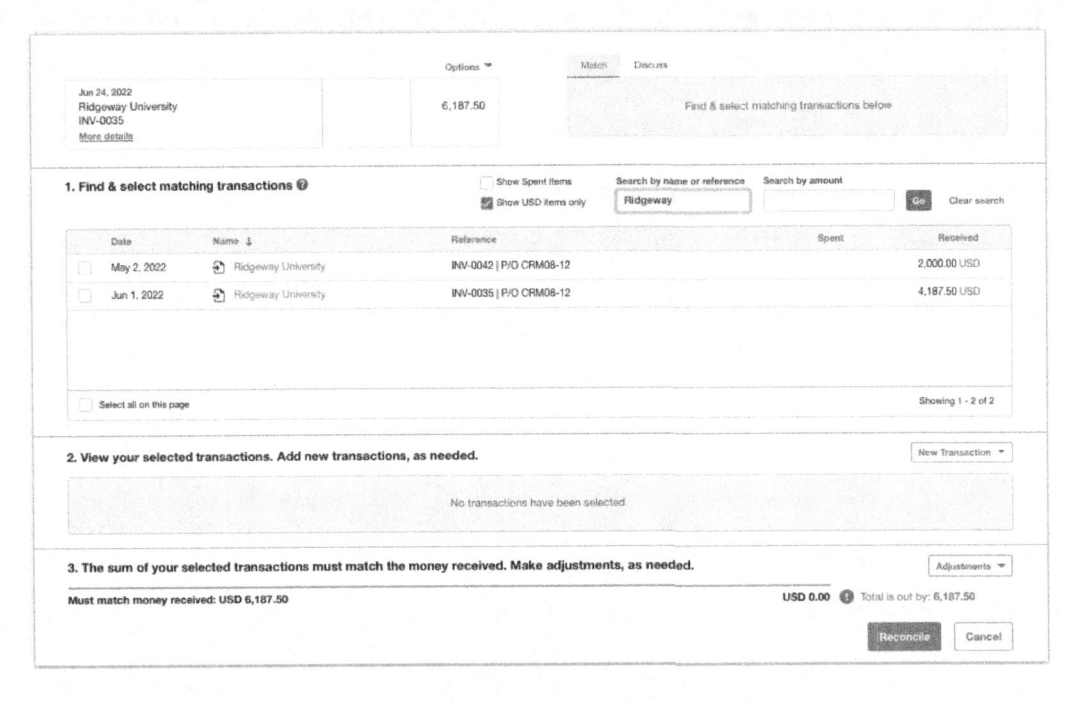

Figure 7.27: The find and match dialog

2. To make it easy, you enter part of the customer's name, `Ridegway`, and you get a search result, showing open invoices that match the search. In this case, it has both of these invoices, as shown in the preceding screenshot. Note the single arrow, which indicates unpaid invoices. We select the two invoices, and now the transaction is *greenlit*.

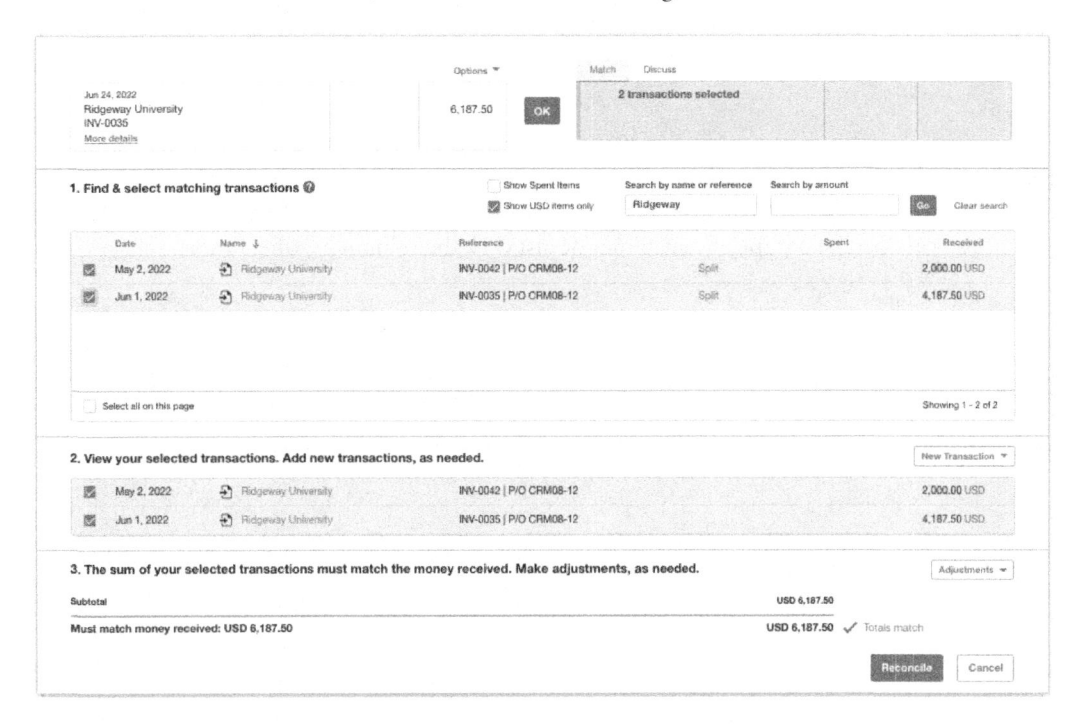

Figure 7.28: The find and matched dialog

3. Now that we have the correct matches and the green highlighted boxes, as seen in *Figure 7.28*, we can click **Reconcile** or **OK**. When we click **Reconcile**, Xero will mark these invoices as paid.

4. The alternative method is to go into each transaction and enter the payment details.

Figure 7.29: The invoice payment dialog

5. Once you click **Add Payment**, Xero marks this invoice as paid. Note in the find and match dialog that the invoice icon shows double arrows, which indicates a payment and not just the invoice.

106   Invoicing and the Sales Process

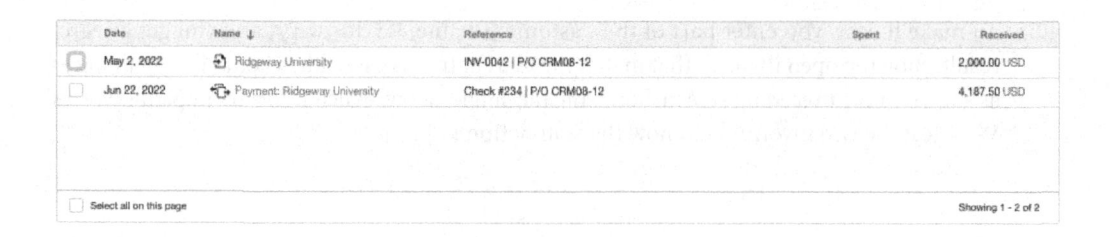

Figure 7.30: The invoice payment icon

6. There is actually a third method to apply payments in bulk, using the **Awaiting Payment** screen. You can search for a specific customer or just click the column heading to sort.

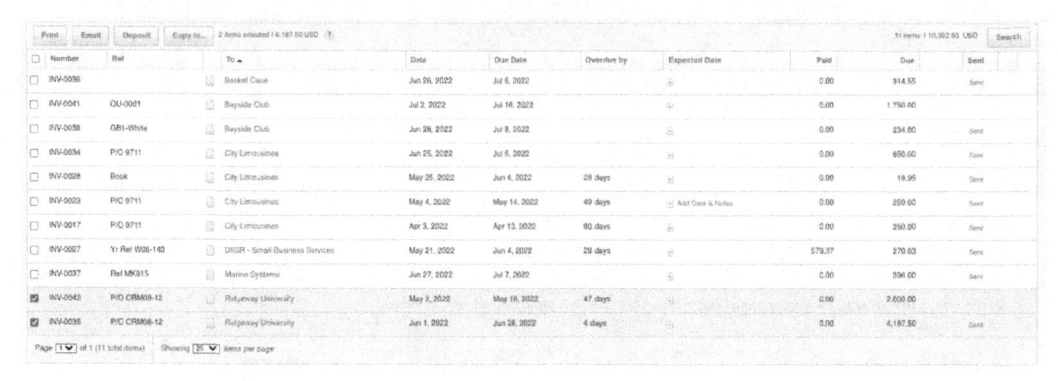

Figure 7.31: Invoices awaiting payment

7. Select the invoices you want to mark as paid; you will want to do this again by using the deposit slip and matching the invoices paid to the payments. Once you have checked the box to the left, you have selected the invoices to be marked as paid, click the **Deposit** button at the top, as seen in *Figure 7.31*.

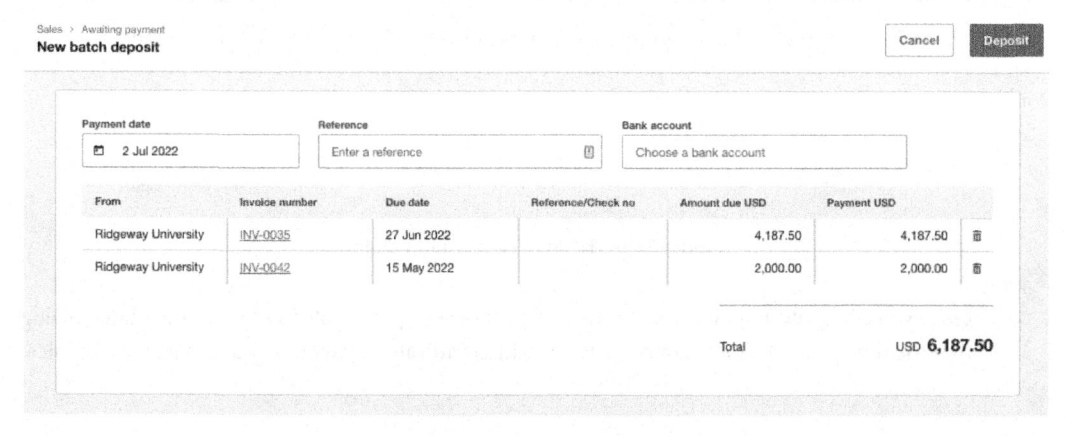

Figure 7.32: New batch deposit

8. Enter the payment date in the **Payment date** box, enter a reference if you do not already have one, enter the deposit date, and choose the bank account you want this payment applied to. Click the **Deposit** button.

Your payments are made, and you are ready to reconcile the bank transactions.

This completes the quote-to-payment process. There was a lot of detail there, but as you begin to use the process, it will become second nature.

Summary

We covered the quote-to-payment process in this chapter, along with products, services, and the setup process to make day-to-day operations in Xero simple and easy. As covered in the chapter, products and services help you stay consistent and make for easy data entry with forms. The invoice and form setup allows you to set up your forms the way you want them to look, with information relevant to your business. Xero makes it super easy to create quotes, convert them into invoices, create new one-time or repeating invoices, and apply payments to these invoices.

If you bill your customers, you will be well prepared for the next Xero topic. We will see you in the next chapter.

8
Managing Bills and Purchases with Procure-to-Pay in Xero

Just as businesses need income to survive, they also need to purchase goods and services! Every business owner must manage bills and payments, along with the associated cash flow. As we saw in the last chapter, some businesses invoice and some don't; the same goes for managing bills through accounts payable. Here, we will show you how to navigate the procurement-to-pay process in Xero for a business. This will ensure you are firmly on the road to success when dealing with the purchase of goods and services, from the Purchase Order stage, all the way through accounts payable, to the eventual payment of the invoice.

In this chapter, we're going to cover the following main topics:

- Exploring the Purchase Order
- Processing accounts payable invoices
- Paying the invoices

By the end of this chapter, you will be able to create a Purchase Order, receive it, convert it to a bill, and pay it. This will allow you to go through the entire procurement-to-pay cycle in Xero.

Exploring the Purchase Order

Just as we discussed in the last chapter, you may or may not use or need to use **Purchase Orders** (**POs**). If you run a cash-based business and just pay all your bills directly, you probably do not need to use a PO or process **Accounts Payable** (**AP**) invoices. The PO, when submitted to a supplier or vendor, is your commitment to purchase a specified good for service at the specified price. You can indicate terms for payment as well, and if the supplier accepts the PO, they have committed to providing the goods or service at the requested price and terms.

By using the PO in Xero, you are using the system, and the items within it, to maintain consistency throughout Xero and your general ledger, as well as adding a level of tracking and approvals for your purchasing.

Let's dive into the *PO* feature in Xero:

1. Let's start by clicking on **Business** in the main menu, followed by **Purchase orders** from the drop-down menu.

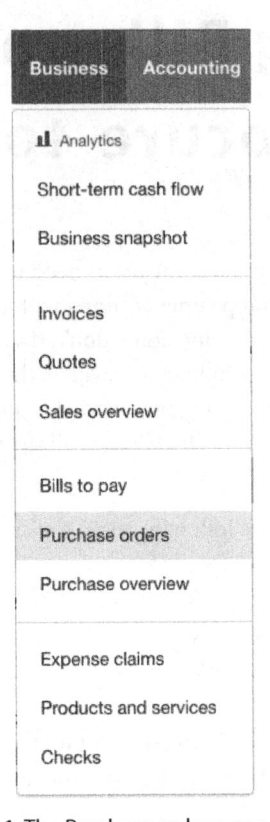

Figure 8.1: The Purchase orders menu option

2. Once on the **Purchase orders** main screen, you will see the familiar tab-focused Xero user experience. On this screen, you can create a new PO and see all POs, including POs in the following statuses (as shown in *Figure 8.2*), based on the tab you select:

    - **Draft**
    - **Awaiting Approval**
    - **Approved**
    - **Billed**

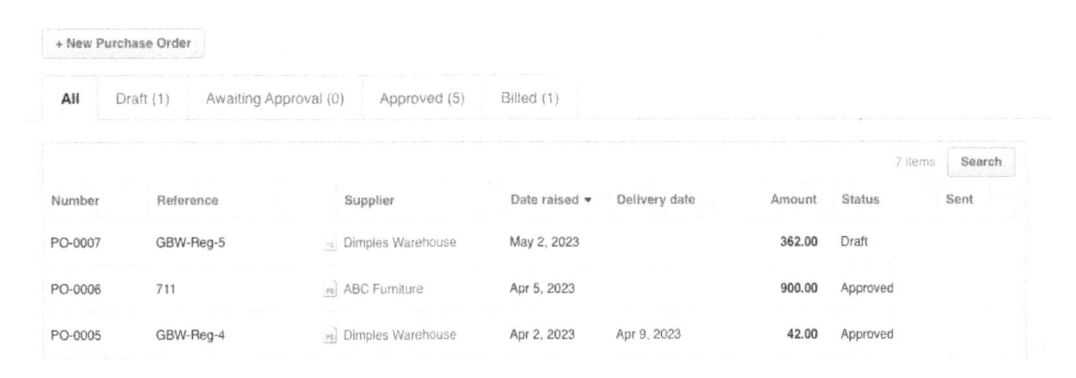

Figure 8.2: The Purchase orders main screen

3. We are going to click on the **New Purchase Order** button (as shown in *Figure 8.2*) and start the purchase process.

    As we saw in the last chapter, the transaction screen has a similar look to the quote, invoice, and bill screens. Again, there may be a field or two specific to the form, but the look, feel, and functions are very similar.

4. As you can see from *Figure 8.3*, we enter the contact details, the date of the PO, the expected delivery date, and the item details, including quantity and price.

Figure 8.3: The PO creation screen

5. You can choose a specific address at the bottom of the PO to specify the delivery, and should you have instructions for the delivery, you can add them in the **Delivery Instructions** box. Should you want to add any documents or pictures to the PO, you can do so by clicking **attach files** and choosing the files you want to attach for the supplier's use.

6. When you are satisfied with your PO, click **Approve**.

   This is what you will see:

   Approved

Contact	Date	Order number	Theme
Bayside Wholesale	Apr 19, 2023	PO-0008	Standard
Phone: 850 5556900			

   Add Address

   No tax

Item	Description	Quantity	Unit price	Disc %	Account	Tax rate	Region	Amount USD
GB1-White	Golf balls - white single. Wholesale catalog item #020812-1	1.00	4.20		500 - Cost of Goods Sold	Tax Exempt (0%)		4.20
GB3-White	Golf balls - white 3 pack. Wholesale catalog item #020812-3	1.00	12.00		500 - Cost of Goods Sold	Tax Exempt (0%)		12.00

Subtotal	16.20
Total No Tax 0%	0.00
Total	**16.20**

   Delivery details

Delivery Address	Attention	Instructions
23 Main Street		
Central City		
Oaktown	Telephone	
NY	800 1234 5678	
12123		
USA		

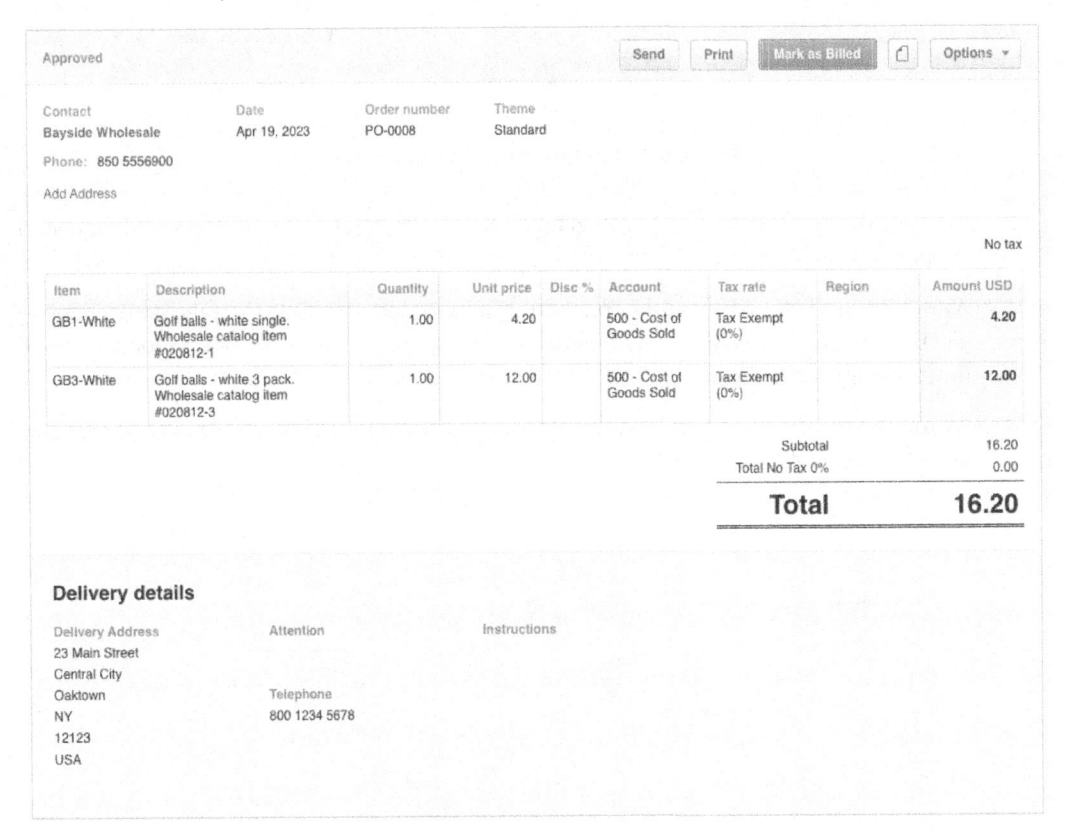

   Figure 8.4: The Approved PO screen

7. When you are ready to send the PO, click on **Send** at the top of the screen. A **Send Purchase Order** box will open, showing the email address and the details of the email going to your customer. All the details in the email can be customized in **Email settings**.

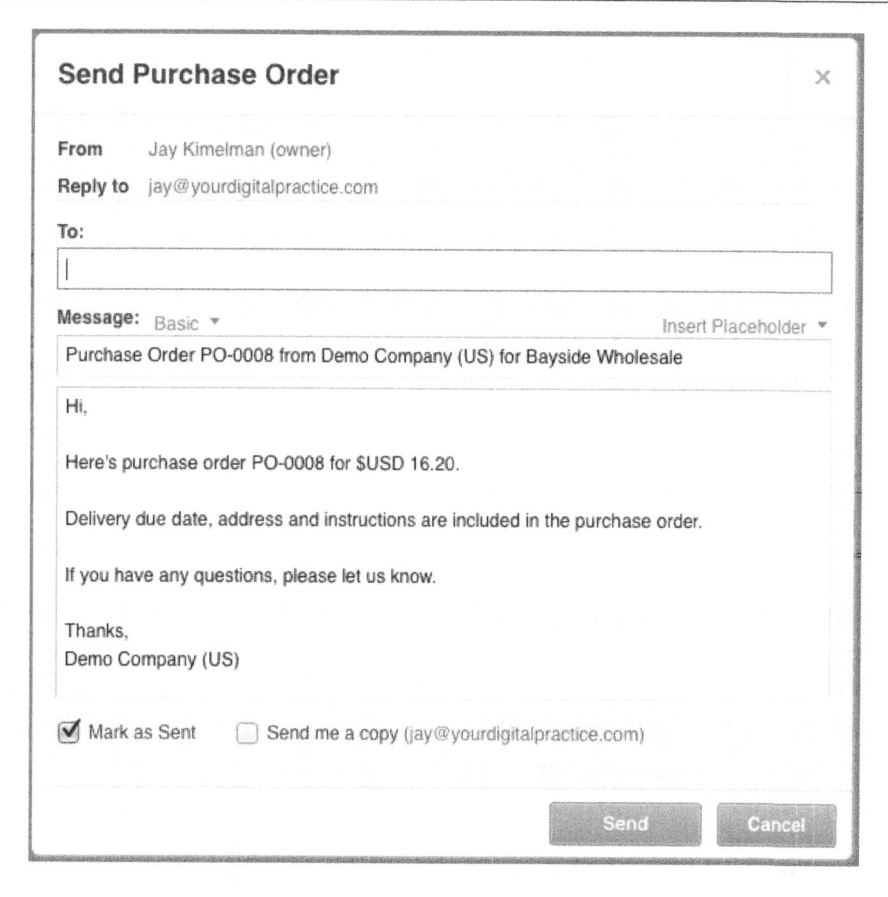

Figure 8.5: The Send Purchase Order screen

8. Once the invoice arrives for your PO, you can click the green **Mark as Billed** button (as shown in *Figure 8.4*). Then, you will see the following screen:

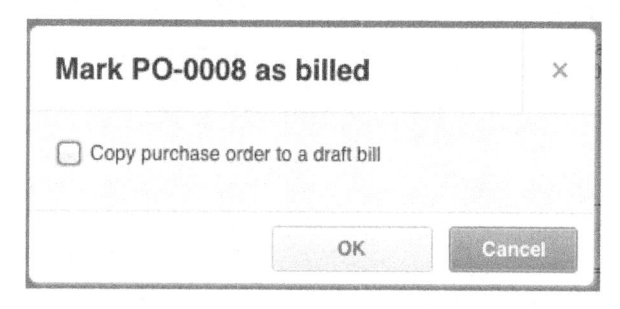

Figure 8.6: The mark as billed PO screen

9. Now, click on the checkbox to the left of **Copy purchase order to a draft bill** to accomplish just that.

Figure 8.7: The draft bill screen

The details of the PO, including the Purchase Order number, are entered into the draft bill. You can approve the bill if it meets all of your requirements. This is accomplished by clicking on the green **Approve** button. Make sure the details of the PO match the invoice. You may need to update the information in the converted bill to match the invoice received from the supplier.

Now that we have completed creating, approving, and sending a bill for a PO, we will look at processing accounts payable bills.

Processing bills and the purchase process

In the last section, we created a PO to begin the procure-to-pay process. In this section, we will dig a bit deeper into the billing process.

Let's look at the bill that was created in the previous section. You can see it in *Figure 8.8*, and it is in the **Awaiting Payment** status.

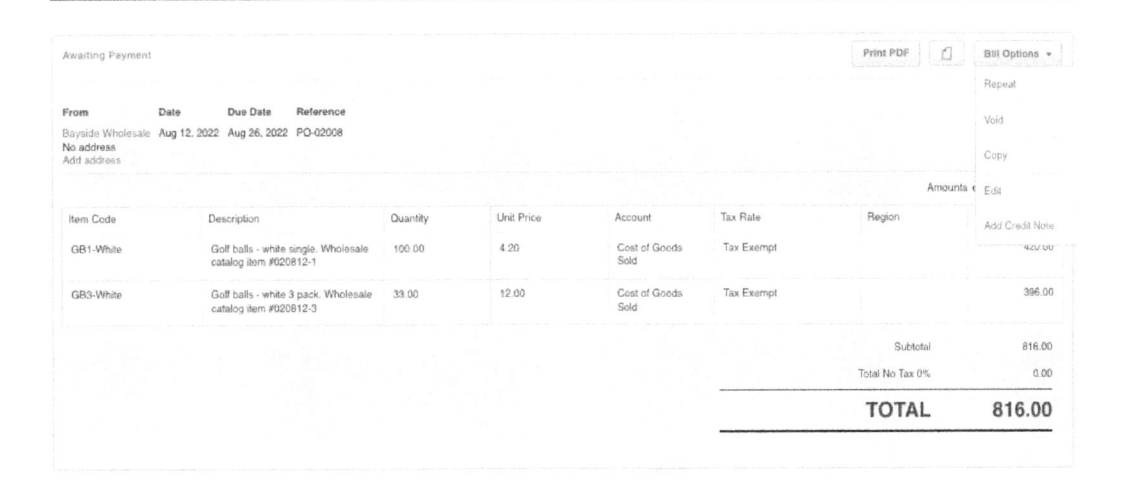

Figure 8.8: The bill options

By clicking on the **Bill Options** button, we can do either of the following:

- Generate a repeating bill
- Void the current bill
- Copy the current bill to a new bill
- Edit the current bill
- Add a credit note

The preceding processes are exactly the same as those we covered in the last chapter for invoices. I suggest you go back to the last chapter to review how those processes are applied, use the same exact steps, and apply them to the bill instead of the invoice.

You have been reading about the similarities of the bill features to the invoice features in Xero. The same can be said of the purchase overview. From the main **Purchases** screen, the familiar Xero tabular menu interface is shown. You can see and search for bills in different statuses, from **All** to **repeating**. Clicking on a status will filter the bills and show only those with that status.

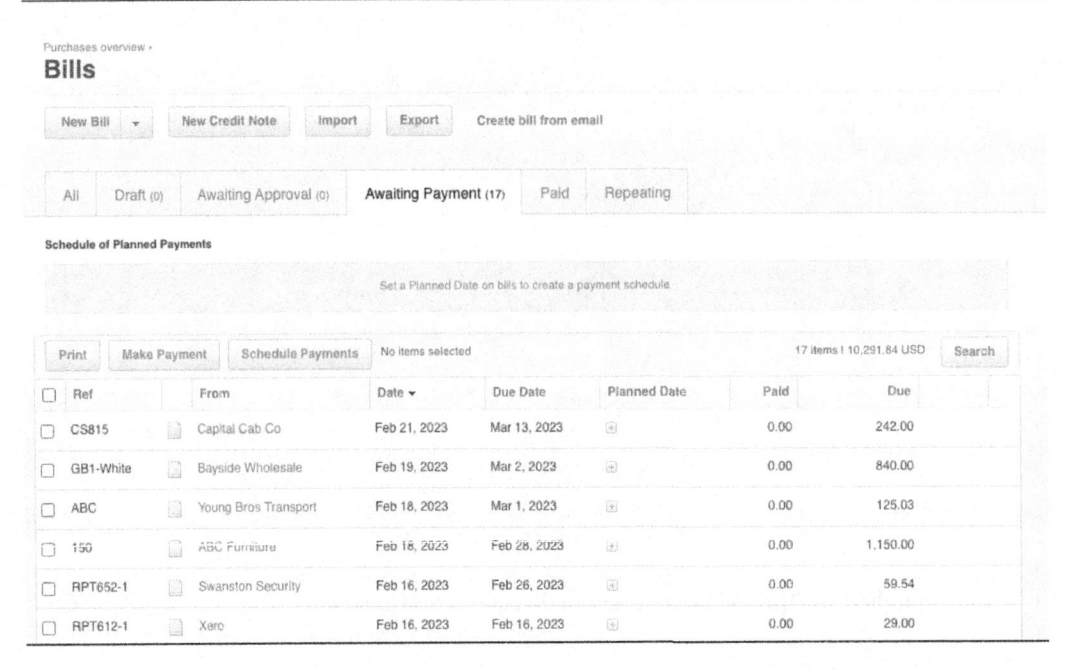

116   Managing Bills and Purchases with Procure-to-Pay in Xero

Figure 8.9: The Bills status screen

As you can see at the top of the status screen, you can create a new bill, a new repeating bill, and a credit note. You can also click **Create bill from email** to provide an email address so that you can submit invoices to your Xero company, and Xero will automatically create a draft bill, as shown in *Figure 8.10*.

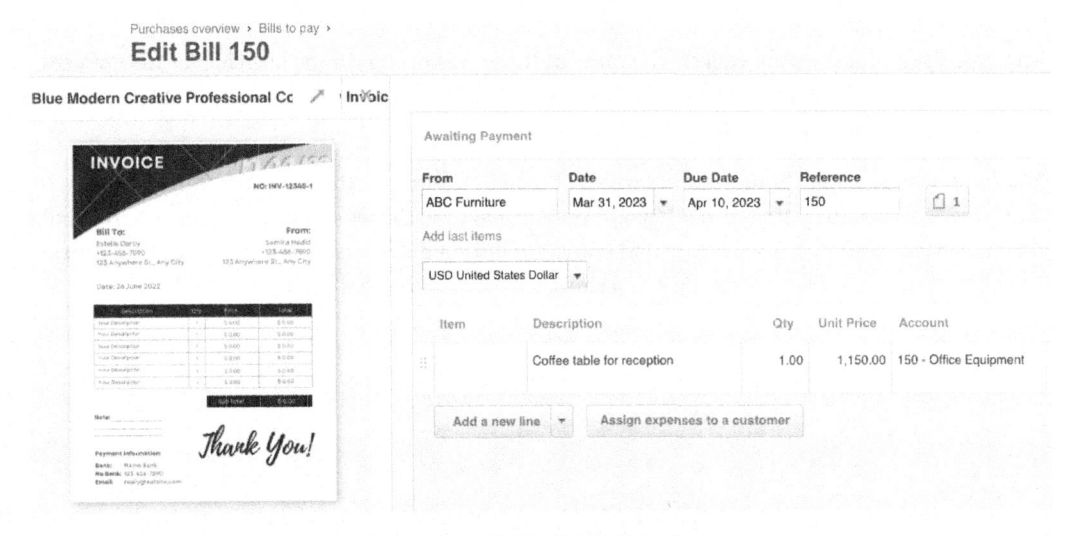

Figure 8.10: The draft bill dialog box

Some details have been added, but you will need to fill in the missing details, such as the contact and the account code. The best part, though, is that a PDF of the bill is attached to the invoice.

We have skirted around the bill creation process, and as you can see, it is indeed the same process as creating an invoice on the sales side, except you are entering a supplier contact and not a sales contact.

You can filter further by clicking the **Search** button, which brings up the search dialog box.

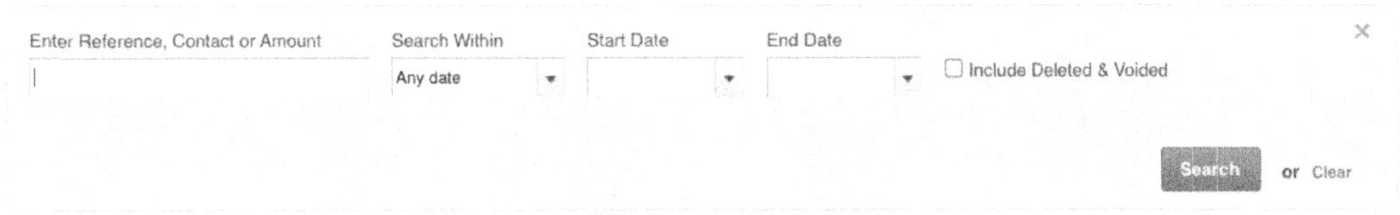

Figure 8.11: The bill search dialog box

In the search box, you can enter a contact or amount, a date range, or both. Click **Search**, and you will see the results.

The one feature I do want to point out is on the **Awaiting Payment** tab, as shown in *Figure 8.12*.

Note the **Planned Date** column. If you click on the + sign, a calendar popup will open. This allows you to enter the date you expect to pay this bill to a vendor. This will update the cash flow features in Xero to give a better indication of the positive cash flow from this transaction. It will also assist in the payment of the bills you have indicated, by creating an additional filter.

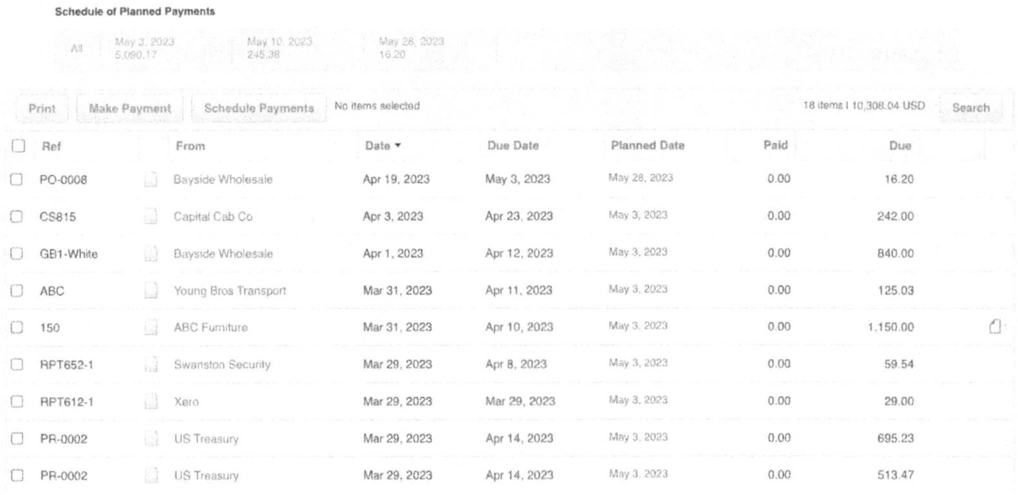

Figure 8.12: The Planned Date column

Now that we have created the bills, it is time to get them paid.

Paying bills is super easy

Paying bills in Xero is easy, whether you are using an app, writing a check, or using your credit card. Let's face it – how many of us actually write checks these days? I see it happening less and less.

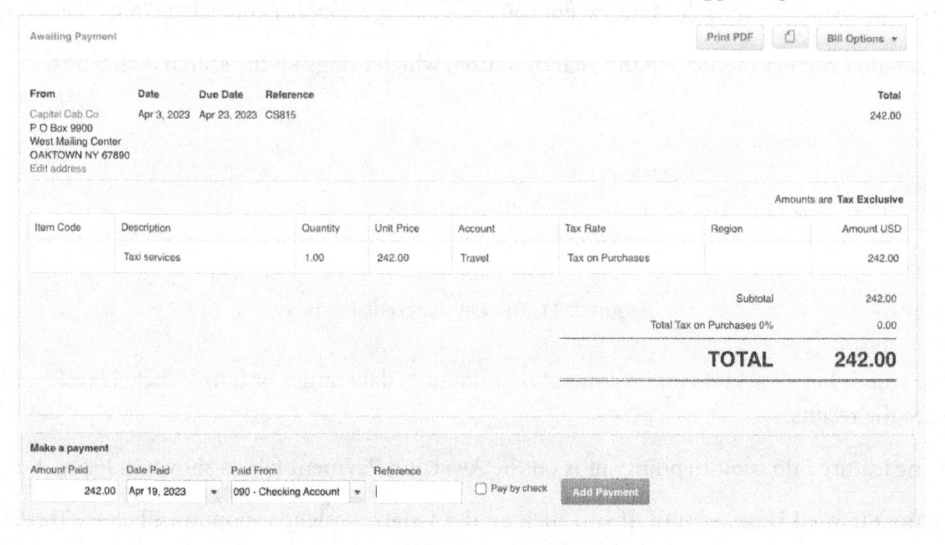

Figure 8.13: The bill payment screen

The quick way to mark a bill as paid in Xero is to go directly from the bill screen. At the bottom of the screen, you will fill in the following fields:

- **Amount Paid**
- **Date Paid**
- **Paid From**

If you are planning on writing a check, ensure you mark the **Pay by check** checkbox, and then click **Add Payment**. You can see all this in *Figure 8.13*.

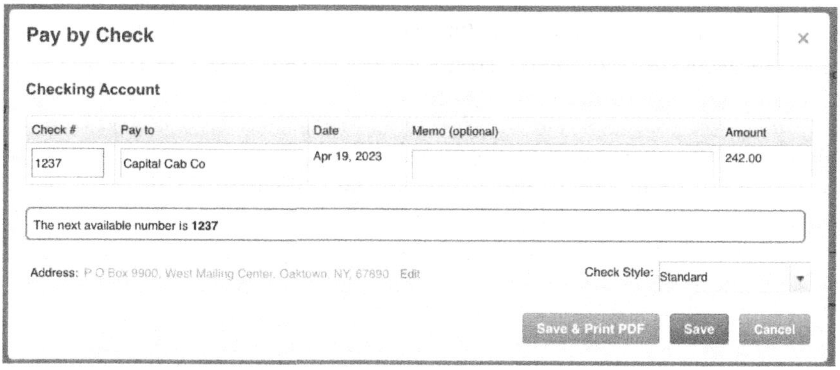

Figure 8.14: The Pay by Check dialog

On the **Pay by Check** screen (*Figure 8.14*), you can enter the check number along with a memo. When completed, click **Save & Print PDF**. If you have a check stock, you can then print the PDF on it. I recommend you use a complete blank check stock and use the **New Check Style** page to set up your checks, as this is the easiest way to have the details appear on your check. Setting up your checks can be accomplished by going to **Check Styles** on the **Settings** menu.

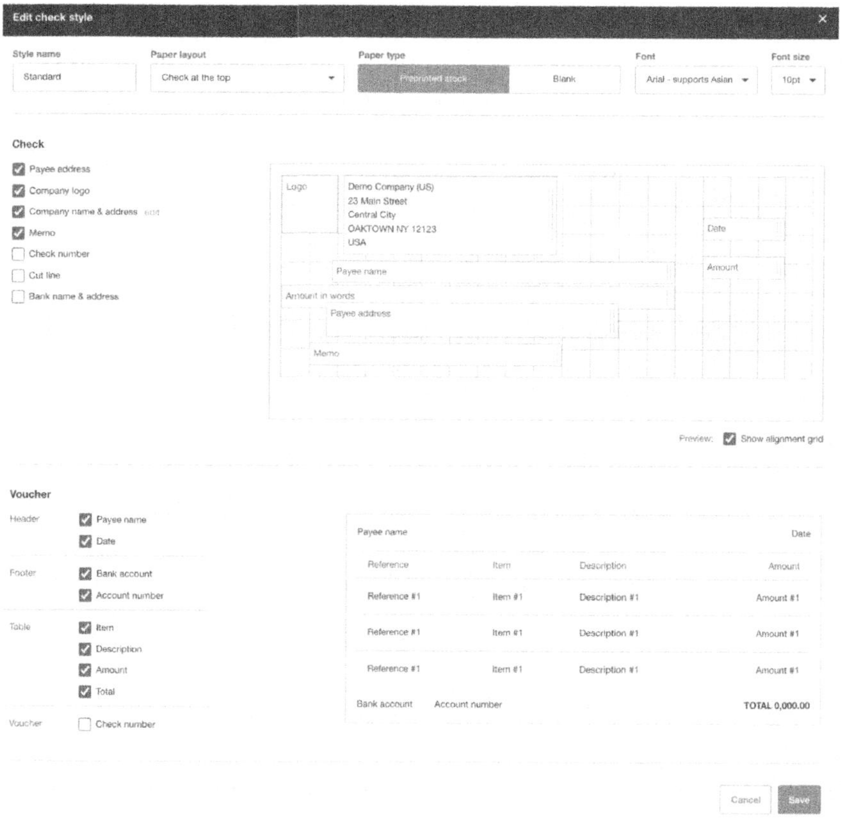

Figure 8.15: The New Check Style setup screen

In *Figure 8.15*, you can see the **New Check Style** screen. Here, you can hide/unhide fields by clicking the box next to the fields, and each field can be moved by drop and drag. From there, it is about testing the fit and making adjustments until it is perfect.

Paying multiple bills is easy as well. From the **Awaiting Payment** tab, you can select individual bills to pay by clicking the box to the left, or you can use the **Planned Payment** dates, click one of the dates at the top of the screen, and then choose all of the bills in the filter.

Figure 8.16: The Schedule of Planned Payments screen

Then, just click the **Make Payment** button (as shown in *Figure 8.16*). You will see the following screen:

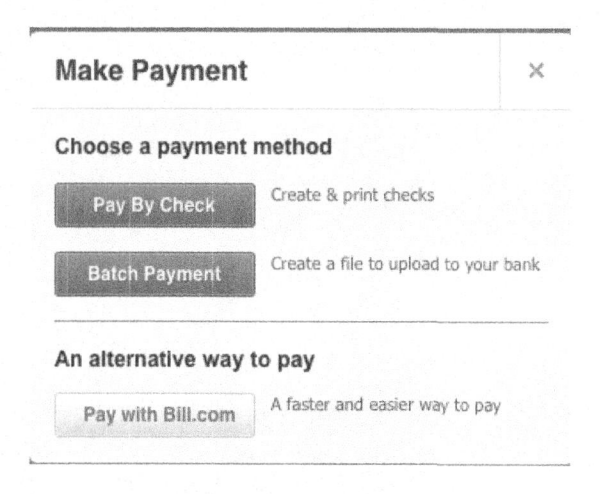

Figure 8.17: The Make Payment screen

To pay by check, click on the **Pay By Check** button and complete the check process, as we did earlier.

To pay by any other means, such as bank checks or credit cards, click on the **Batch Payment** button. This will take you to the **New Batch Payment** screen. The most important thing is to pick the correct bank account from where the funds will be withdrawn. Click **Make Payments** when you are ready.

> **Note**
>
> When paying to an account other than a Xero bank account, such as a clearing account (current asset), ensure that the **Enable payments to this account** box is checked in the chart of accounts for this account.

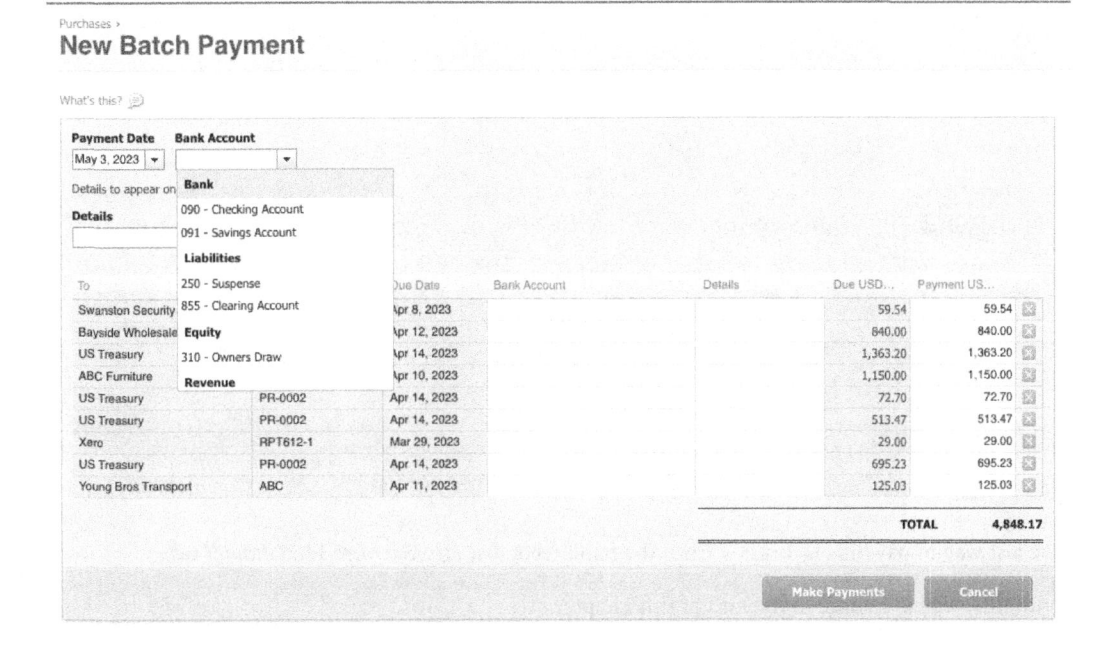

Figure 8.18: The New Batch Payment screen

Once completed, you will get a confirmation screen showing the payments and amounts paid (*Figure 8.19*). You can also create remittance reports from this screen to send to the suppliers. All you need to do is to click the **Send Remittance** button.

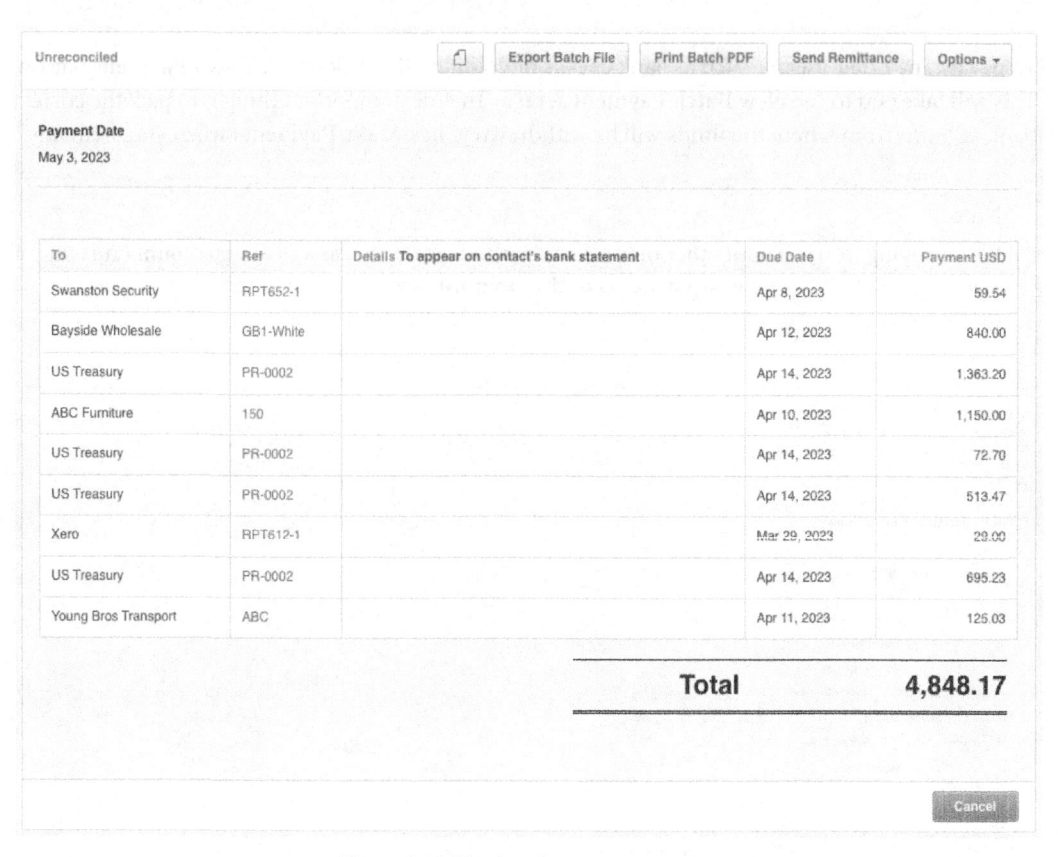

To	Ref	Details To appear on contact's bank statement	Due Date	Payment USD
Swanston Security	RPT652-1		Apr 8, 2023	59.54
Bayside Wholesale	GB1-White		Apr 12, 2023	840.00
US Treasury	PR-0002		Apr 14, 2023	1,363.20
ABC Furniture	150		Apr 10, 2023	1,150.00
US Treasury	PR-0002		Apr 14, 2023	72.70
US Treasury	PR-0002		Apr 14, 2023	513.47
Xero	RPT612-1		Mar 29, 2023	29.00
US Treasury	PR-0002		Apr 14, 2023	695.23
Young Bros Transport	ABC		Apr 11, 2023	125.03
			Total	**4,848.17**

Figure 8.19: The batch payment screen

The last way to pay bills is directly from the bank feed, just as we covered in *Chapter 6*.

With this, we have come to the end of this chapter.

Summary

Wow! We have really covered a lot in this chapter – from creating a PO, approving and sending it, creating a new purchase invoice, and converting from a PO to the scheduling and further payment of bills, via check or other methods. Now, you should have the procure-to-pay process down, and you are ready to run your own business and keep the cash flow going.

In the next chapter, we will make things mobile. We will show you how to use Xero on the go.

9
Using Xero on the Go

Xero is not just a browser-based accounting tool that you use from the comfort of your office or home. You can use the browser on your phone and tablet. I have done that plenty of times, but you can get more usability in the field using the mobile app for your device. We will show you how to do just that throughout the chapter.

In this chapter, we're going to cover the following main topics:

- Using the Xero mobile app and the features available to you
- Creating and sending invoices on your iOS and Android devices
- Reconciling bank transactions on the go with your mobile device

Xero mobile on the go

The Xero Accounting app allows you to do many of the daily tasks you do from behind your desk while you are away from it, using your mobile device. That mobile device may be your iPhone or iPad, or your Android phone or tablet. Irrespective of the type of mobile device used, the mobile app has you covered for the daily tasks you need to do while you are on the go. The iOS and Android apps are very similar, with the same functions or features. The main differences are in how the device operates. We will cover the similarities and differences here as we go through this chapter.

The mobile app is great if you are a business owner or an accountant and you are a road warrior who's always or often traveling. If you have your phone with you, you can reconcile your bank or send that invoice, all without having to pull out your laptop.

A few years back, I had a client tell me how much he loved Xero, especially how he could reconcile his bank account transaction while he drove to work. We paused, and he then clarified – he did it while at stop lights when he wasn't moving. We shared with the client we were glad he was able to be so productive but did warn against distractive driving, and he assured us he would never work on his phone while actually moving in his vehicle.

So that was a win-win.

We previously mentioned reconciling bank transactions in Xero accounting. In the next section, we will dive a little deeper into using the mobile app and the various features available in Xero.

Xero features on the go

The Xero Accounting app contains a dashboard that gives a snapshot of details that every business owner looks for, containing overall bank balances, bills, and so on. With the help of the app, you can convert quotes into invoices, create invoices directly, and then send them to your customers to get paid. You can create purchase bills, edit them, and mark them as paid. And as we said earlier in the chapter, you can even reconcile your bank transactions.

As we go through the rest of this chapter, we are going to highlight how each of the aforementioned features works in the Xero Accounting app.

The mobile dashboard

The dashboard of the Xero Accounting mobile app gives you a quick peek at the numbers you want to know about your business. Starting at the top of the page, you have the **Overall cash balance** section, along with the number of bank accounts you have active in the Xero organization. The bank account section shows the bank accounts, along with some details of the accounts, such as **Balance in Xero** and **Statement balance**.

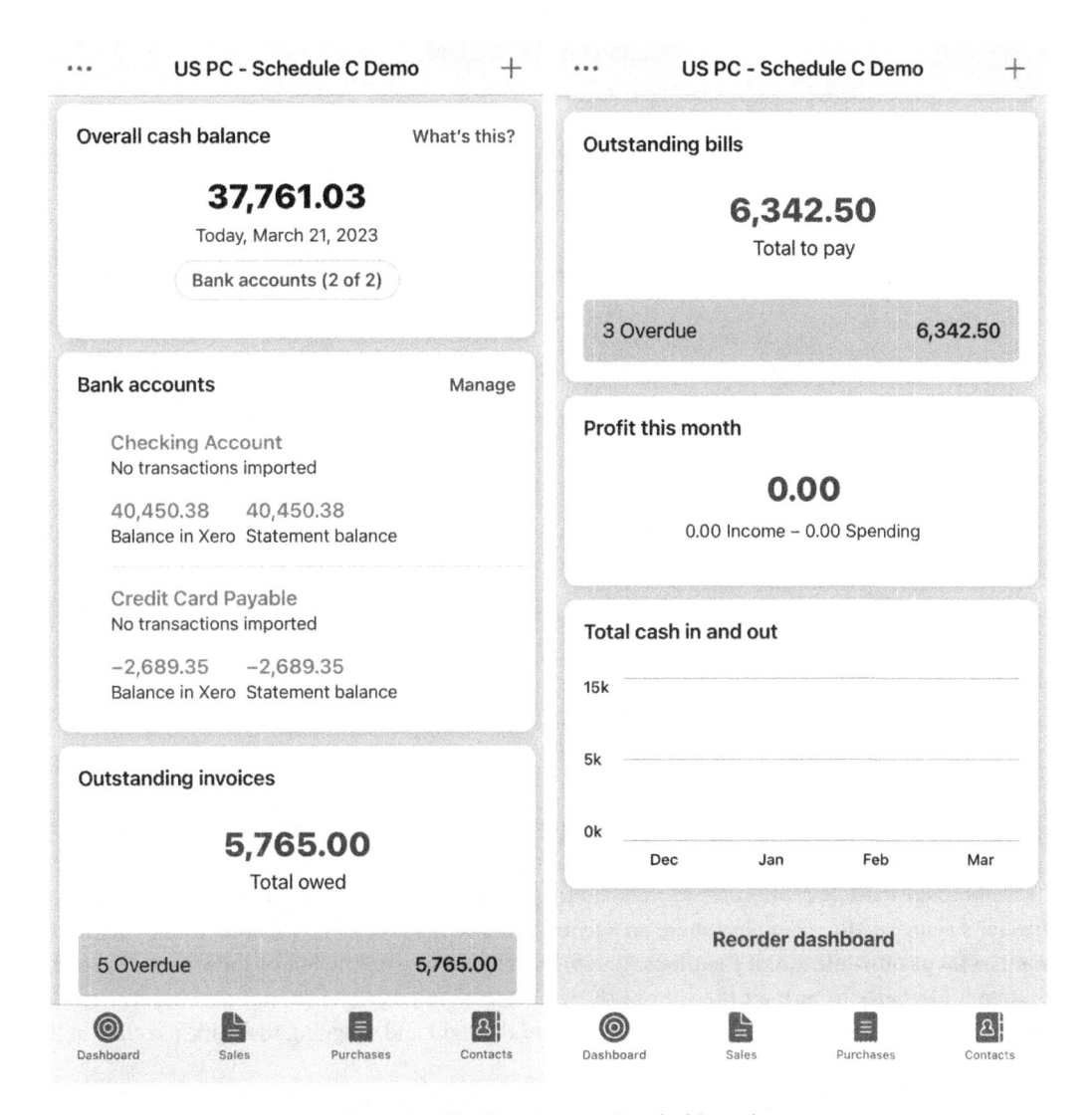

Figure 9.1: The Xero Accounting dashboard

You can click on **Manage** at the top right of the **Bank accounts** section to change what is seen in this section.

| Close | **Manage bank accounts** |

Balances

Choose what you want displayed on your dashboard

Balance in Xero

Statement balance

Balances explained

List order

Hold and drag your bank accounts to choose how they are ordered on your dashboard

Checking Account
987654321

Credit Card Payable
**** **** **** 1234

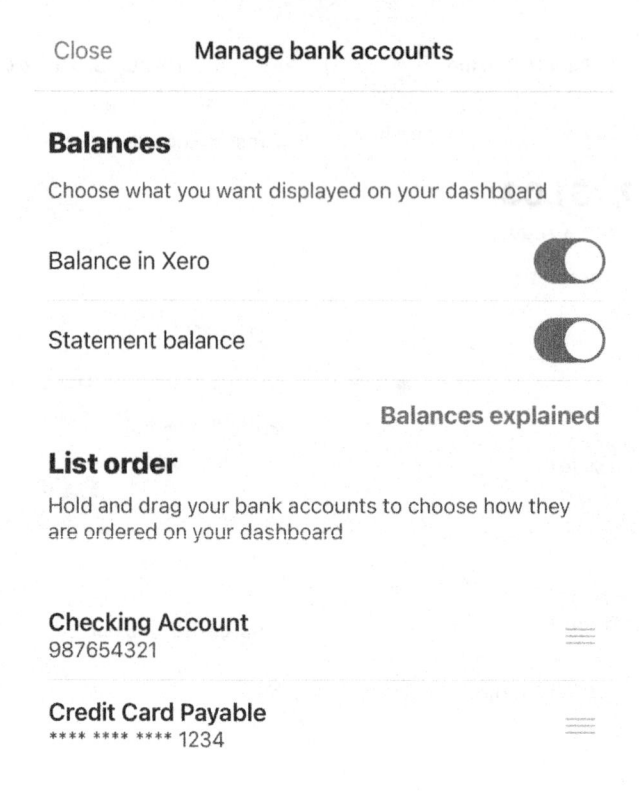

Figure 9.2: Xero Accounting Manage bank account screen

In the **Manage bank accounts** screen, you can toggle off the balance details if you do not wish to see specific balances – for example, where an account may be inactive or is just something you do not want to focus on while out of the office. Just toggle the buttons to the left of **Balance in Xero** and **Statement balance** to turn off the view of those balances. You can also change the display order of the bank accounts by touching the three-line icon to the right and dragging the bank accounts in the order you wish to see on the dashboard.

Click on **Balances explained** to see the Xero definition of the specific balances and for an explanation as to why the **Balance in Xero** and **Statement Balance** balances may be different. Click the **Close** button to close this screen, and then click **Close** at the top of the screen to close the **Manage bank accounts** screen. As we go back to the dashboard, we can see the number of unreconciled transactions in each account.

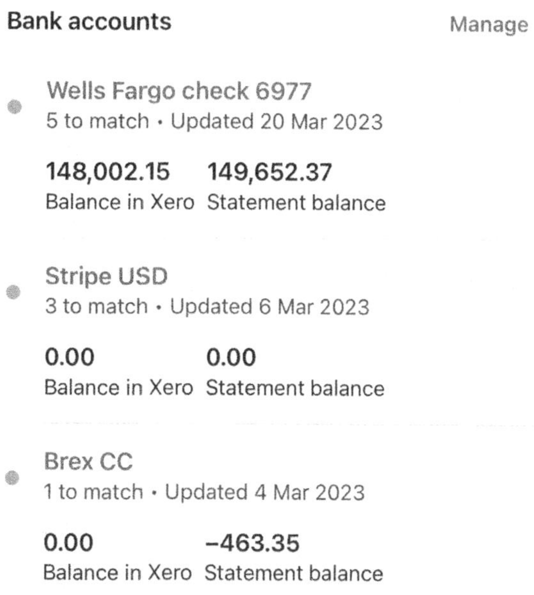

Bank accounts   Manage

- Wells Fargo check 6977
  5 to match • Updated 20 Mar 2023

  148,002.15   **149,652.37**
  Balance in Xero   Statement balance

- Stripe USD
  3 to match • Updated 6 Mar 2023

  0.00   **0.00**
  Balance in Xero   Statement balance

- Brex CC
  1 to match • Updated 4 Mar 2023

  0.00   **−463.35**
  Balance in Xero   Statement balance

Figure 9.3: Bank accounts

As you can see, you can easily view the details of your bank accounts. In the next section, we shall dive into reconciling your bank and credit card accounts on the go.

Xero banking on the go

If we click on the account we wish to view or reconcile – in this case, the Wells Fargo check 6977 account – we can see the details of the transactions. As you can see in the following screenshot, the **STRIPE** deposit to the Wells Fargo account shown in it is clearly a transfer. However, if you wanted to reconcile the transaction some other way, you could drag the screen to the right, as indicated by the two small dots at the bottom of the screen.

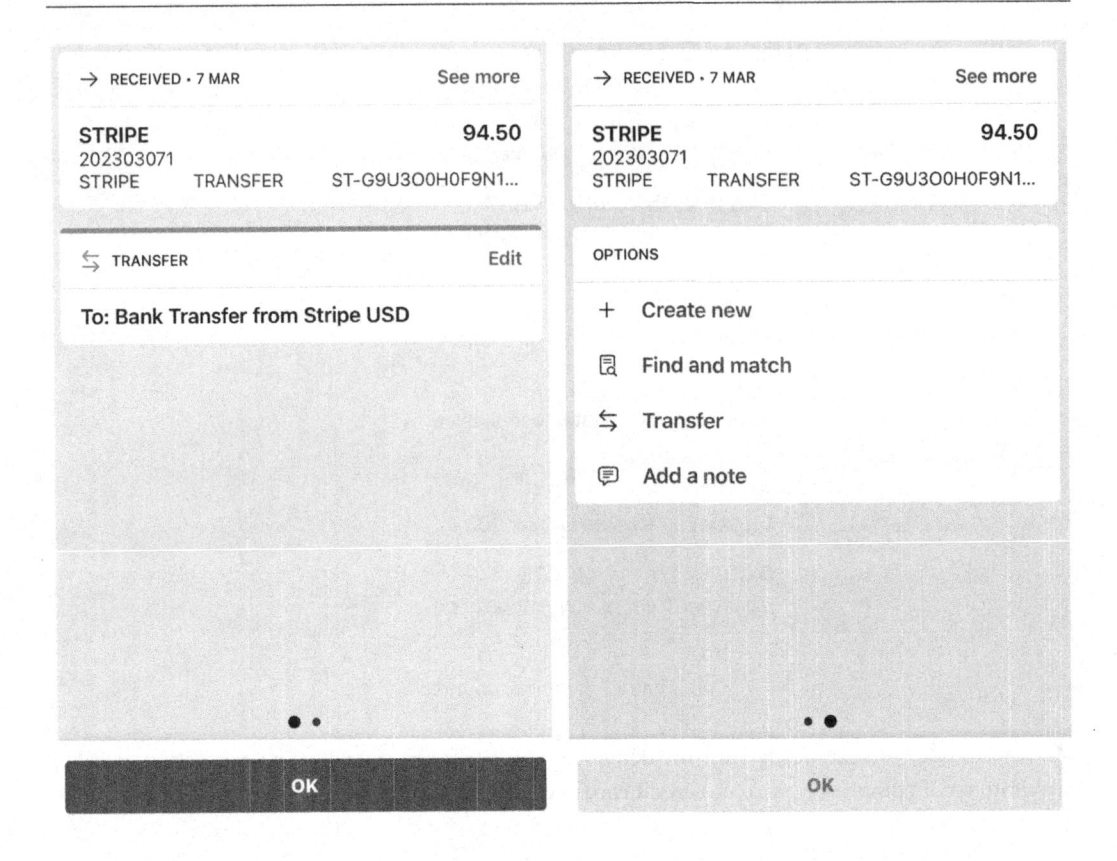

Figure 9.4: Xero Accounting bank reconciliation

Continuing this example, on the **STRIPE** account, to accept the transfer, click the blue **OK** button, as displayed on the left side of *Figure 9.4*. To change the selection, use the right side of the image by sliding your finger to the right, just like we did on the preceding checking account. Here, on the right side of that transaction, you can create a new transaction by clicking + **Create new**, as we discussed in the preceding example. As you can see in *Figure 9.4*, by doing so, you can even match to an existing transaction. Just click the selection and enter the details, just like you do with the banking transactions in the browser. When you click **OK**, the transaction turns green and disappears, bringing up your next transaction. Reconcile until you have reconciled all of your transactions or hit a stopping point.

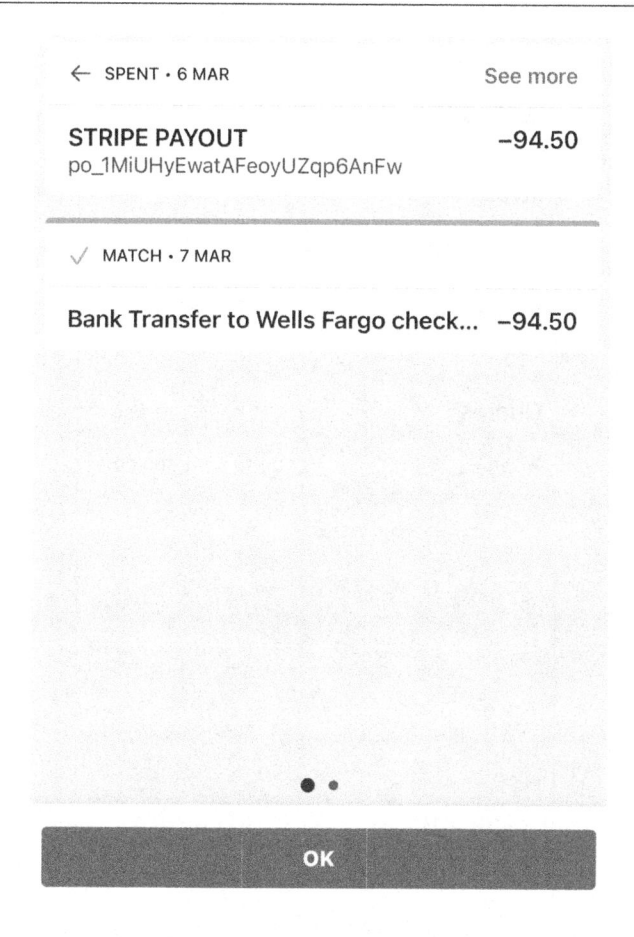

Figure 9.5: Matching a transfer

Let's reconcile transactions in another account. Let's click on the Stripe account from the dashboard. As you can see in *Figure 9.5*, this is the Stripe side of the transfer we recorded in the Wells Fargo account earlier. You can see that Xero has matched it; all you need to do is click **OK**.

That is all there is to banking in the Xero Accounting app. It is super easy and available to you wherever you may need it. Next, we will look at invoicing in the mobile app.

Invoicing on the go

Going back to the main dashboard, the **Sales** dashboard gives you a snapshot of your unpaid invoices and your quotes. You can also see those in the draft status.

Sales

Invoices	See all
• 5 unpaid	5,765.00 >
• 5 overdue	5,765.00 >

Quotes	See all
• 1 sent	1,500.00 >

Dashboard | Sales | Purchases | Contacts

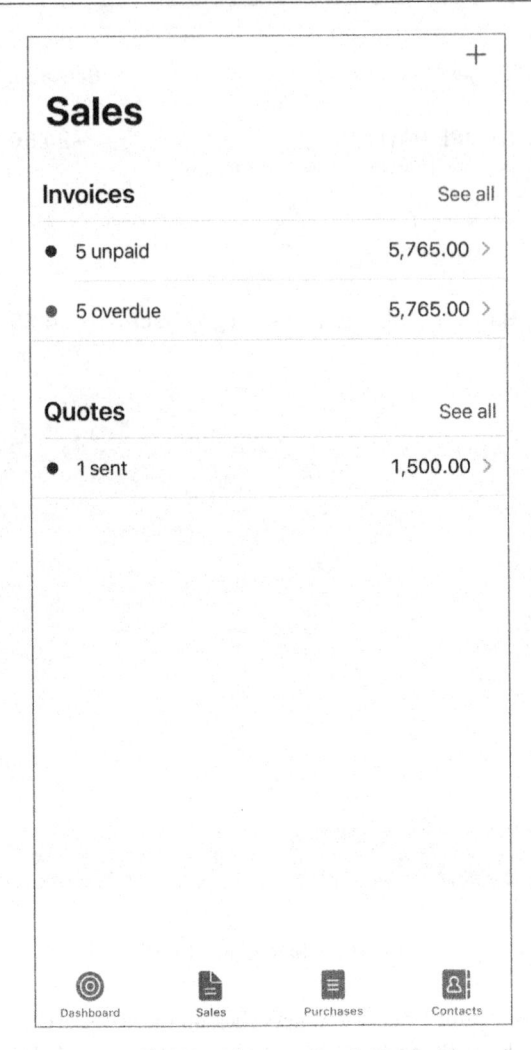

Figure 9.6: The Xero Accounting Sales dashboard

Note the + symbol in the upper-right corner of the sales dashboard; this allows you to create an invoice or quote.

Create Invoice

Create Quote

Cancel

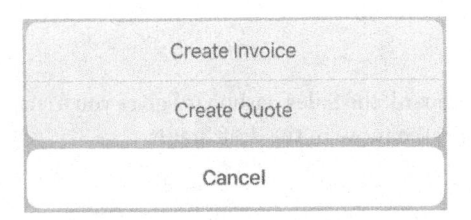

Figure 9.7: Sales dashboard options

The process of creating invoices and quotes via the app is pretty much identical to doing so in the browser. Use the techniques you learned in creating invoices and quotes, and you will find it super easy.

You can see in *Figure 9.6* that there are currently five invoices unpaid, and they are all overdue. You can click the amount to see the invoices.

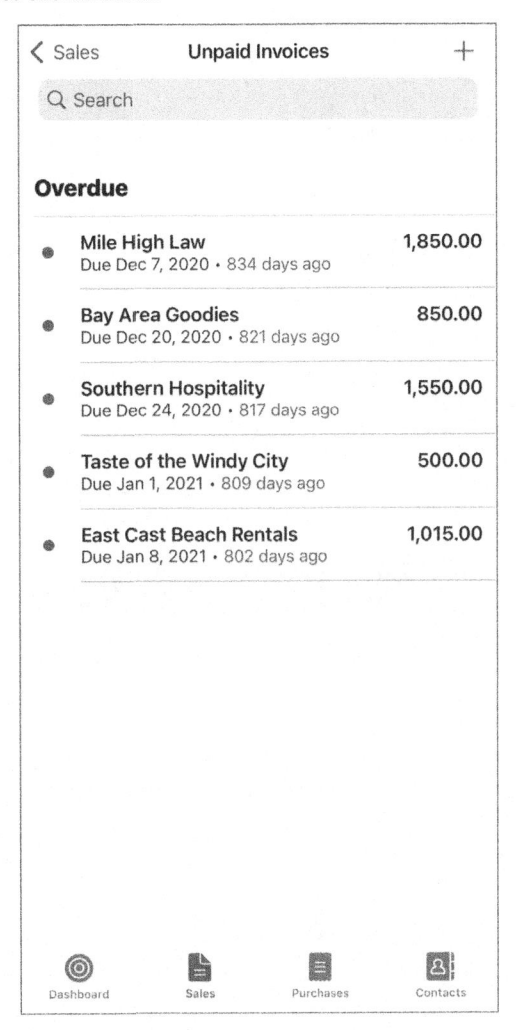

Figure 9.8: Unpaid invoices

132　Using Xero on the Go

You can then click on each invoice to view the details, make changes, add an attachment such as a picture, or even add a payment. However, I would recommend that if you are going to add a payment, do it through the bank reconciliation process we discussed earlier in the chapter.

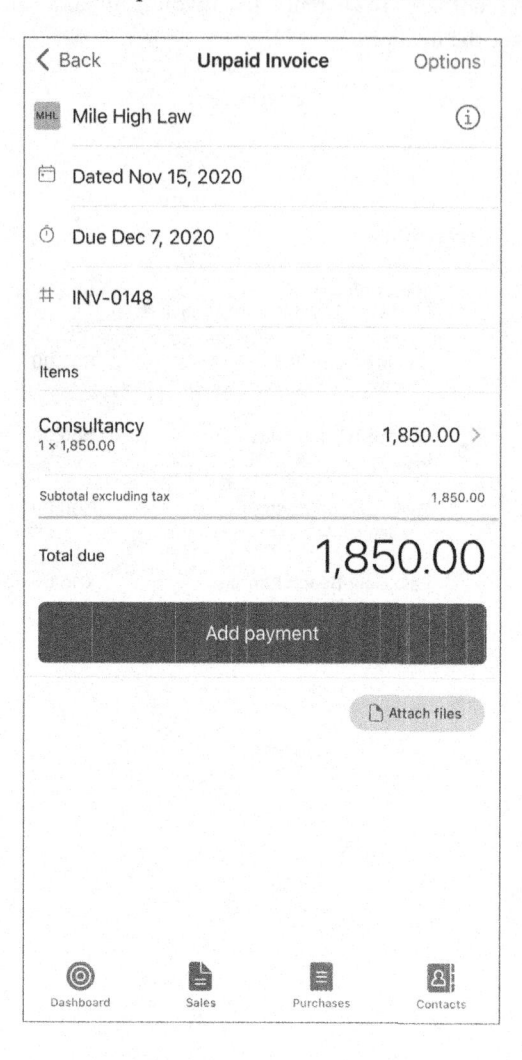

Figure 9.9: Invoice details

In the upper-right-hand corner of the invoice screen, you can see the **Options** button.

This gives you the ability to send, share, get a preview of, edit, copy, and attach files to an invoice.

```
Send

Share

Preview

Edit

Make a Copy

Attach Files

Cancel
```

Figure 9.10: Invoice options

Most of those options are self-explanatory. However, I do want to discuss the send versus share dilemma. The **Send** option will send an email to the email address on the record of the contact, just like it does in the browser. The **Share** option sends a link to the invoice to your messaging app and allows you to text the invoice to the recipient. They are both very good options, although I do find that sharing via text gets the invoice paid faster.

Invoicing on the Xero Accounting app makes it simple and easy to send invoices. This is especially true when you are providing services out in the field and want to provide your customer with an invoice while you are there. This helps to get paid faster.

Payables on the go

The payable feature in the mobile app is just like the invoice feature, and it works just like it does in the browser. The biggest benefit to you is having the ability to process these documents while you are on the go. Just like I said regarding the invoices, I would not mark a bill as paid. I would use the bank reconciliation feature and match the bill to the bank feed transactions.

Figure 9.11: Purchases and Bills

The **Purchases** feature is handy but, in my opinion, not as important as the invoicing feature. The payables can be processed at the desk, and it will not make you pay them faster. Invoicing on the go via the app gives you the ability to deliver the invoice immediately, and the shareability sends a text and almost implies the customer should pay immediately. This is sure to increase your cash flow.

So, we have looked at the features of the mobile app and the efficiencies you will gain. In the next section, we shall look at the differences between iOS and Android apps.

Battle of the apps in different operating systems

For the most part, the features of the iOS app and the Android app are very similar. The differences come into play in how the apps work with the operating system. You saw earlier that when we clicked an option or the + menu in the iOS app, the menus appeared at the bottom (see *Figure 9.7* and *Figure 9.11*). On Android, the menus come down from the top.

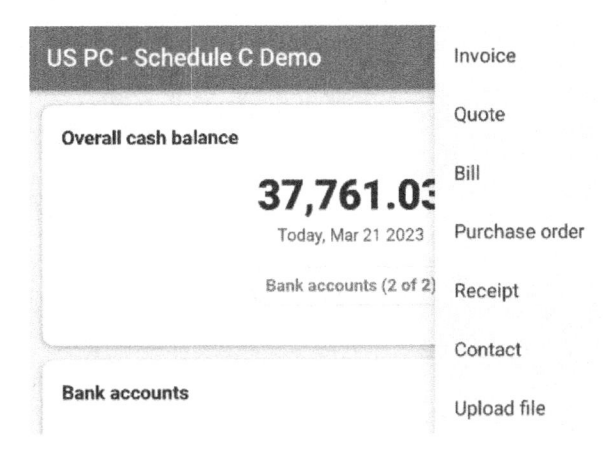

Figure 9.12: The Android menu system

Again, the features are the same; it is just how the operating system interacts with the app.

Having used both the Android and iOS apps for the purpose of writing this chapter, I can say that there really is no loser in this battle. They both work super well, and again, it comes down to the device you are using in your everyday life.

Summary

As you can see, the Xero mobile app is an easy tool to learn and use. It comes in handy when you are traveling or working in the field and you want to be able to see your stats at a glance, send an invoice to get paid, or even reconcile your bank accounts. And whether you use an Apple device or an Android, your Xero needs will be well taken care of.

In the next chapter, we will look at the Fixed Asset management system in Xero.

Part 3: Closing Out the Accounting Period

The objective of this section is to familiarize you with some of the more advanced topics and features on closing out accounting periods on the platforms.

This section comprises the following chapters:

- *Chapter 10, Managing Fixed Assets in Xero*
- *Chapter 11, All You Need to Know About Manual Journals in Xero*
- *Chapter 12, Correct Your Mistakes with Find and Recode*

10
Managing Fixed Assets in Xero

Businesses purchase goods and equipment every day. The majority of these purchases are regular expenses and are handled as shown in previous chapters throughout the book. Then, there are capital assets, or what we will refer to as **fixed assets**. These assets generally have a useful life of over 1 year and cost $2,500 or more. Here, we will show you how to handle the fixed asset process in Xero for a business, which includes the addition and disposal of assets as well as running depreciation. The understanding of the processing of assets, as well as the topics of bank transactions and bills, which we covered in previous chapters of this book, ensure that you have the knowledge to handle all of a business's expenditures.

In this chapter, we're going to cover the following main topics:

- Adding new assets
- Processing depreciation
- Disposal of assets

Let's begin the journey by taking an in-depth look at fixed assets.

Exploring fixed assets

What exactly is a fixed asset, you ask? Whether called a **capital asset**, **long-term asset**, **fixed asset**, or something else, it is a tangible item with a useful life of over a year. This would include items such as buildings, land, computers, production machinery, furniture, and vehicles.

The **Internal Revenue Service (IRS)** rules, effective from January 1, 2016, set the *de minimis* safe harbor, an administrative convenience, at $2,500 per invoice or item. What that means is that expenses under $2,500 are considered **expenses** and those over $2,500 are to be capitalized and treated as **fixed assets**.

Let's jump into Xero and learn how to handle fixed assets. Start by clicking on **Accounting** to activate the menu and then choosing **Fixed assets**:

Managing Fixed Assets in Xero

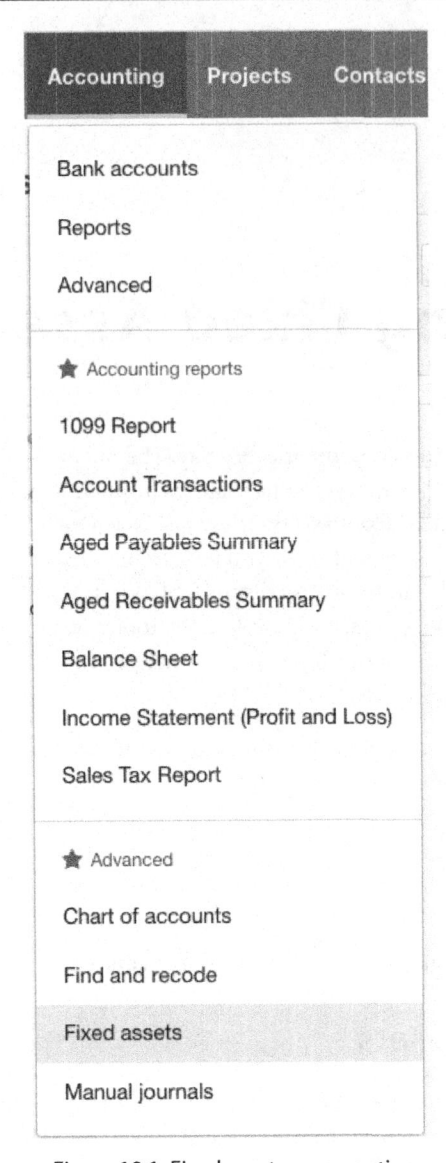

Figure 10.1: Fixed assets menu option

This takes you to the main **Fixed assets** screen. It has the familiar Xero look with menu buttons at the top and the tabs (**Draft**, **Registered**, and **Sold & Disposed**) for each page below.

Fixed assets

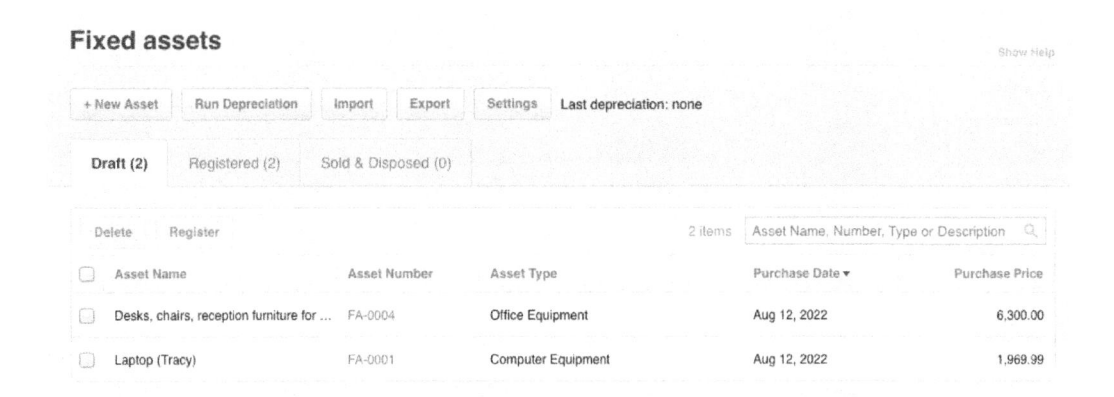

Figure 10.2: Fixed assets main screen

We will start by looking at the setup. This setup is usually a *do it once when you get started* process unless you are adding an additional asset type, so let's begin here by clicking the **Settings** button.

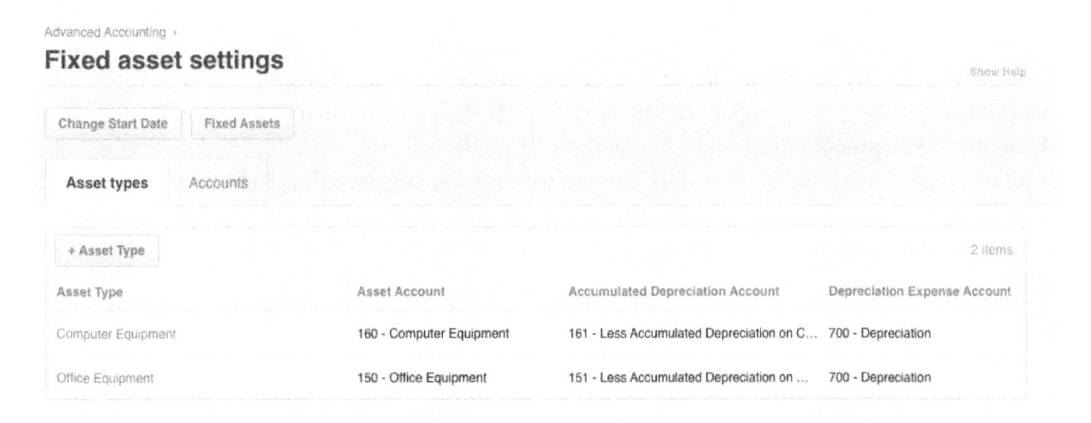

Figure 10.3: Fixed asset settings screen

From the **Fixed asset settings** page, you can edit the date from which you want to start depreciating your assets. Click the **Change Start Date** button and enter the date to begin your depreciation. It should probably be the business start date or the first day of the current year. Clicking the **Fixed Assets** button will take you back to the **Fixed assets** main page.

As you can see in *Figure 10.3*, we have two asset types already set up. We are going to look at the **Computer Equipment** asset type by clicking on **Computer Equipment**. This is the same screen you would get if you clicked on + **Asset Type**, except here we have the details completed for you.

Figure 10.4: Asset Type screen

As seen in *Figure 10.4*, you have several fields to complete. Start by entering the type of asset (you can choose things such as `Computer`, `Office Equipment`, `Building`, `Vehicle`, etc.) in the **Asset Type** field. The next lines are all dropdowns containing chart of account options. Choose the appropriate option for the company for each of the fields: **Asset Account**, **Accumulated Depreciation Account**, and **Depreciation Expense Account**; these are the accounts where the asset and subsequent transactions will be recorded. Next, let's jump down to **Book Depreciation Default**. We will use the dropdowns to choose **Depreciation Method** and **Averaging Method**. Choose the appropriate option for the company, keeping in mind these are used to record the depreciation on the books, not tax. The last thing you need to enter is the useful life of the asset and then click **Save**.

> **Note**
> Depreciation is the systemic reduction in the value of an asset based on time and wear. It can be calculated based on time (useful life) or even units produced.

The last part of the fixed asset setup process is to click **Accounts** on the main setup screen. This will allow us to choose the accounts for use when disposing of assets. I suggest setting up an account in your chart of accounts called `Gain (Loss) on Disposal of Assets` and using that. You can create an account for each option, **Capital Gain on Disposal**, **Gain on Disposal**, and **Loss on Disposal**. Just make sure you click **Save** when you are finished:

Figure 10.5: Account setup screen

Now that we have completed the setup of fixed assets, let's look at adding assets and the rest of the asset cycle.

Adding assets to Xero

You can add a new asset to Xero by clicking the **+ New Asset** button from the main **Fixed assets** menu. I can probably say with 100% certainty that you have recorded the asset purchase either through a **spend money** or a **purchase bill** transaction. If you record those transactions to an asset account that was previously set up in **Asset Type**, the base details are set up for a new asset in **Draft**, as shown in *Figure 10.6*:

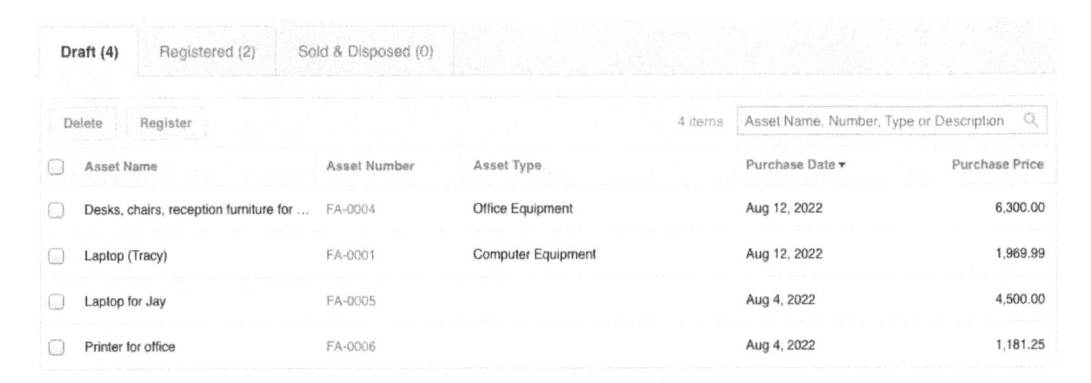

Figure 10.6: Draft fixed assets screen

Let's jump into one of the assets, **FA-0006**, and complete the asset addition. The basic information from the original transaction is filled in for you. You should update that information with the correct details. If you need more information, you can access the original Xero entry by clicking on the **See original transaction** link just below the **Options** button. This will take you to the original transactions, where you can see a receipt or invoice with details of the transaction that may have been attached to the transaction in Xero:

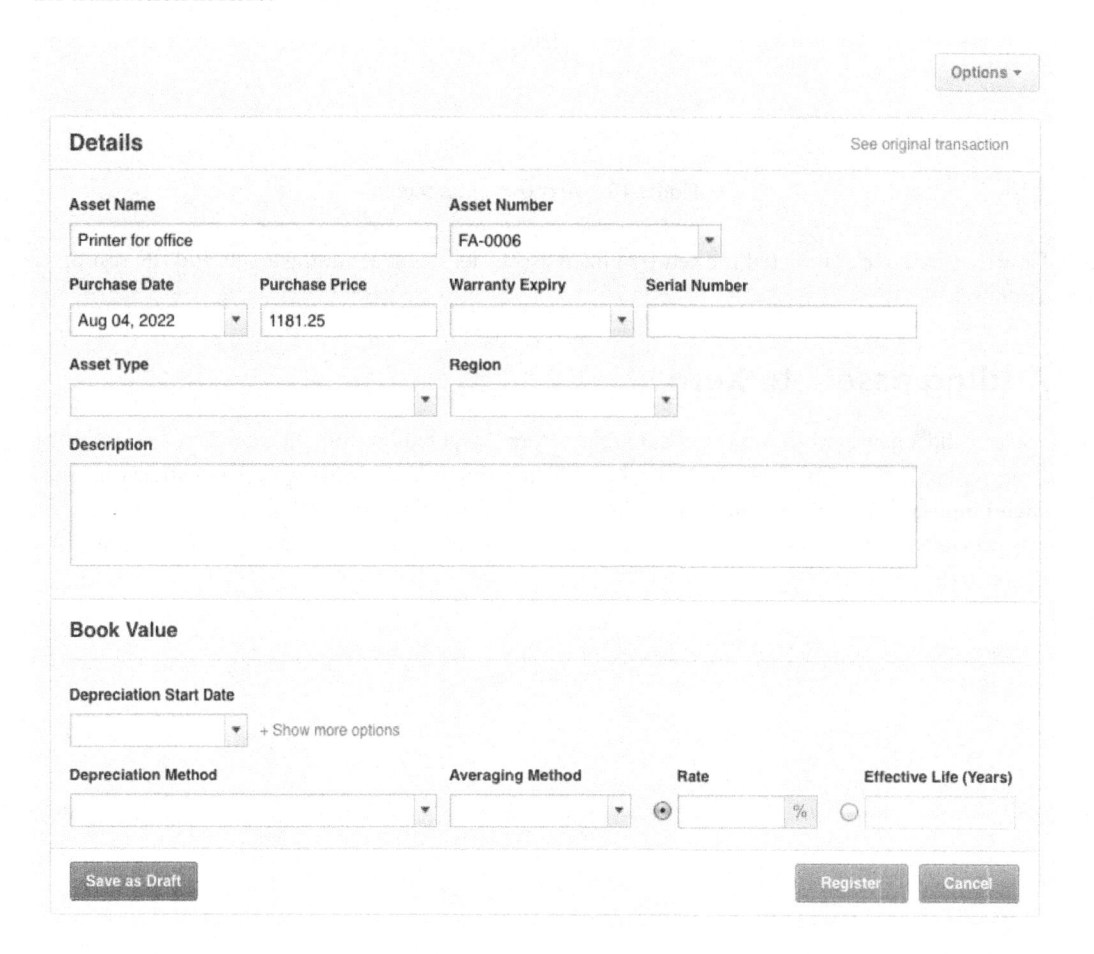

Figure 10.7: Asset Details screen

Make the required changes, by entering the **Asset Type** details of this asset, adding the warranty expiration date (if known), the serial number, a description (if needed), and the date you want depreciation to start. Then, click on **Register**. That's it, your asset is set up. Xero recently released an update to this process and has simplified it greatly. You can see the completed asset in *Figure 10.8*:

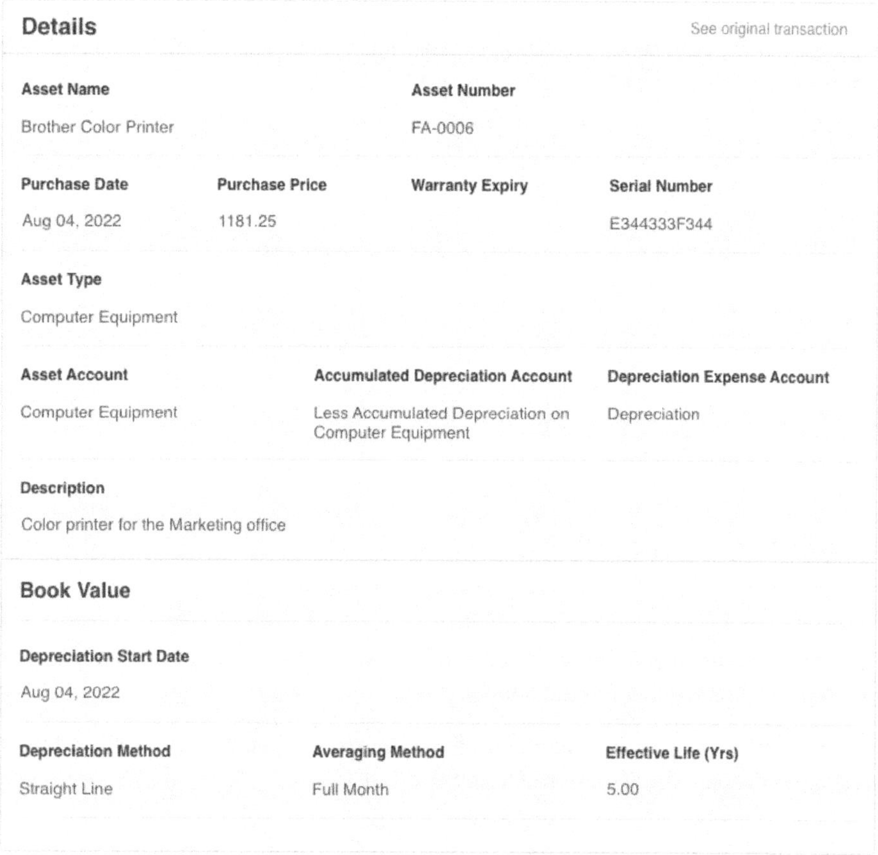

Details

See original transaction

Asset Name	Asset Number
Brother Color Printer	FA-0006

Purchase Date	Purchase Price	Warranty Expiry	Serial Number
Aug 04, 2022	1181.25		E344333F344

Asset Type
Computer Equipment

Asset Account	Accumulated Depreciation Account	Depreciation Expense Account
Computer Equipment	Less Accumulated Depreciation on Computer Equipment	Depreciation

Description
Color printer for the Marketing office

Book Value

Depreciation Start Date
Aug 04, 2022

Depreciation Method	Averaging Method	Effective Life (Yrs)
Straight Line	Full Month	5.00

Figure 10.8: Completed asset screen

As you can see, adding assets in Xero is pretty simple. All that is left is to run the depreciation.

Depreciating those assets

Now that we have added our assets, let's run the depreciation.

You can start by clicking on the **Run Depreciation** button from the main **Fixed assets** screen. This brings you to the **Depreciate** screen.

Once there, select the **To** date that you want to run depreciation through. This can be done monthly or annually. Xero will record the depreciation expense monthly for each asset. We have chosen to run depreciation through the end of 2022, as shown in *Figure 10.9*:

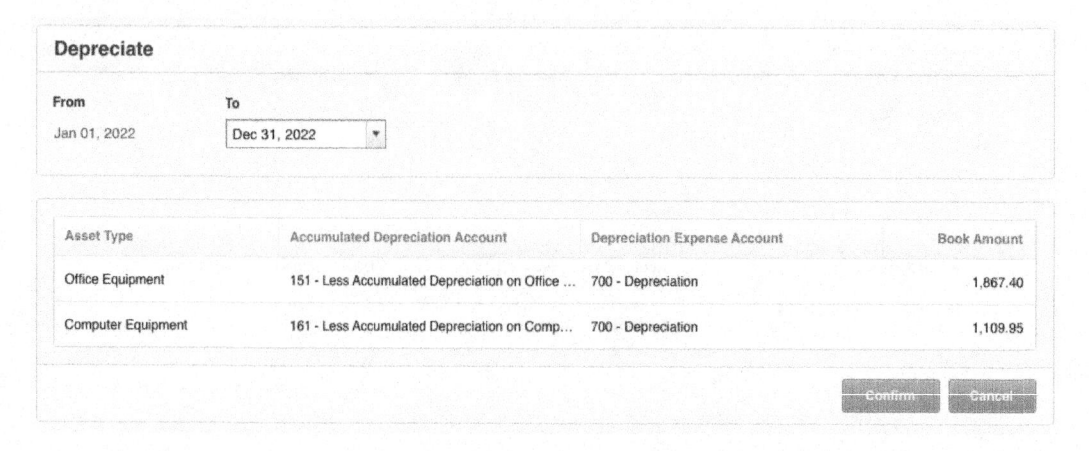

Figure 10.9: Depreciate screen

After depreciation is run, if you find a missed asset, no worries, you can roll back depreciation, thus removing all depreciation entries to the point you select.

You can start this process by clicking on the **Rollback Depreciation** button on the **Run Depreciation** screen. Just enter the date you wish to roll back to and click **Save**:

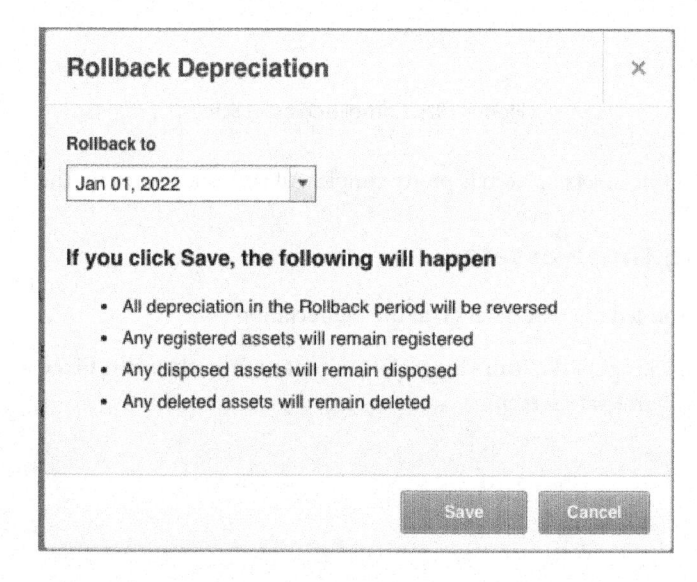

Figure 10.10: Rollback Depreciation dialog box

This will basically reset the depreciation and allow you to rerun depreciation and include any missed assets that were added after the original depreciation run.

If you go back to the asset details and click on the **Value** tab, you will see the details of the asset showing its original value, current book value, and its depreciation details:

Figure 10.11: Asset detail value

We have added an asset and run depreciation; let's look at closing the asset process by looking at disposing of assets next.

Disposing of assets

The purchase cycle of assets includes not only the acquisition but also the disposal of assets. You may trade, sell, or dispose of the assets when they stop meeting the needs of your business. Let's walk through the process of disposal:

1. We start by clicking the **Options** button on the asset **Details** screen and selecting **Dispose** from the drop-down menu under it:

Figure 10.12: Asset Options

2. When the **Disposal** screen pops up, enter the date of the transaction and the amount you received for the item, and then under **Sales Proceeds**, enter the asset account this account was previously coded to.

3. If you haven't run depreciation, you can select to run depreciation and set the date to run depreciation through the sale date. Click the **Show Summary** button:

Figure 10.13: Dispose asset screen

The summary will show you the details of the transactions, including adjustments to depreciation and the amount of the gain and loss. You can adjust the dates or any other setting on this screen and click **Update** to see those changes.

4. Click the **Review Journals** button when you are ready to finalize the transaction:

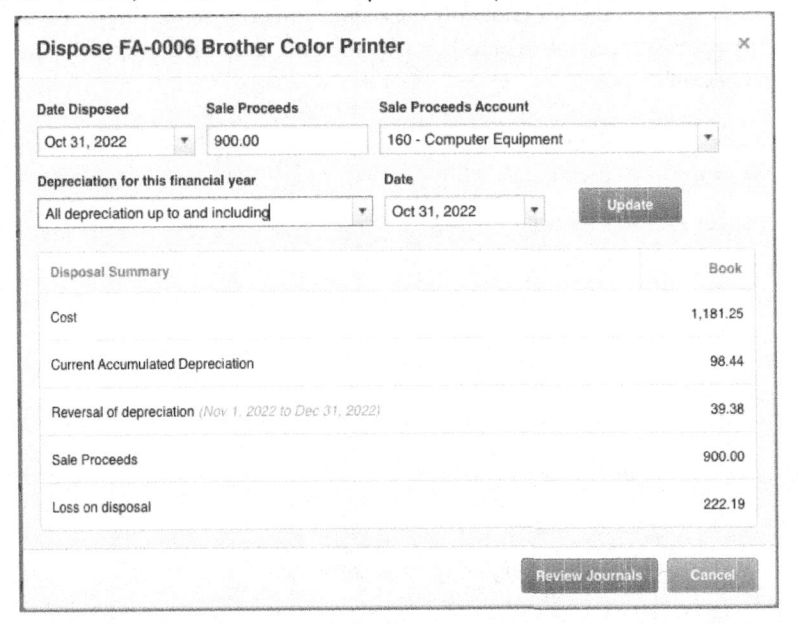

Figure 10.14: Dispose summary screen

The journal review is your last chance to check the entry and to ensure the loss or gain is going to the correct account.

5. If you are satisfied with the entry, click the **Post** button to finalize the disposal:

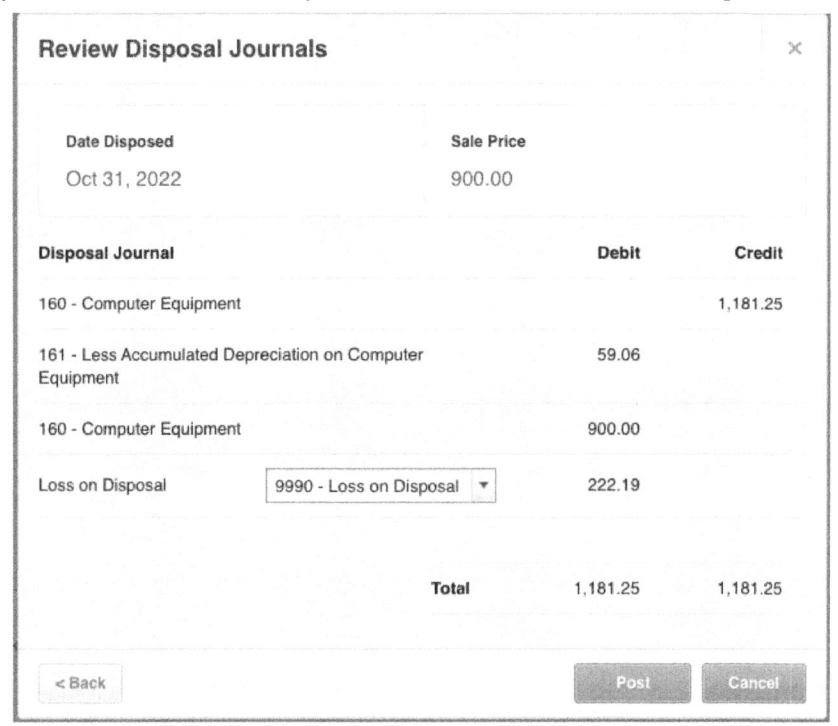

Review Disposal Journals			
Date Disposed Oct 31, 2022	**Sale Price** 900.00		
Disposal Journal		**Debit**	**Credit**
160 - Computer Equipment			1,181.25
161 - Less Accumulated Depreciation on Computer Equipment		59.06	
160 - Computer Equipment			900.00
Loss on Disposal	9990 - Loss on Disposal	222.19	
	Total	1,181.25	1,181.25

Figure 10.15: Disposal journal screen

There you have it; we have disposed of an asset, as well as added assets and ran depreciation earlier in this chapter.

Summary

Fixed assets are an essential part of most businesses. Having assets tracked in Xero is helpful for the business owner, as they know what assets they have, their depreciation, their age, and so on. Come tax season, it also helps you provide your tax professional with the details of all your asset additions and disposals easily. In this chapter, we went through the process of setting up Xero for your fixed assets; we added a new asset, depreciated it, and then disposed of it. We covered the entire cycle, and now you should have the confidence to perform this on your books or for your clients.

So far, everything we have done has booked the entries into Xero for us. In the next chapter, we will dive into manual journals, the key to posting adjustments and changes in Xero, and we're taking things mobile! We will show you how to use Xero on the go.

11
All You Need to Know about Manual Journals in Xero

Every accountant must have a few tools in their toolbelt. The journal entry is probably the #1 most-used tool. Whether it is to record expenses, liability accruals at the end of the month, or to process prepaid expenses, the journal entry is one of the most widely used tools in accounting. Xero makes the entry process simple with **manual journals**. Throughout this chapter, we will give you the knowledge of when and how to use manual journals like an expert so you can confidently record your journal entries with ease.

In this chapter, we're going to cover the following main topics:

- The Xero rules for the manual journal
- Standard manual journal entry
- Repeating journal entry

The manual journal

Most accounting platforms are composed of a **general ledger** (**G/L**) and journals that post to the G/L. Those journals are usually sales journals, purchase journals, and so on, and the entries into these journals (and subsequently, the G/L) are created from transactions in the system, such as invoices or accounts payable bills or purchases. Well, sometimes you need to post an entry to the G/L to correct or record something that you could not do with a system transaction, and that is where the manual journal comes into play in Xero.

Xero has a regular/standard manual journal where you can either set up a one-time entry or a repeating entry that can be created at given intervals. We will jump into the specifics shortly.

Xero's rules for creating manual journals

Xero has set up several parameters around the manual journal to maintain the integrity of the underlying data. Too many times, you see all entries posted via journal entries, and no system entries have been used at all. So, to avoid unnecessary chaos, here are the Xero rules for manual journals:

- You must have the *advisor* or *standard + all reports* user role to create or post a manual journal.
- You cannot post a manual journal to a bank account. The bank feed should keep the bank account balance and allow you to record any needed transactions via *spend* or *receive money* transactions. Conversion balances can adjust the starting balance of bank accounts.
- You cannot post a manual journal to a system account. These are accounts set by Xero that have underlying journals, and all transactions posted to a system account must be posted via system transactions such as an invoice or a bill.

System account	Allows transactions or manual journals
Accounts Payable	No*
Accounts Receivable	No*
Bank Revaluation	No
Current Earnings	No
Historical Adjustments	Yes
Realised Currency Gains	Yes
Retained Earnings	Yes
Rounding	Yes
Sales Tax	Yes
Tracking Transfers	No
Unpaid Expense Claims	No
Unrealised Currency Gains	No

Figure 11.1: Xero system accounts (Source: Xero Central)

Getting into the manual journal

Let's jump into Xero and take a look at the manual journal. Start by clicking on **Accounting** to activate the menu, and then choose **Manual journals**.

This takes you to the **Manual journals** dashboard screen (as seen in *Figure 11.2*), where you see the familiar Xero tab format. Here, you can create a new journal and select the different statuses of the journal to view. We will go through these selections as we talk more about manual journals throughout the remainder of this chapter.

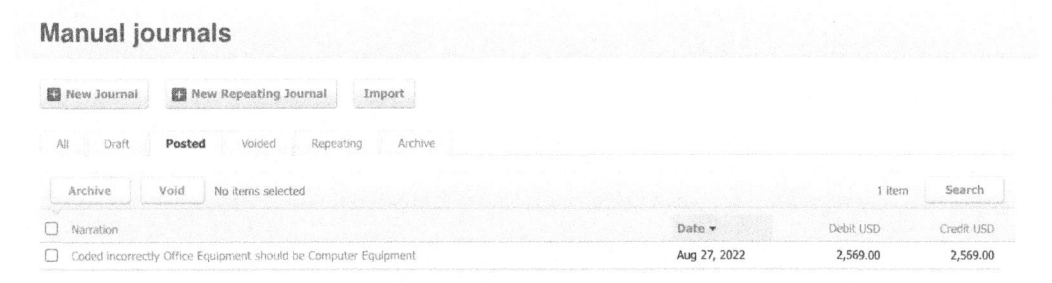

Figure 11.2: Manual journal dashboard

We have now covered the *about* section of the manual journal. In the next section, we will jump into the creation and posting of manual journals.

Creating manual journals

We start by clicking the **New Journal** button. This will allow us to create a standard one-time or one-off journal entry. If we wanted to create a recurring or repeating entry, we could click the **New Repeating Journal** button. We will get to the differences in the creation soon, but let's move forward with the one-off entry.

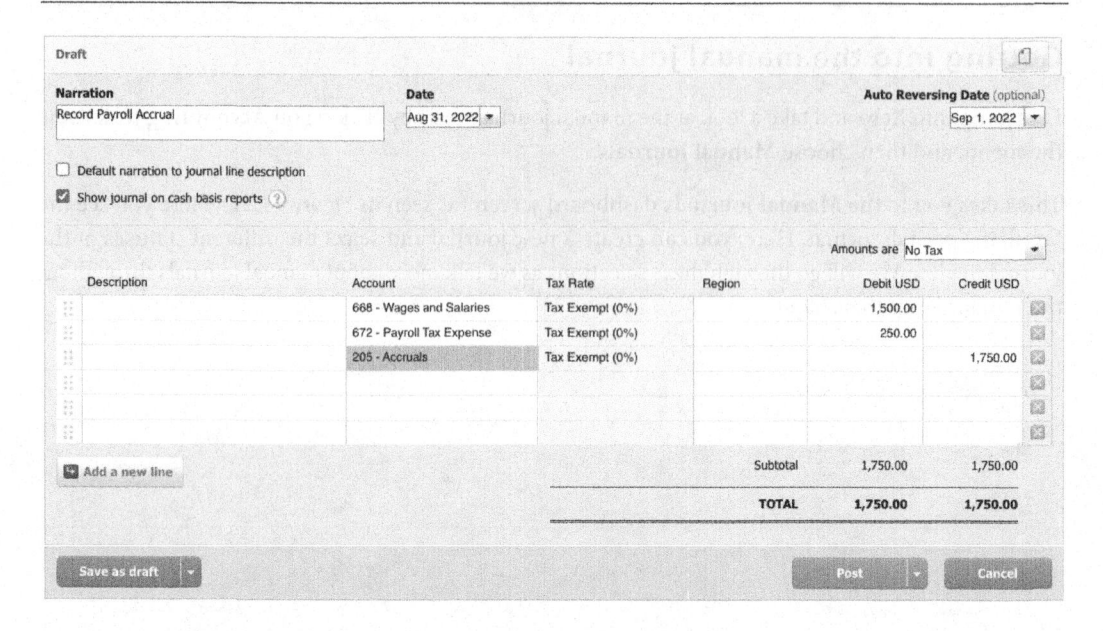

Figure 11.3: Manual journal screen

Let's walk through the fields of the manual journal as shown in *Figure 11.3*:

- All entries must have a **Narration** field, which is the description of the entry.
- **Date** is the date on which you are posting the journal to the G/L.
- **Auto Reversing Date** is the date you want this entry to post an automatic reversal of the original entry you are creating. You would use this on a payroll accrual, for example.
- **Default narration to journal line description** – I always remove that check from the box. Leaving it will push the narration to the description and it will show twice.
- **Show journal on cash basis reports** – Use this on any transaction you want to appear on a cash basis.
- **Amounts are** is usually set to **No Tax**. This is unless you are adjusting sales accounts and the company is calculating sales tax. This may require a sales tax change, but I do not recommend changing that here. Try to edit the source entry to ensure your sales tax is correct:
  - Here, we are talking about manual journals in USD. If we were to need to post in another currency, it would be posted in the base currency. If you must post in a currency other than the base currency, you must convert it first to the base currency.

- **Description** can be used to add a further description to the transaction, adding to **Narration**.
- **Account** is your account from the chart of accounts.
- **Tax Rate** is the appropriate tax rate based on the tax settings that were created during setup.
- **Region** is your tracking category; remember you may have up to 22 categories showing there.
- **Debit USD** is the amount you want to post as a debit to the account chosen in US dollars.
- **Credit USD** is the amount you want to post as a credit to the account chosen in US dollars.
- **Add a new line** allows you to add a new blank line to your entry.

When you have entered all of your data, the required transaction lines ensure your totals match at the bottom of the debit and credit columns. When done, click **Post**; if you are not ready to post your entry, you may want to save a draft. To do that, just click the **Save as draft** button. The draft will be saved, and you can view it again to update or post by clicking on the **Draft** tab. Like most other transactions in Xero, you can drag a PDF or other file to the manual journal to save in Xero files. This is helpful for accrual or other source documents for the transactions.

From any of the journal dashboard tabs, you can search for your specific entry.

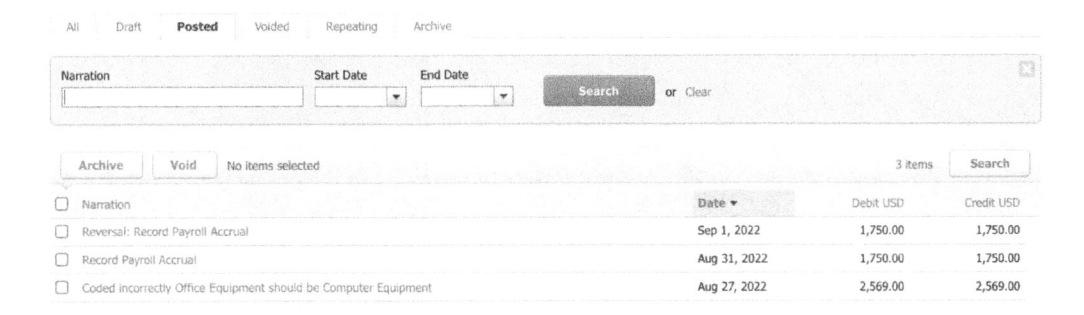

Figure 11.4: Posted journal screen

As seen in *Figure 11.4*, you can see the entry I posted along with the reversal. As we look at the posted original entry in *Figure 11.5*, you can see it says **Posted** and there is a link to view the reversal. If you click on the **View Auto-Reversed Journal** link, it will take you to the linked reversal. Likewise, from the reversal, there is a link to the original transaction.

156 All You Need to Know about Manual Journals in Xero

Manual Journals >
Posted Manual Journal #562

	Posted View Auto-Reversed Journal			Print PDF	Journal Options ▼

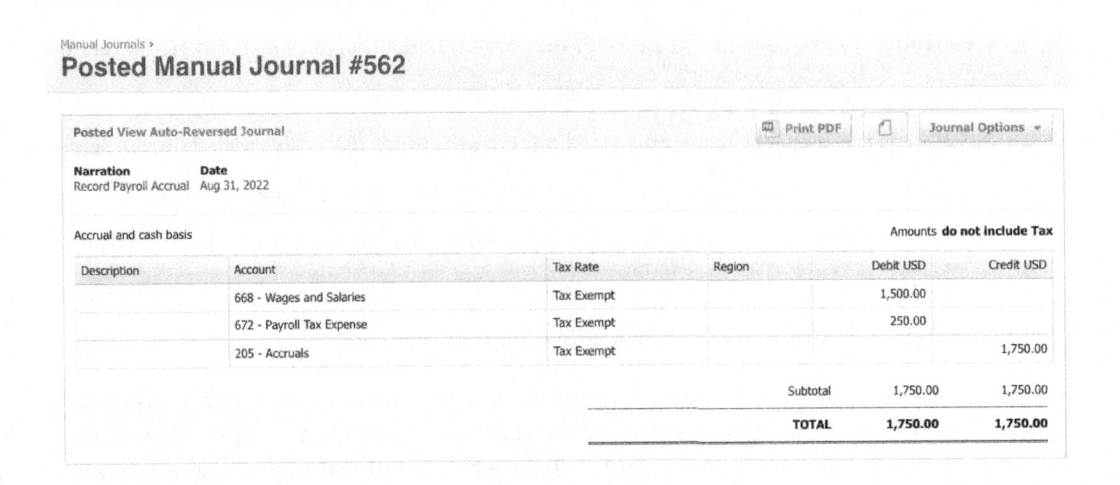

Narration   **Date**
Record Payroll Accrual   Aug 31, 2022

Accrual and cash basis   Amounts **do not include Tax**

Description	Account	Tax Rate	Region	Debit USD	Credit USD
	668 - Wages and Salaries	Tax Exempt		1,500.00	
	672 - Payroll Tax Expense	Tax Exempt		250.00	
	205 - Accruals	Tax Exempt			1,750.00
			Subtotal	1,750.00	1,750.00
			TOTAL	**1,750.00**	**1,750.00**

Figure 11.5: Posted manual journal screen

Let's look at the options we can use on this posted entry. By clicking the **Journal Options** button, we find the following options:

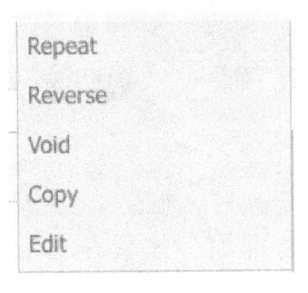

- Repeat
- Reverse
- Void
- Copy
- Edit

Figure 11.6: Journal Options

Let's look at those options:

- **Repeat** allows us to convert the one-off entry to a repeating journal. We will go through that process shortly.

- **Reverse** allows you to post a reversal if you forgot to originally or now need to reverse a previously posted entry.

- **Void** will remove the posting from the G/L.

- **Copy** allows you to make a duplicate of the original entry. This is helpful for the occasional similar entry but not on a regular schedule, when you may want to use a repeating journal.

- **Edit** allows you to do just that: edit the original transaction.

- **Show History** and **Add Note** allow Xero users to communicate and pass information regarding the transactions:

    - In the bottom-left corner, click on **Show History**. The user can see the history (audit log) of this journal according to the date and time.

    - Using notes, the accountant/bookkeeper can place important notes regarding this journal and required explanations for the future. Click the **Add Note** button to enter your note and click **Save** to save the note to the entry.

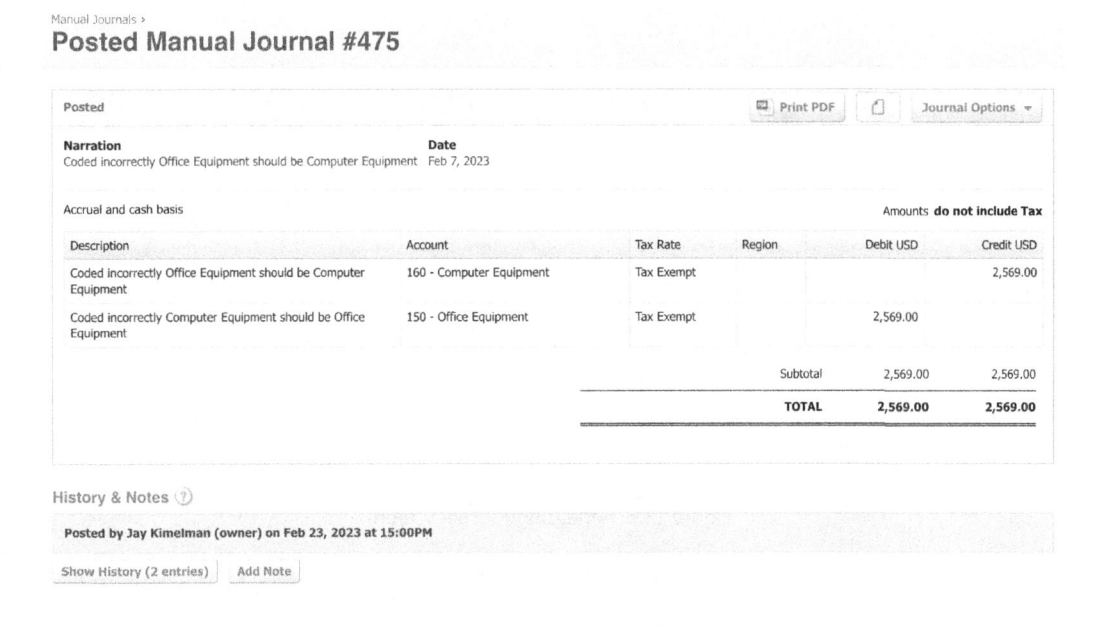

Figure 11.7: Posted manual journal

As you can see, manual journal entry is a powerful tool. In the next section, we look at adding efficiency with the repeating manual journal entry.

The repeating journal entry

The repeating journal entry is great for those entries you post on a regular (monthly, quarterly, or annual) basis. You build the skeleton of the entry and update the amounts as needed when you are ready to post the entry.

The process is fairly similar whether you convert a one-off entry or create a new one.

Let's walk through it now.

158 All You Need to Know about Manual Journals in Xero

When I click **Repeat** from the journal options from the posted one-off entry, the **Narration**, **Account**, and **Amount** details carry over. We just need to do some editing.

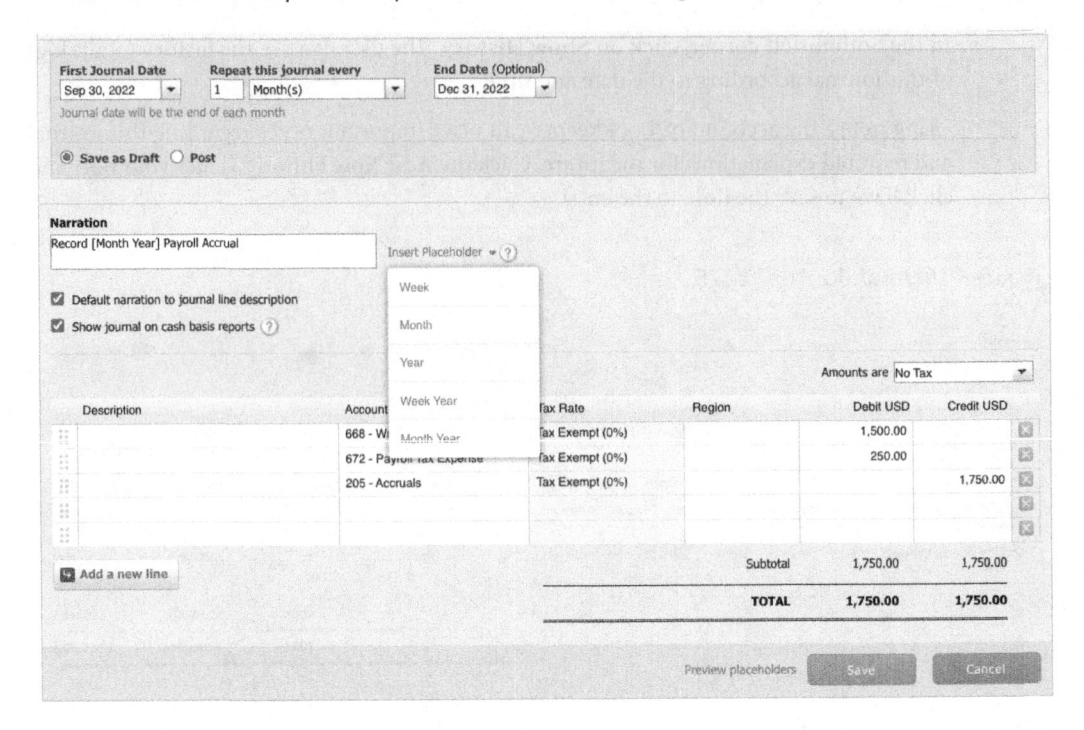

Figure 11.8: Repeating journal screen

As you can see in *Figure 11.8*, there are many similarities between the repeating journal and the manual journal.

I am going to highlight the differences for you here.

The repeating journal has the following additional fields:

- **First Journal Date** is the date the entry will first post to the G/L.
- **Repeat this journal every** is the cadence the entry will repeat, such as **1 Month**.
- **End Date (Optional)** is the date you may enter to end the repeating process. Keep in mind that if the date you enter in the **First Journal Date** field is prior to the current date, the entry will be created and placed in draft or posted based on the setting.
- Speaking of that, you can use **Save as Draft** in order to update the amounts if needed each month or period.
- You should select **Post** if your amounts will not change with each period.

- The last difference is the placeholders, as you see in the figure. You can use the placeholder to add the week, month, or year automatically in your repeating entry. All you have to do is click **Save**.

Importing your journal

You might have seen the **Import** button on the screenshots relating to the manual journals. Yes, you can import your data to create your journals. You can build templates to pull data and copy that data easily to the manual journal import template.

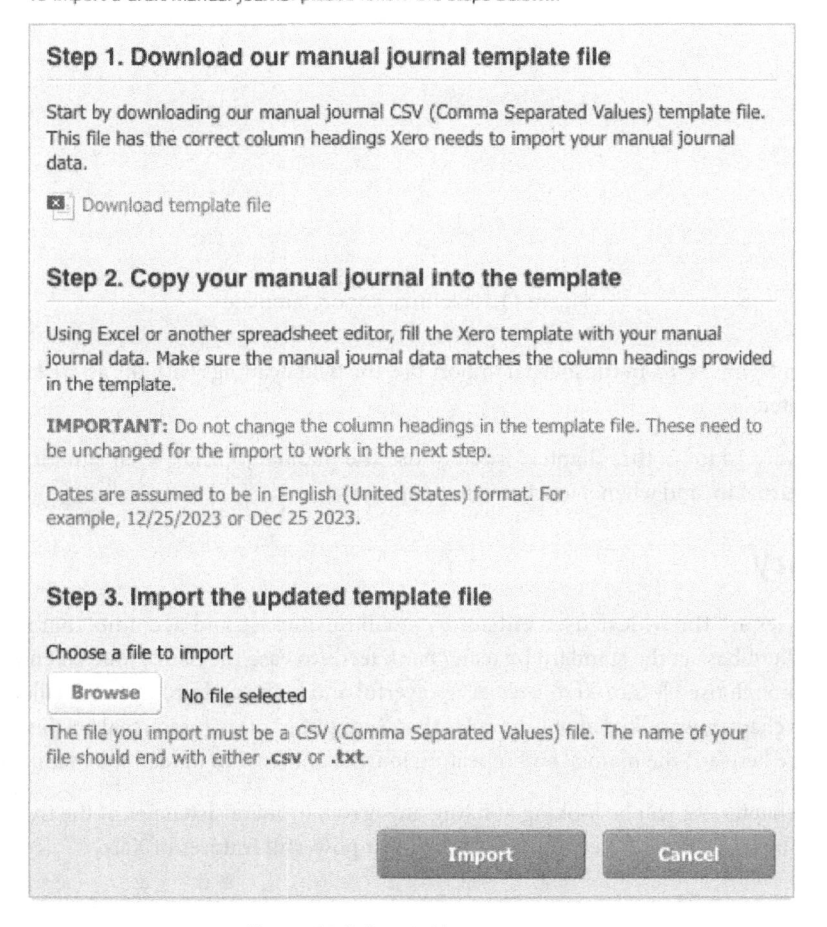

Figure 11.9: Journal import screen

As you can see in *Figure 11.9*, you can download the official template right from the import screen. You can see the fields are very similar to those in the manual journal screen. Those with asterisks (shown in *Figure 11.10*) are required fields. You can have up to 300 lines in a manual journal import. When entering details into the import file, if you leave the **Narration** and **Date** cells blank, Xero will treat those lines as if they are associated with the same journal above it. You can post multiple entries here – just change the date and it will create a separate entry for each date. When you are done, click **Browse** on the import screen, select your file, and click **Import**. Review the message and click **Complete Import**. The entries will be saved as a draft that you can view, edit, and make changes to before posting.

	A	B	C	D	E	F	G	H	I	J	K
1	*Narration	*Date	Description	*AccountCo	*TaxRate	*Amount	TrackingNa	TrackingOpti	TrackingNa	TrackingOption2	
2											
3											
4											
5											
6											
7											
8											
9											
10											
11											
12											
13											
14											
15											
16											
17											

Figure 11.10: Journal import template

As you see in *Figure 11.10*, in the journal import file, the field headings with the asterisks are required to be populated.

We have covered a lot in this chapter: when to use the manual journal, what situations to use the repeating journal in, and when a journal is not appropriate.

Summary

Journal entries are the widest-used entries by small businesses and accounts that service small businesses. Xero has set the standard by using bank feeds to ease the use of journal entries. Manual journals, although used less in Xero, are very powerful and help you become more efficient in using Xero. In this chapter, we talked about the rules that Xero put in place for journal entries. You learned the difference between the manual and repeating journal and how to upload the manual journal.

In the next chapter, we will be looking at fixing any errors or inconsistencies in the transactions we have posted by using **Find & Recode**, one of the most powerful features of Xero.

12
Correct Your Mistakes with Find and Recode

Find & Recode was one of the earlier major feature enhancements to hit Xero. It was highly requested and anticipated by the global Xero user community. It allows the *Advisor* user to make coding changes in bulk. When it arrived, it was positively accepted and extensively used for multiple reasons. Other than the intended use to correct miscoded transactions, it was also used as a global search function before the global search function was introduced by Xero sometime later. Let's jump right in and show you why **Find & Recode** is so powerful.

In this chapter, we're going to cover the following main topics:

- What transactions you can adjust with **Find & Recode**
- How to process **Find & Recode** to perfection

The basics of Find & Recode

Find & Recode allows users with the *Advisor* role to search for transactions with specific criteria and change particular aspects of the transactions. A standard user cannot access the **Find & Recode** feature. The common changes you can make are as follows:

- Change the account
- Change the tax rate
- Change the contact
- Change or add a tracking category

Find & Recode works on most of the Xero transaction types; here is a list of the supported transactions:

Transaction type	Transaction status	Transaction abbreviation
Spend money	Reconciled, unreconciled, and marked as reconciled.	SM
Receive money	Reconciled, unreconciled, and marked as reconciled.	RM
Prepayments (bills and invoices)	Unpaid, paid, reconciled, and unreconciled.	PR
Expense claims	Awaiting payment, paid and archived.	EC
Sales invoices, repeating invoices and credit notes	All - draft, awaiting approval, awaiting payment, and paid.	AR/CR
Purchase bills, repeating bills, bill credit notes	All - draft, awaiting approval, awaiting payment, and paid.	AP/CR
Manual journals	Draft and posted. You can also search for archived journals but you can't recode them.	MJ

Figure 12.1: Xero-supported transactions for Find & Recode courtesy of Xero Central

Transaction types not searchable with **Find & Recode** are as follows:

- Voided transactions of any type
- Fixed assets
- Purchase orders
- Quotes
- Bank transfers
- Overpayments
- Tracked inventory

Any transactions of the preceding types will need to be manually edited individually.

System accounts, such as Accounts Receivable and Tracked inventory, as well as bank transactions, cannot be recoded by **Find & Recode**, similar to the restrictions to manual journals we discussed in *Chapter 11*.

Find, the ultimate Xero search tool

As we said earlier in the chapter, **Find & Recode** is a very powerful tool. The **Search** or find function allows you to find transactions meeting specific criteria. Let's jump in and carry out a search:

1. We start by clicking **Accounting** and selecting **Find and Recode**. If you do not see **Find and Recode** in the **Accounting** menu, click **Advanced** to go to the **Advanced accounting** menu and click the star next to the features you want on the menu:

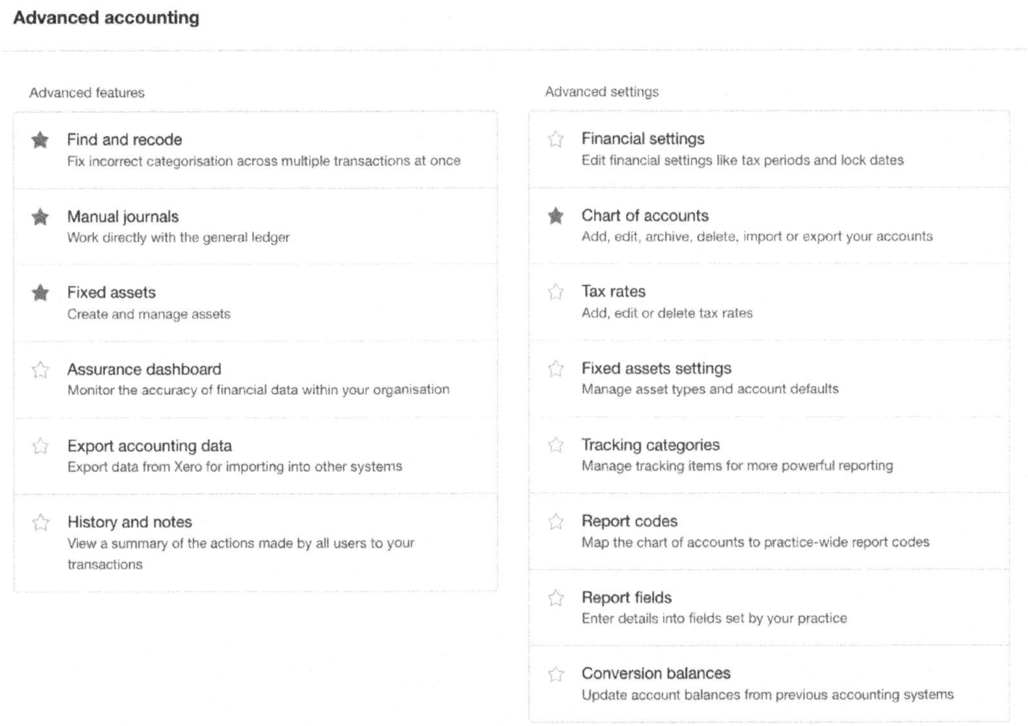

Advanced accounting

Advanced features

★ Find and recode
Fix incorrect categorisation across multiple transactions at once

★ Manual journals
Work directly with the general ledger

★ Fixed assets
Create and manage assets

☆ Assurance dashboard
Monitor the accuracy of financial data within your organisation

☆ Export accounting data
Export data from Xero for importing into other systems

☆ History and notes
View a summary of the actions made by all users to your transactions

Advanced settings

☆ Financial settings
Edit financial settings like tax periods and lock dates

★ Chart of accounts
Add, edit, archive, delete, import or export your accounts

☆ Tax rates
Add, edit or delete tax rates

☆ Fixed assets settings
Manage asset types and account defaults

☆ Tracking categories
Manage tracking items for more powerful reporting

☆ Report codes
Map the chart of accounts to practice-wide report codes

☆ Report fields
Enter details into fields set by your practice

☆ Conversion balances
Update account balances from previous accounting systems

Figure 12.2: Xero Advanced accounting features

2. Click **Find and recode** on the **Advanced accounting** menu:

Figure 12.3: Find and recode main screen

3. Click the **Find and recode** button.

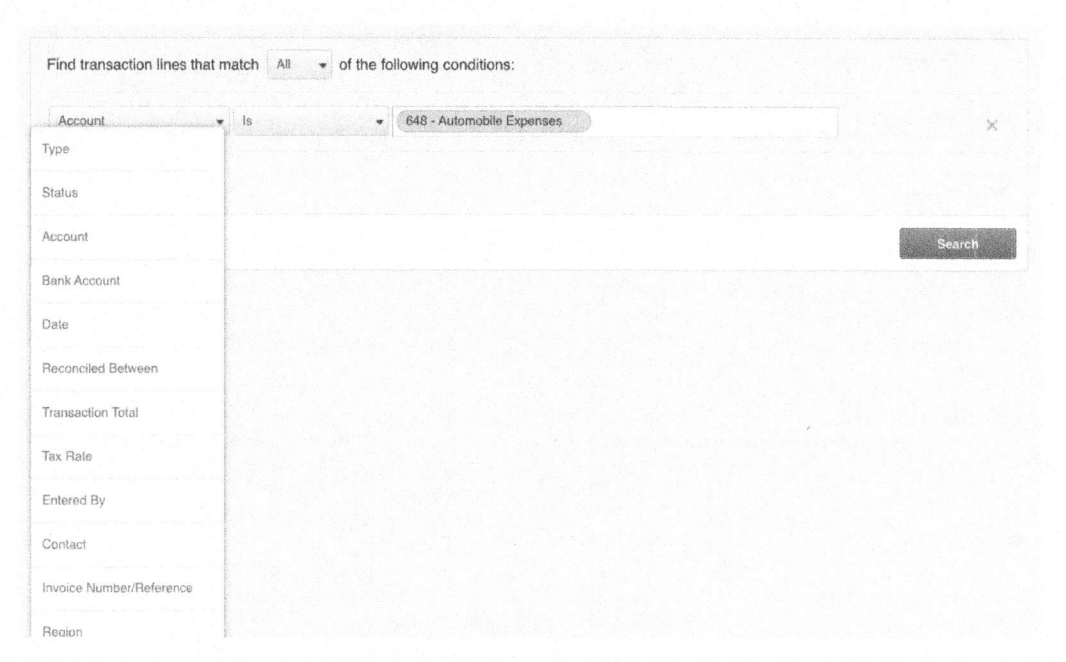

Figure 12.4: Find and recode find screen

As seen in *Figure 12.4*, I chose **Automobile Expenses** as the search criteria or condition. You can see there are other types you can choose from. They are detailed here:

Category	Search Conditions
Type	All supported transaction types.
Status	All transactions lines with statuses matching Draft, Awaiting Approval, Awaiting Payment and Paid. When you search for Awaiting Payment transactions, the search results will include transaction lines for spend money and receive money.
Account	Can't search accounts receivable, accounts payable, unpaid expense claims, tracking transfers, bank revaluations, unrealised currency gains, bank accounts, fixed assets, tracked inventory accounts or archived accounts.
Reconciled Between	Select a date range to find transaction lines that were reconciled within the two dates.
Bank Account	Select one or more bank accounts that contain the transaction lines.
Date	Transaction lines created on a specific date or within a certain date range. You can't search for transaction lines created prior to a lock date, unless a lock date was set for all users except advisers.
Transaction total	Amounts equal to, less than or more than a specific transaction total.
Tax rate	All active and archived tax rates.
Entered by	User that created the transaction.
Contact	Active contacts, but not archived contacts.
Invoice Number / Reference	The specific invoice number or reference of an invoice or bill.
Tracking	If you've created a tracking category you can also search for transaction lines that haven't been assigned a tracking category.

Figure 12.5: Xero transaction types courtesy of Xero Central

Account is the most widely used search type but there are many useful ones to choose from. I have used **Entered by** to check the coding of a new staff member of the firm or a client. **Contact** is a good one to check for coding consistency.

When we have the conditions set, we click the **Search** button. Xero returns the search results:

Figure 12.6: Find and recode search results

You can further dial in your search by adding additional conditions and clicking **Search** again. If you have what you are looking for, we are ready to recode.

Correcting mistakes with Recode

Now that we have **Find** taken care of, we can select the transactions we need to recode:

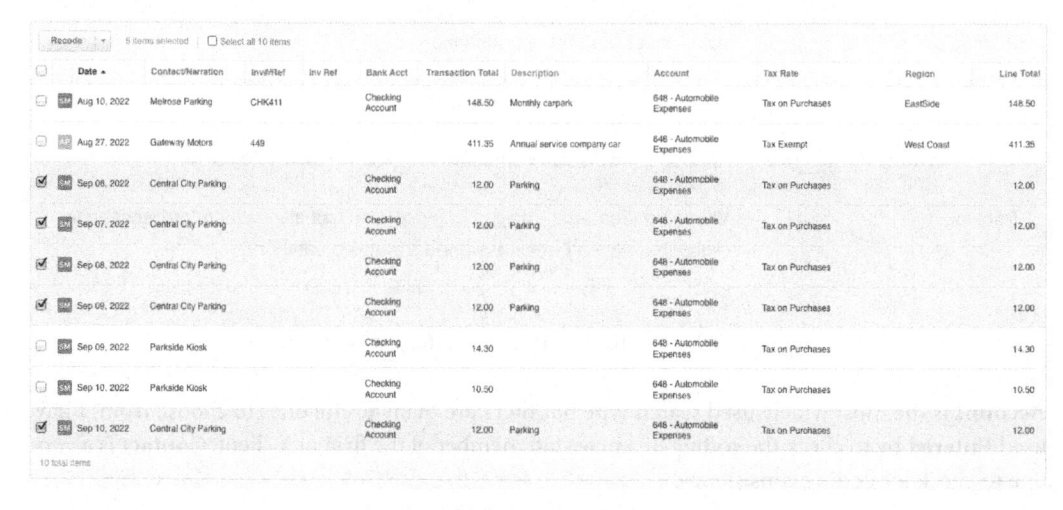

Figure 12.7: Search results screen updated

Correcting mistakes with Recode   167

Here, in our case, we have found that transactions for **Central City Parking** were coded to **Automobile Expenses** and we want to recode them to **Parking and Tolls**. This is an example to illustrate the use of **Find and recode**. We add a checkmark to each of the transactions we want to recode. If we wanted to recode all of the transactions in the search results, we could click next to **Select all 10 items** at the top of the search result. You will notice that once you add a selection, the **Recode** box will activate:

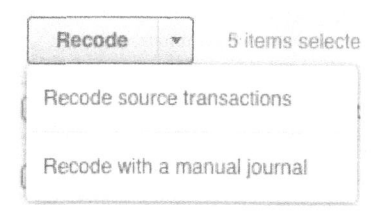

Figure 12.8: Recode options

Clicking **Recode** will show you the options for your recode. You can select **Recode source transactions** or you can create a manual journal. I think I have 100% chosen to modify the source transactions. I know what you are thinking: what about an audit trail? Yes, Xero will leave a detailed trail of the history of this transaction.

We click the **Recode source transactions** option and enter **Parking and Tolls** as the new account to use for the selected transactions. Click **Review**:

Figure 12.9: Recode Transactions screen

After clicking **Review**, you go to the **Confirm** screen:

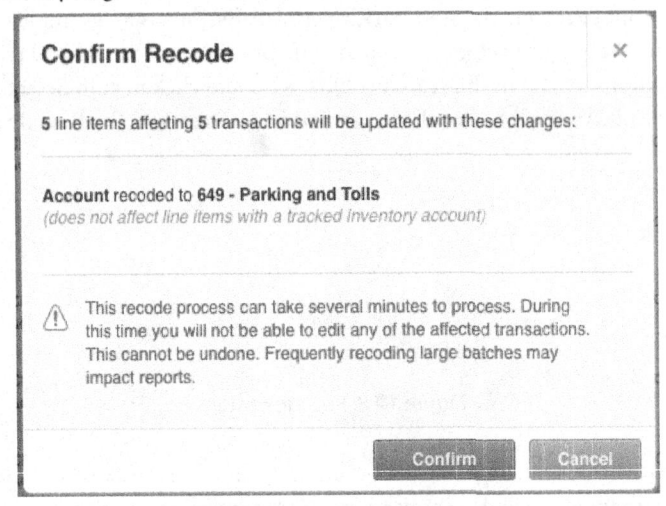

Figure 12.10: Confirm Recode screen

The confirmation screen tells you the number of transactions you are recoding and the changes you are making. Click **Confirm** when you are ready to post the changes to Xero.

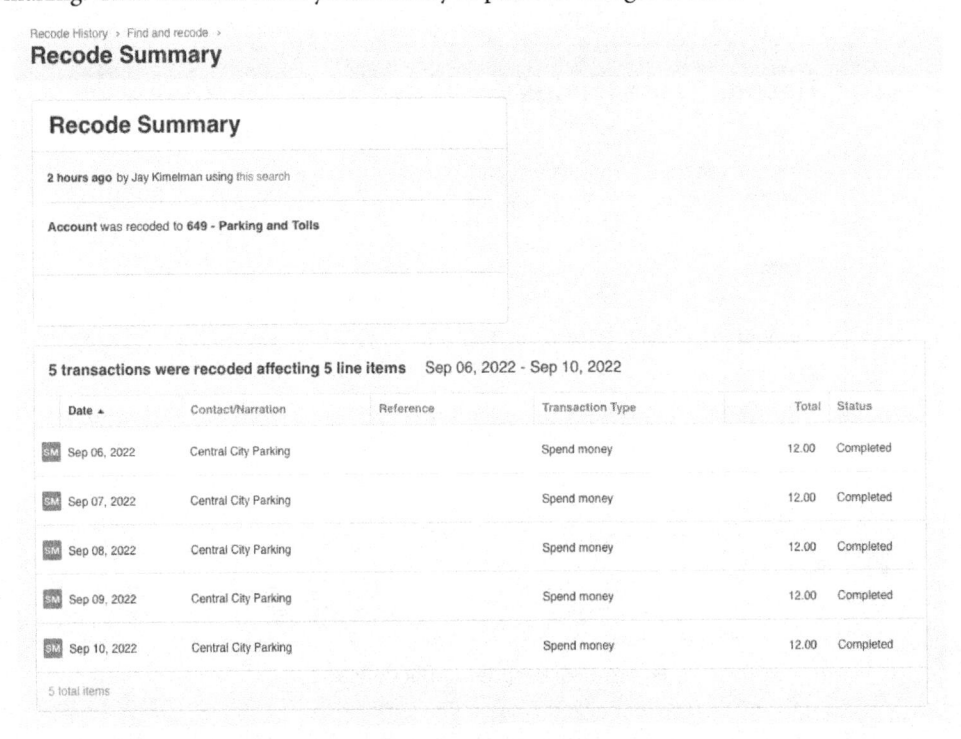

Figure 12.11: Recode Summary screen

Recode Summary shows you the transactions that you have modified and their statuses. With one exception, I have always received a **Completed** status. If you wanted to run the same search again to modify something else, you can click on the **this search** link at the top of the summary section.

Summary

Find & Recode is one of the most powerful tools built into Xero. It has many uses, from searching transactions to modifying transactions in bulk. It is a time-saver and a life-saver in one. In this chapter, you have learned what you can and cannot search using **Find & Recode**. You have also learned how you can modify posted transactions in bulk, changing multiple fields in the original transactions.

In the next chapter, we will begin to look at reporting in Xero, one of the most used features of Xero.

Part 4: Reporting – Knowing About the Performance of Your Business (KPIs)

The objective of this section is to familiarize you with the reporting capabilities built into Xero, as well as how to customize the reports to gain the most information for your business. We will also look at the built-in insight tools, which all Xero users will find useful.

This section comprises the following chapters:

- *Chapter 13, Running and Customizing Basic Reports in Xero*
- *Chapter 14, Business Analytics with Business Snapshot and Short-Term Cash Flow*
- *Chapter 15, Creating Custom Reports in Xero Using the Layout Editor*

13
Running and Customizing Basic Reports in Xero

You have invoiced, posted, paid, been paid, and reconciled. Now that we have transactional data, we can produce reports in Xero to tell the story of how your business is operating. We will be able to see the revenues and expenses that give you your net income, as well as your cash balance, other assets, liabilities, and your equity accounts as of a given date. This gives you the ability to see your results and make sound, timely business decisions. Here we will discuss just how easy Xero makes it to produce reports such as the income statement and balance sheet. So, let's jump right in and get at it.

In this chapter, we're going to cover the following main topics:

- Producing the basic reports
- Using the prebuilt customized report options
- Saving your reports

Reporting in Xero

Reporting in Xero has become one of its main strengths. It coupled with the bank feeds, and ease of use is what makes Xero the great platform it is today. Xero has several pre-built reports that are ready to be used with a click of the mouse. These are standard basic and some not-so-basic reports that you can use immediately. If you have a more complex reporting requirement, you can customize the Xero reports using **Layout Editor**, which we will cover in *Chapter 15*. The pre-built reports apply to each Xero company individually. Xero also has report templates only available to advisors that can be applied at the firm level. We will cover report templates in *Chapter 17*.

174 Running and Customizing Basic Reports in Xero

Now that we have that out of the way, let's take a deeper look at reporting in Xero. We will run a report, modify the settings, and review the report. Let's begin:

1. To get to reports, we click **Accounting**, followed by the **Reports** option below it.

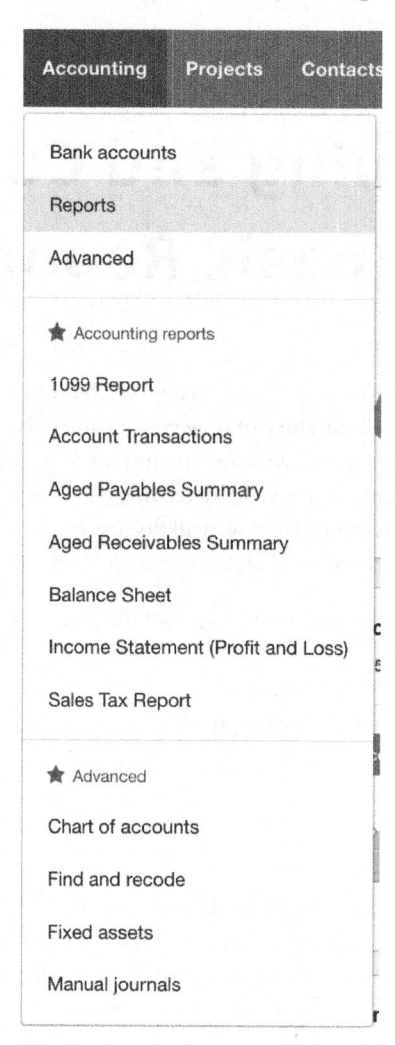

Figure 13.1: Xero Accounting menu

This will take you to the **Reports Home** page or main menu (*Figure 13.2*).

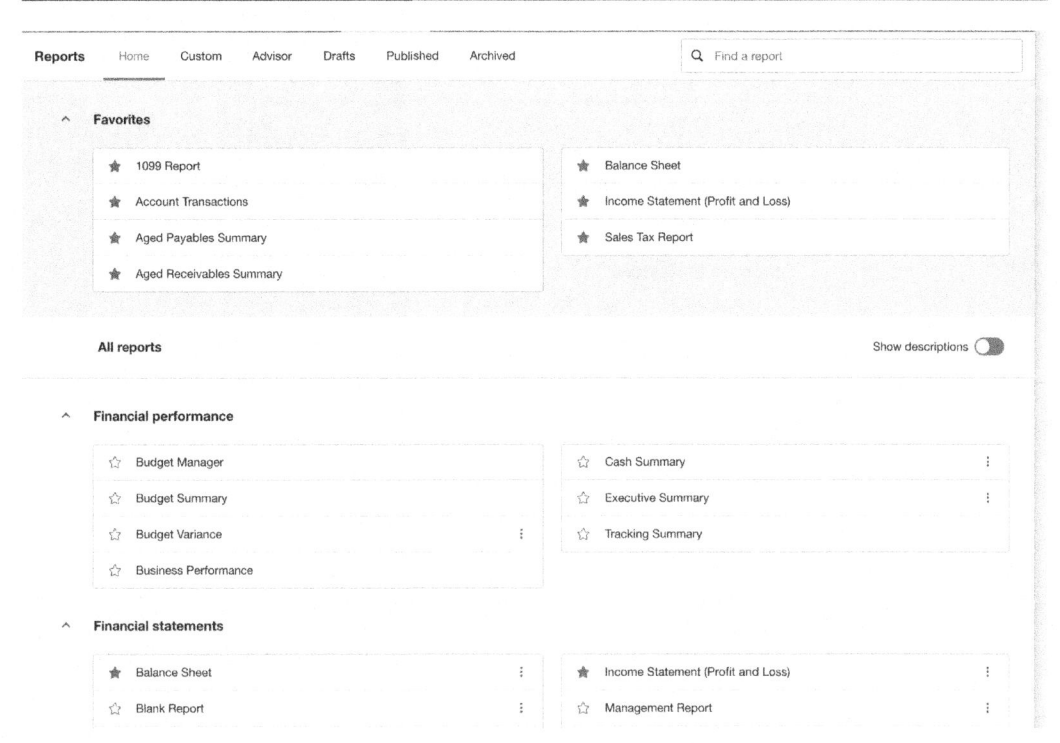

Figure 13.2: Xero Reports main menu

2. You see the reports that have been favorited at the top of the **Reports Home** page. Just like other sections of Xero, you click the start to the left of the selection to favorite it. Also, if you refer to *Figure 13.1*, you will see **Favorites** on the accounting menu.

   Jumping to the top of the **Reports** main menu, you can see **Reports** is comprised of six tabs, very similar to the user interface in other features within Xero. The **Reports** tabs are **Home**, **Custom**, **Advisor**, **Drafts**, **Published**, and **Archived**.

   As we look at the **Home** tab, you will see **Favorites**; those are the reports that have been starred below, and also show on your menu. Below that, you will see the remaining prebuilt reports sorted by report type.

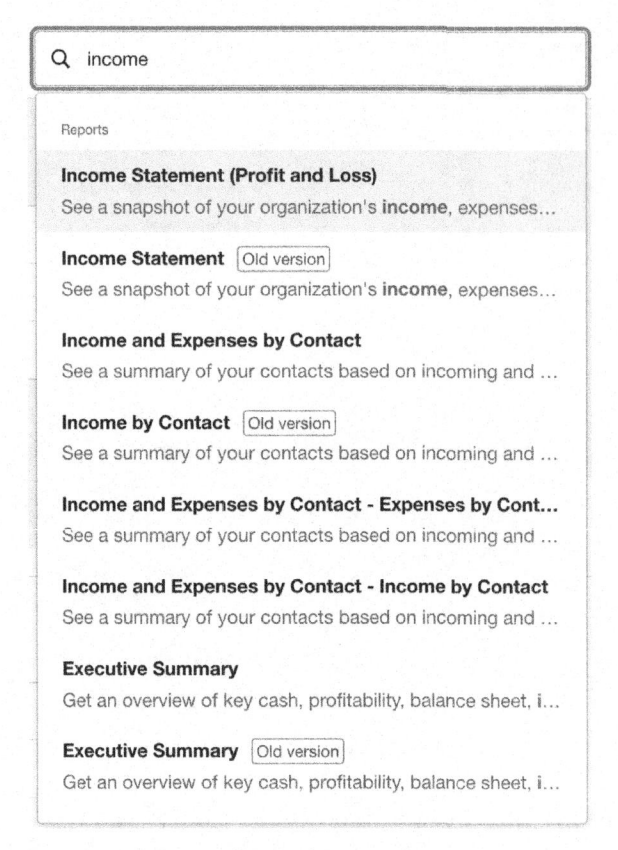

Figure 13.3: Find a report Search

3. At the top right of the screen, you see the **Find a report** search bar; let's search for the income statement.

   We start by typing `income` in the search box. Xero will return the reports with income in the name. You may notice a note on some reports: *Old Report*. These are Xero's original format reports and are set to be phased out at some time in the future.

   To get a clearer idea about which report shows what kind of data, we can activate **Show Description**.

4. Let's click on **Income Statement (Profit and Loss)** to start our reporting journey.

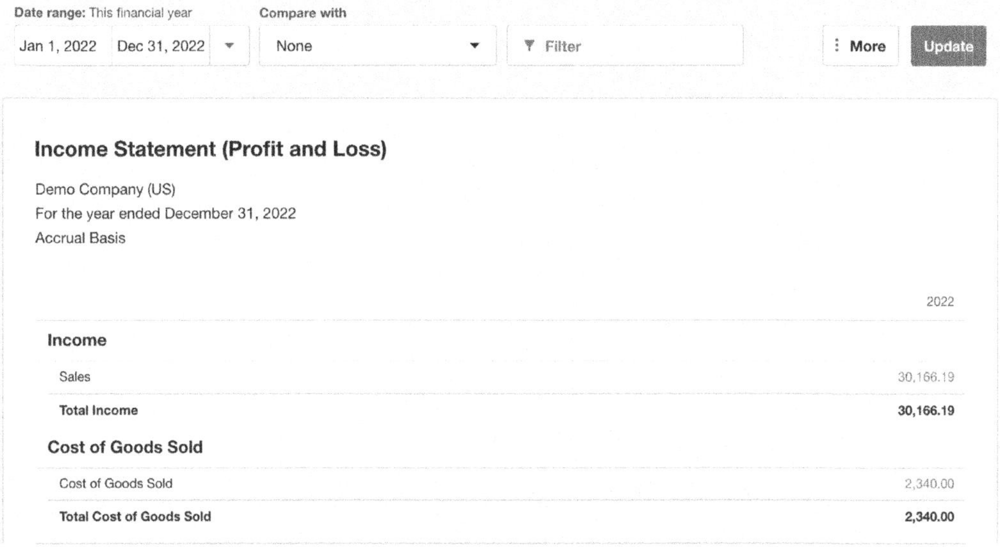

Figure 13.4: Income Statement criteria selection

5. As seen in *Figure 13.4*, at the top of the page is the report criteria selection area. Here we can set **Date range**. Pick a comparison period using **Compare with**, use **Filter** on the data, and select **More**.

The first thing you must do is set the date you wish to run your report on; this is based on your closing period, your needs, the needs of your client, and so on. When I am creating my first report for my clients, I usually set **Last Month** as the date range, but this can be a range of months and you can click in the beginning or ending date fields and select the date range you need if it is not in the list of dates. You would click on the arrow down triangle to the right of the end date to pick a set date range.

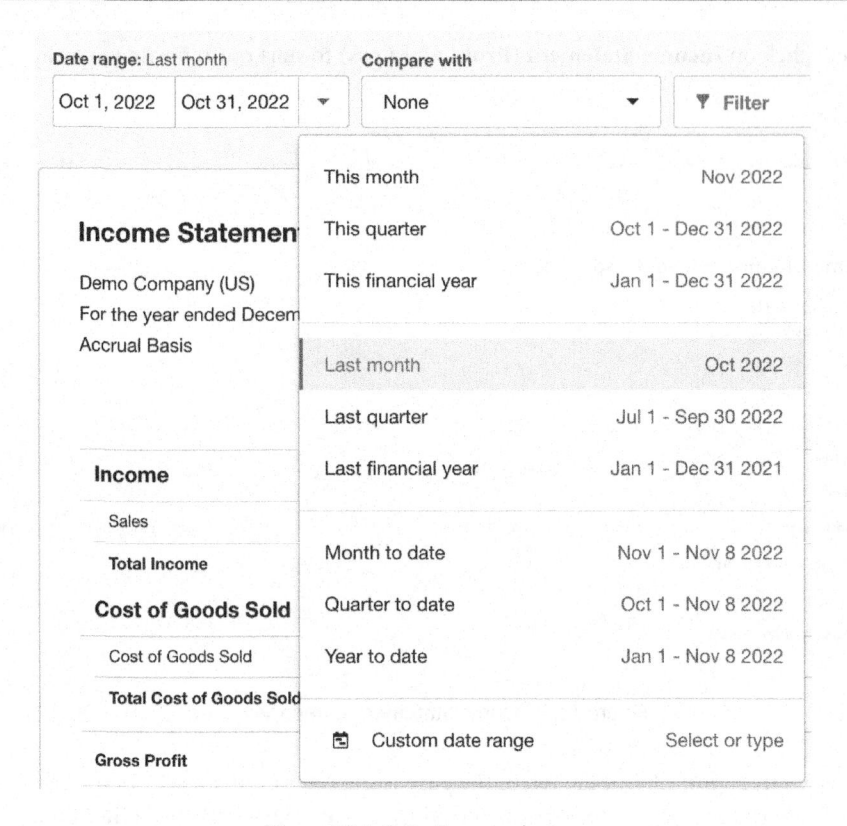

Figure 13.5: Date Range selector

6. Next, we can choose a period to compare with the current results. We click on the arrow down triangle to the right of **Compare with**. You can choose a **Month**, **Quarter**, or **Year** comparison period by selecting the radio button to the left. You can then choose the number of comparison periods.

Compare with

[Compare with 1 year ▼] [▼ Fil]

Comparison period(s)

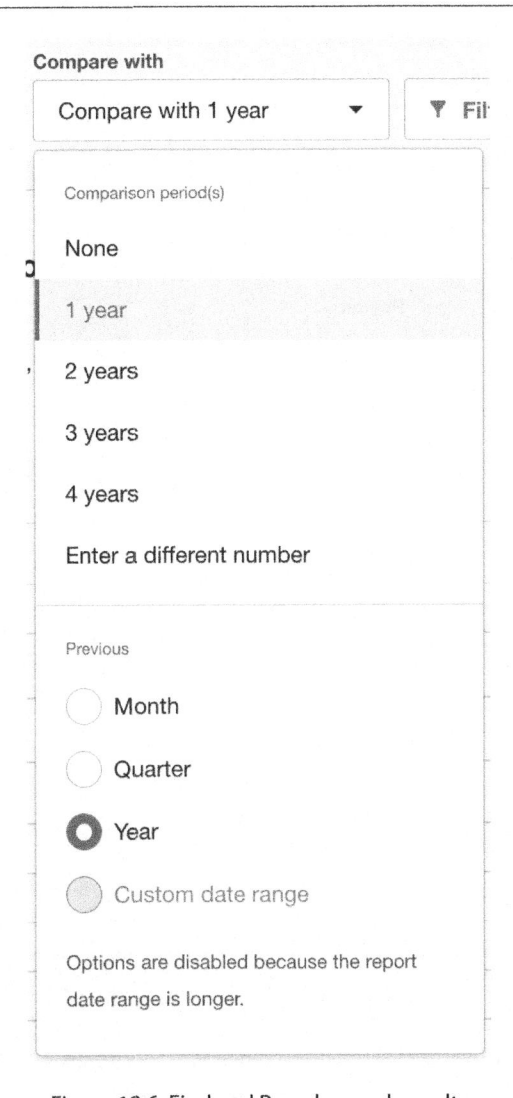

None

1 year

2 years

3 years

4 years

Enter a different number

Previous

○ Month

○ Quarter

● Year

○ Custom date range

Options are disabled because the report date range is longer.

Figure 13.6: Find and Recode search results

7. Xero also allows you to filter the data in your report by **Tracking Category**. Click the **Filter** button to make your filter selections. Select the tracking options by clicking the checkbox and selecting the options you wish to report on and click **Apply**.

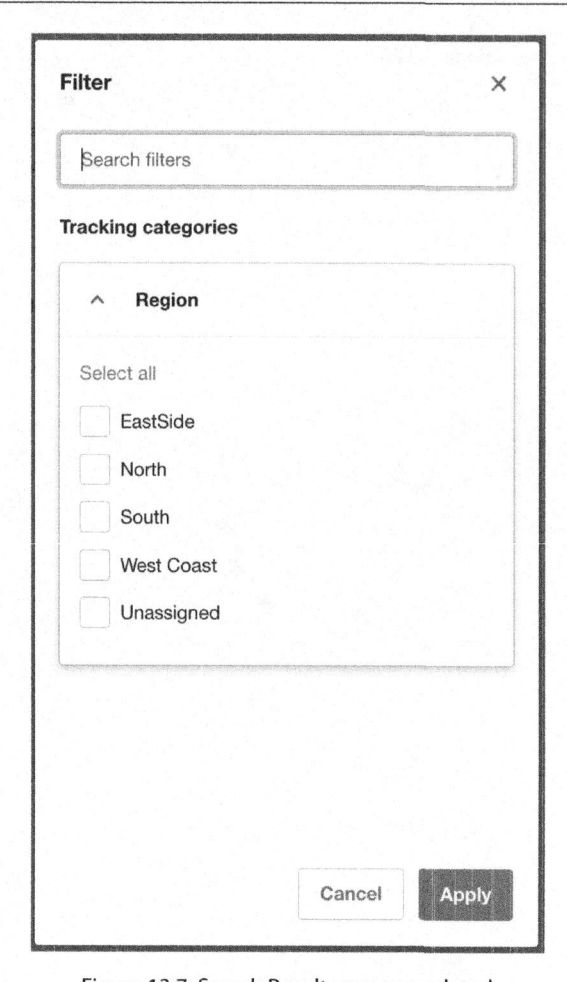

Figure 13.7: Search Results screen updated

8. The **More** button give you a few more options. You can choose the basis on which to run the report, **Cash** or **Accrual**. You can add **Percent of income**, **Total**, and **Year to Date** columns by selecting the checkboxes to the left of the options you wish to add.

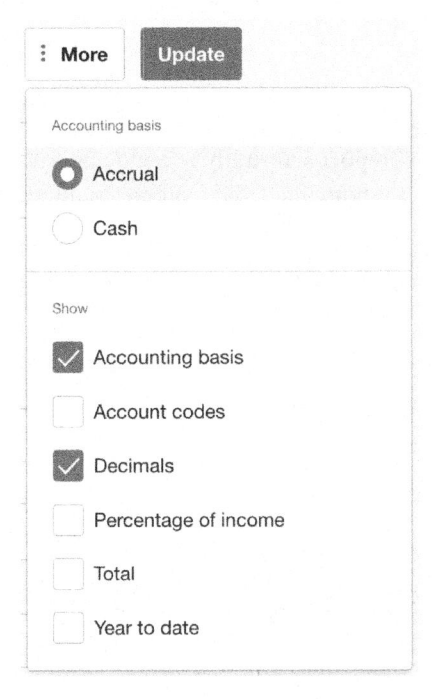

Figure 13.8: Report options

9. Once you have the sections you wish, click the **Update** button.

Income Statement (Profit and Loss)

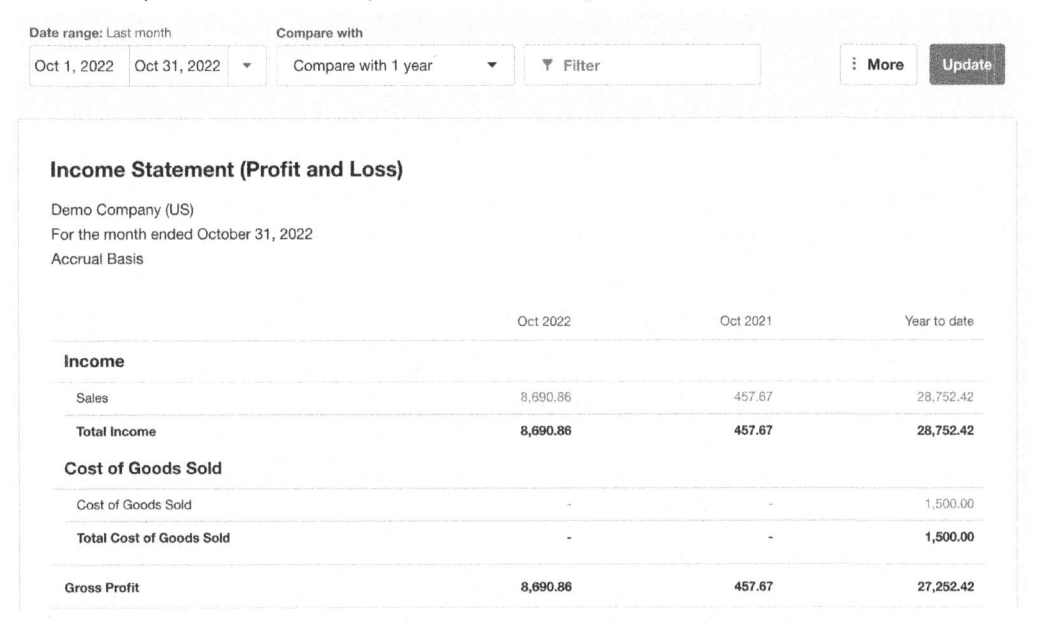

Demo Company (US)
For the month ended October 31, 2022
Accrual Basis

	Oct 2022	Oct 2021	Year to date
Income			
Sales	8,690.86	457.67	28,752.42
Total Income	**8,690.86**	**457.67**	**28,752.42**
Cost of Goods Sold			
Cost of Goods Sold	-	-	1,500.00
Total Cost of Goods Sold	**-**	**-**	**1,500.00**
Gross Profit	**8,690.86**	**457.67**	**27,252.42**

Figure 13.9: Income Statement report with selected criteria

> **Note**
> If there are multiple currencies in use, reports are generated in the base currency.

10. In the left margin of the **Report** screen, there are quick-select options for common report formats. These formats are shortcuts to the customizations we just configured with the setup of the income statement.

    Just click the option you are looking for and the report will update.

Xero standard report

Income Statement (Profit and Loss)

Common formats

Budget Variance

Current and previous 3 months

Current fiscal year by month

Month to date comparison

Year to date comparison

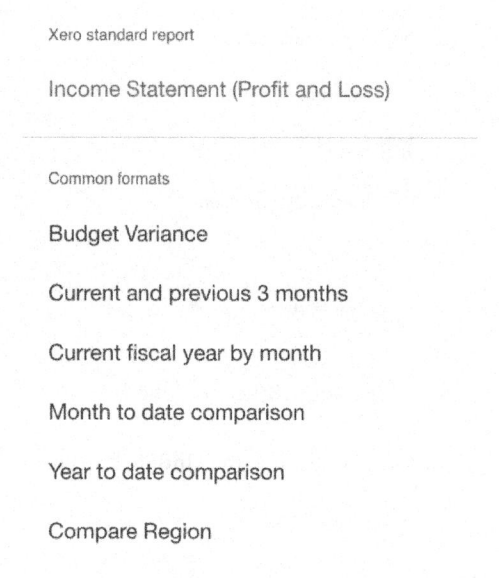

Compare Region

Figure 13.10: Prebuilt Report Customizations screen

At the footer of the report page, there are other options to further customize your reports, as well as options to save and export the report. We will cover the customization options later in *Chapter 15*.

Edit layout | Insert content ▼ | Compact view | Save as ▼ | Export ▼

Figure 13.11: Other report options

You made an effort to customize your reports; now it's time to ensure you can reuse them. In the next section, we will talk about saving reports.

Saving reports in Xero

You can save your reports as a **Draft**, **Published**, or **Custom**. This will save the report in the tab of the same name. Published reports save the report as a snapshot of the time the report was generated and allows the user to drill down into the details. **Custom** will save the report with the current settings and is available to use over and again. I recommend you star the custom reports you will use often.

Figure 13.12: Save as options

Of course, we also want to use this report in other ways. You can **Export** to **PDF**, **Styled PDF**, which is available only to Xero practice users, **Excel,** or **Google Sheets**.

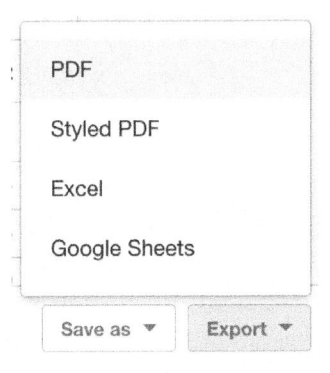

Figure 13.13: Export Options

The other reports are set up very similarly to **Income Statement**.

Summary

We have now gone through the entire cycle from data entry to reports. The Xero reports are super easy to use and very flexible. We have just touched on the flexibility and ease of running the basic reports in Xero, setting them up for the reporting period, and also looked at some of the common prebuilt customized options available. These reports make it easy to understand how your business is functioning and whether it is profitable. We will cover the additional customizations of Xero reports in *Chapter 15*.

In the next chapter, we begin to look at Data Analytics and the Business Snapshot tools in Xero.

14
Business Analytics with Business Snapshot and Short-Term Cash Flow

In the previous chapter, we learned how to produce, run, and customize reports. In this chapter, we will dive a little deeper into reports with business analytics, a newly added feature in Xero to give advisors and business owners actionable details on a business. Let's get right into it.

In this chapter, we're going to cover the following main topics:

- How to produce and read the short-term cash flow report
- Utilizing the business snapshot to analyze your business

Analytics in Xero

The best predictor of the future is the past. Using past data and trends, Xero will use AI to predict how your business will perform in the future. To accomplish this, Xero released **Analytics** and **Analytics Plus**. Analytics comes with a standard **Early** or **Growing** plan, whereas Analytics Plus, which is an expanded form of Analytics, requires an upgrade to the Established plan. Features that are included in the Analytics Plus version of short-term cash flow are not available in trial organizations. We will detail what is included in each of the features as we describe the features.

Short-term cash flow

As we previously said, cash is the lifeblood of business, and knowing your cash position is central to all business decisions. To help business owners, Xero has the **Short-Term Cash Flow** (**STCF**) tool. Let's take a look at the tool in Xero. To get to STCF, we click on the **Business** menu, followed by the **Short-term cash flow** option below it.

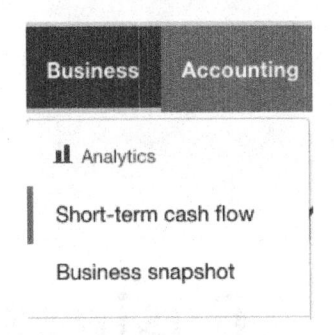

Figure 14.1: The Xero Business menu

This will take you to the STCF main menu.

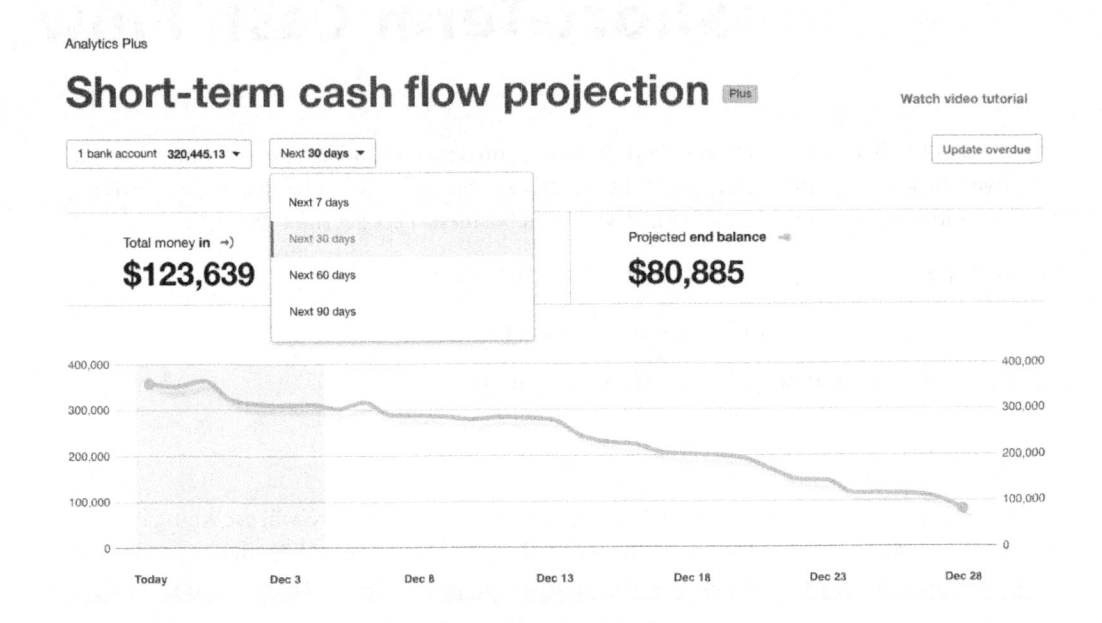

Figure 14.2: A STCF projection

You will need to select your operating cash account(s) and select the time frame for your cash projection. Analytics allows 7 or 30 days, whereas Analytics Plus gives you an additional option of 60 or 90 days for your cash flow projection. The STCF tool will show you future cash based on the invoices and bills in Xero. You will be able to see the impact of scheduled invoices and bills. With Analytics Plus, you get predicted cash flow based on **Spend** and **Receive Money** transactions, and you can add one-off amounts to see the effect on your cash flow and the projections.

⚠ Projections are only based on invoices and bills entered in Xero

Figure 14.3: The Analytics limitation disclosure

Further down the page, below the projection, you will see the projection breakdown. This breakdown can be grouped by **All**, **Day**, **Week**, and **Invoices / bills**.

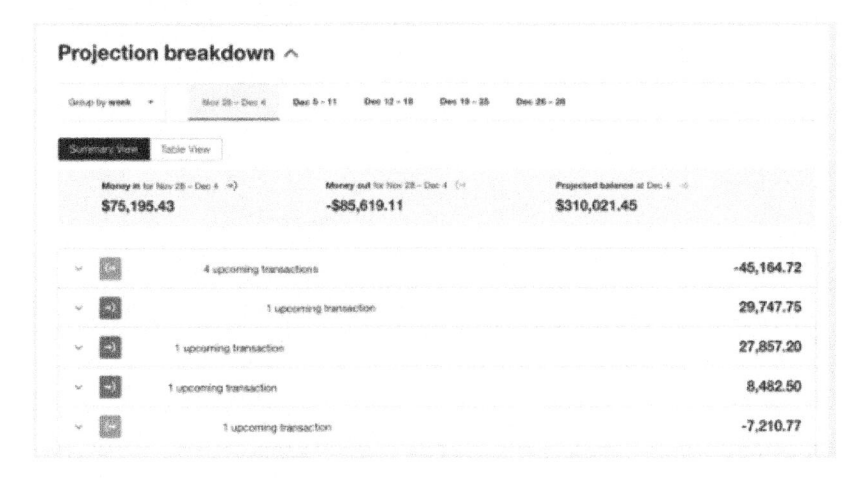

Figure 14.4: The STCF projection breakdown

If you click on any line, you will see the predicted transactions for that breakdown.

Figure 14.5: The line projection detail

To further drill down, click on the date, as shown in *Figure 14.5*, and it will reveal the transactions that make up the projection.

Review prediction

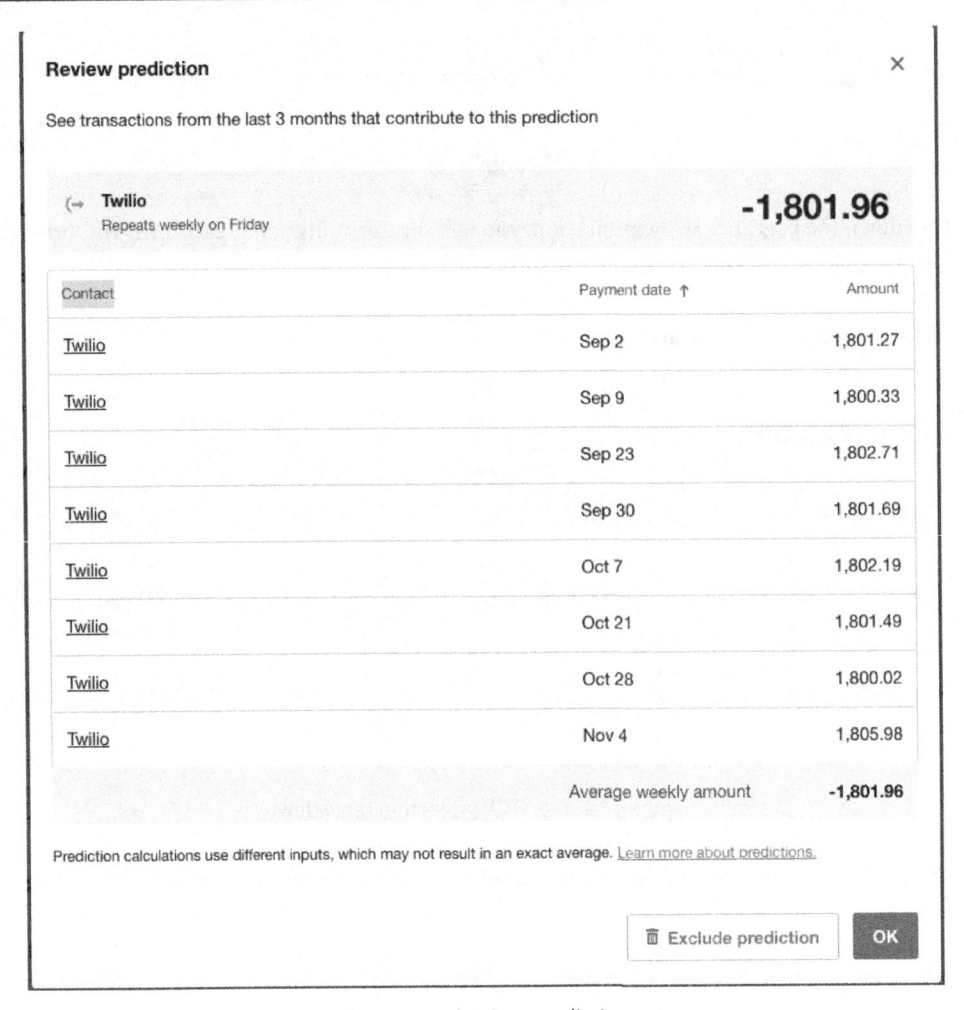

See transactions from the last 3 months that contribute to this prediction

Twilio
Repeats weekly on Friday — **-1,801.96**

Contact	Payment date ↑	Amount
Twilio	Sep 2	1,801.27
Twilio	Sep 9	1,800.33
Twilio	Sep 23	1,802.71
Twilio	Sep 30	1,801.69
Twilio	Oct 7	1,802.19
Twilio	Oct 21	1,801.49
Twilio	Oct 28	1,800.02
Twilio	Nov 4	1,805.98
	Average weekly amount	**-1,801.96**

Prediction calculations use different inputs, which may not result in an exact average. Learn more about predictions.

Figure 14.6: Review prediction

If you wish to exclude this certain prediction, click the **Exclude prediction** button. This will remove this specific line from the projection.

You will be taken to this confirmation screen:

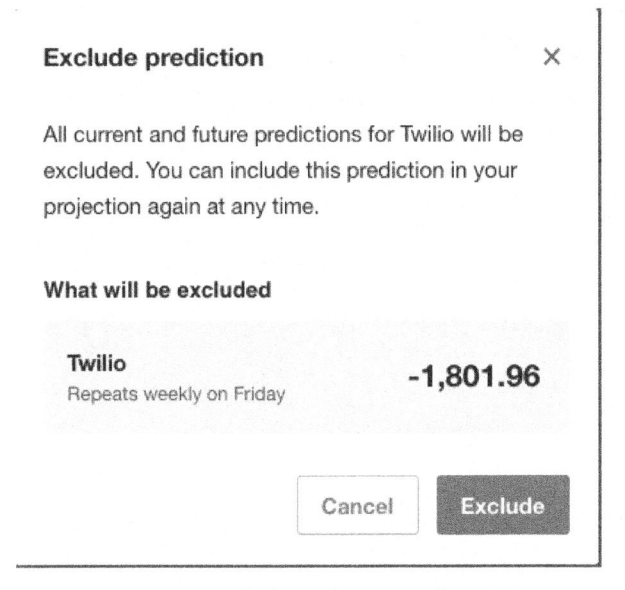

Figure 14.7: Exclude prediction confirmation

At the bottom of the screen, click **View excluded predictions** to see all of the items you excluded from this projection.

In the top-right corner, there is an option called **Update overdue**. With its help, we can edit our projection. There, we can edit bills and invoices' expected payment dates and planned payment dates.

Further down the page, we have **Suggested actions**.

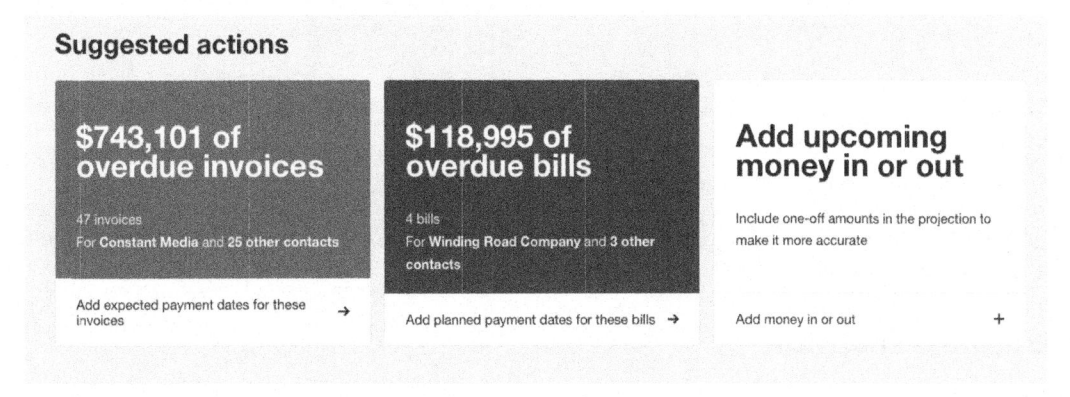

Figure 14.8: Suggested actions

Xero detects invoices and bills with no expected payment date. You should add expected payment data to give you a more accurate cash projection. You can do that by clicking **Add expected payment**

dates for these invoices or **Add planned payment dates for these bills** and entering the expected payment dates. To avoid this, add payment terms to customers and suppliers in their contact records to give Xero an estimate of when to expect the payments.

You can also use **Add upcoming money in or out** when you do not have a transaction in Xero at the time of the forecast.

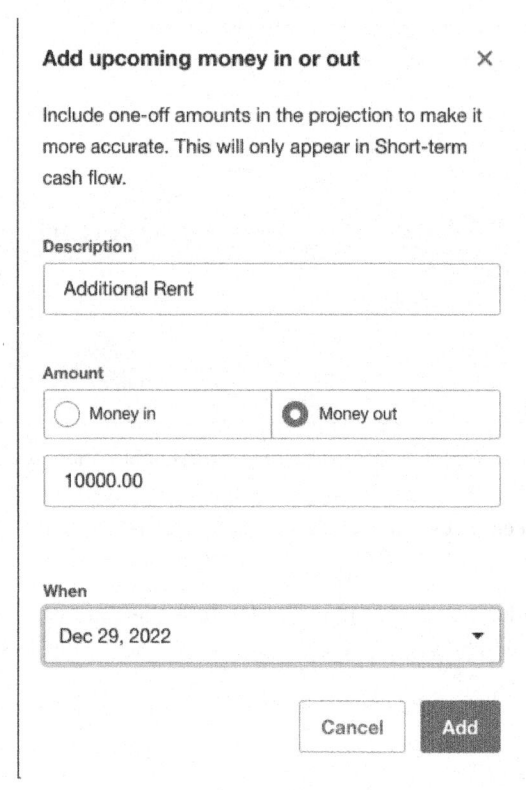

Figure 14.9: Money in or out

Click **Add**, and the entry will be added to your cash projection.

The Xero STCF tool, whether in Analytics or Analytics Plus, is an easy-to-use and very flexible tool that provides you with the details you need to run your business.

Business snapshot

As we said earlier, cash is the heartbeat of the business, but having information about other details of the business is just as important. To help business owners, Xero has the *business snapshot* tool. Let's take a look at the tool in Xero. To get to the business snapshot, we click on the **Business** menu, followed by the **Business Snapshot** option below it.

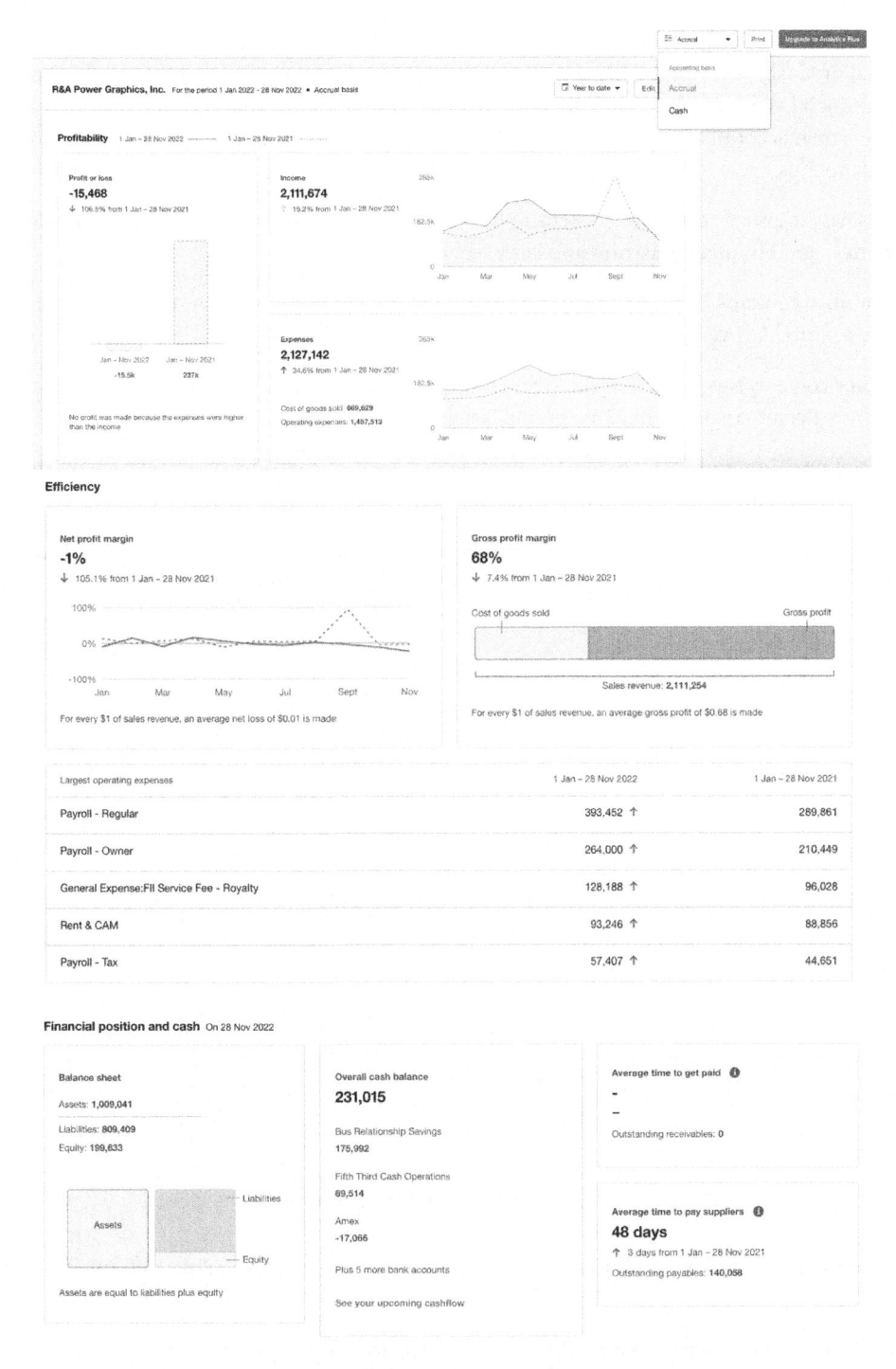

Figure 14.10: A business snapshot in Analytics Plus

If you are not on the Plus version, the snapshot is fairly static. You can choose your accounting basis, **Accrual** or **Cash**, and you can choose from preselected time intervals, **Last month**, **Last quarter**, **Last financial year**, and **Year to date**. For any more granularity, such as custom date ranges, or to choose which accounts to use in the calculations and which expenses to include, you will need to upgrade to Plus.

The business snapshot, regardless of whether on the Plus version or not, is broken down into **Profitability**, **Efficiency**, and **Financial position and cash** sections.

Profitability contains **Profit or Loss**, **Income**, and **Expenses** sections. It shows the difference from the same period last year.

Efficiency contains **Net profit margin**, **Gross profit margin**, and **Largest operating expenses** sections, again with a comparison to the same period last year.

Financial position and cash contains a rudimentary balance sheet, your overall cash balance, and some metrics on how long it takes to pay and be paid.

The data on the snapshot, whether on Analytics or Analytics Plus, is capable of being drilled down. Any amount will take you to the appropriate report, giving you details of what transactions comprise the amount.

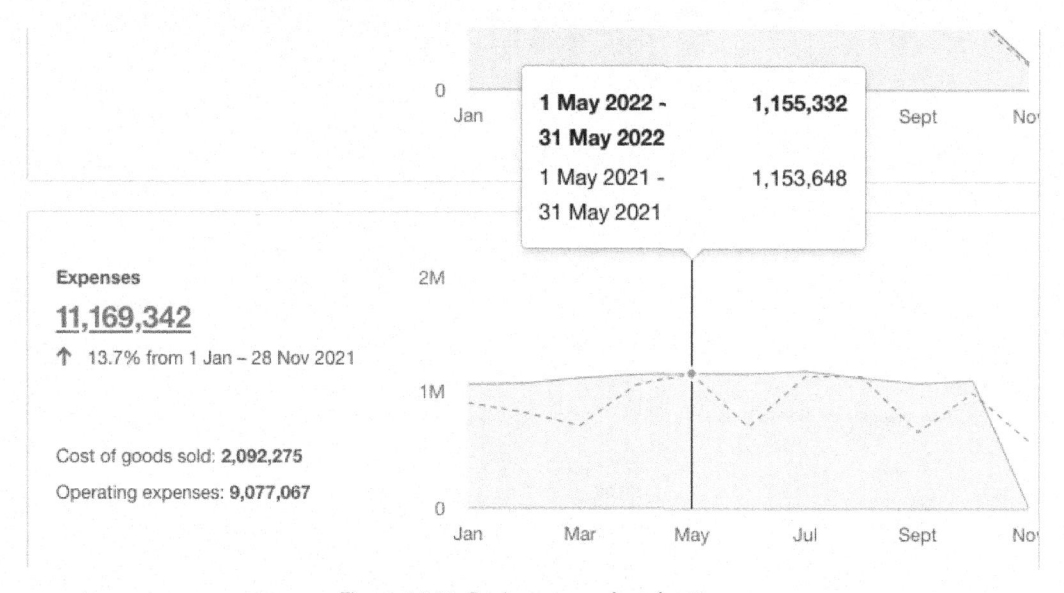

Figure 14.11: Business snapshot details

In addition, if you move your mouse over the graphs, it will give you a breakdown for the period you hover over.

As you can see, the business snapshot gives you a lot of actionable data to use in your business.

Now that we know about the STCF tool and business analytics, we have a much clearer picture of where a business is and where it is heading in terms of cash flow. We also have maximum actionable data, thanks to the two tools, that shows how we can improve our business. This now brings us to the end of the chapter.

Summary

In the chapter, we touched on the basics of Xero reporting and business analytics. The STCF tool and business snapshot give you a glimpse into the past of your business and also show you a clear path forward. These are things every business owner needs to run and manage a successful business.

In the next chapter, we will go back to our Xero reports and begin to customize them with the **layout editor**.

15
Creating Custom Reports in Xero Using the layout editor

As you have seen in *Chapter 13*, Xero does a great job of giving you the basic reports. Now, they even have common formats – which we introduced in *Chapter 13*, (see *Figure 13.10*) – that you can choose and use immediately, but sometimes you need more. You may need to build a summary of Profit and Loss or a specialized schedule, which is like a report on certain balance sheet accounts, and all of that can be done with the layout editor, a reporting design tool embedded in Xero. So, to create custom reports, in this chapter, we will learn how to use the layout editor, customize basic reports, design a schedule using a blank template, and save reports. Let's jump right in and take a look.

In this chapter, we're going to cover the following main topics:

- Exploring the layout editor
- Customizing the basic report
- Starting from a blank slate
- Saving your reports

Exploring the layout editor

The layout editor is a tool built into Xero that allows you to add, remove, and group data in your Xero reports. It gives you the flexibility to meet the needs of different industries and deliver to the business owner's needs.

To access the layout editor, we first must open the basic report:

1. Click **Accounting** followed by the **Reports** option below it.
2. Choose **Income Statement (Profit and Loss)** as our starting point.

3. Set the report parameter that you are looking for. In this case, we will run a report for the current year, with no comparison periods, and we will report on an accrual basis.

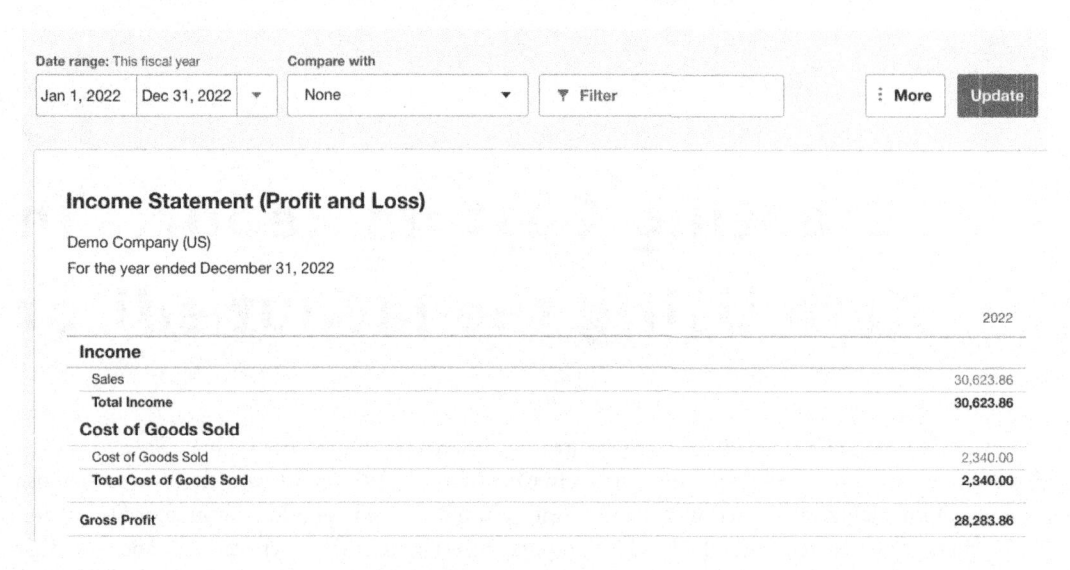

Figure 15.1: Xero Income Statement

4. To open the layout editor, click the **Edit Layout** button in the lower left of the report screen.

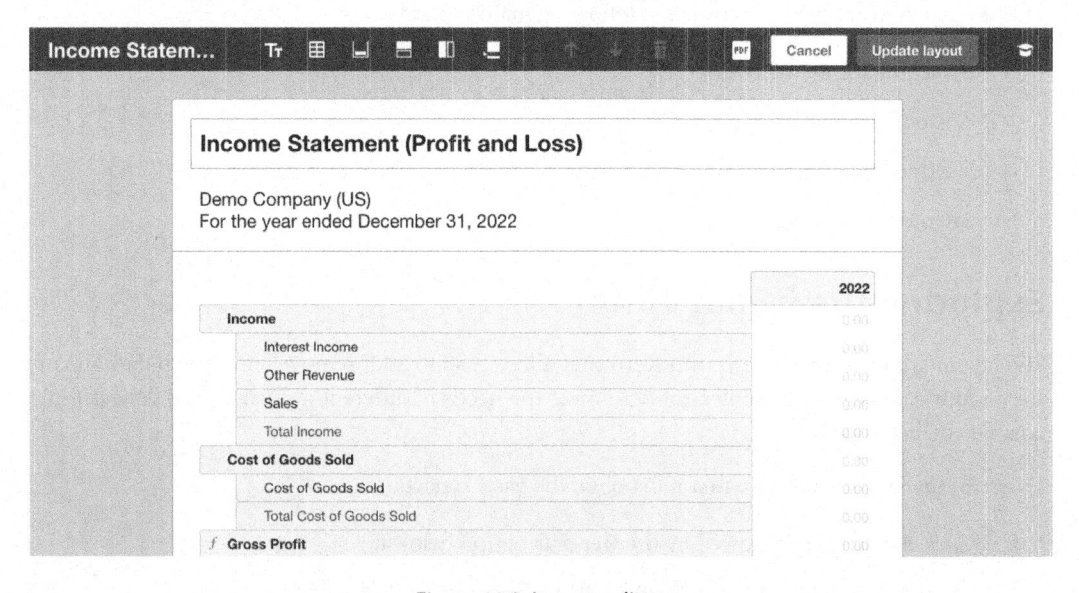

Figure 15.2: Layout editor

The layout editor functions from left to right in the upper menu are as follows:

- **Text block**
- **Schedule**
- **Footer**
- **Rows**
- **Columns**
- **Page break**
- **Move up**
- **Move down**
- **Delete**

For the remainder of this chapter, we will put these features to work.

Customizing the basic report

Let's begin customizing the basic report by adding two columns:

1. To do that, click the **add Columns** icon and then click the type of column you wish to add. In this case, we will want to add one **Date** column and one **Variance** column.

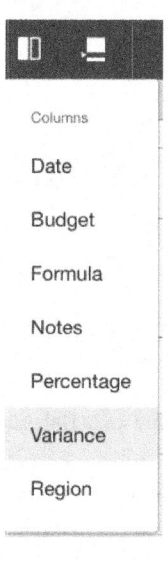

Figure 15.3: Column addition choice types

2. Next, we will click on **Date** and **Variance**, and the layout editor adds them to columns.

	2022	2022	Variance
Income	0.00	0.00	0.00
Interest Income	0.00	0.00	0.00
Other Revenue	0.00	0.00	0.00
Sales	0.00	0.00	0.00
Total Income	0.00	0.00	0.00
Cost of Goods Sold	0.00	0.00	0.00
Cost of Goods Sold	0.00	0.00	0.00
Total Cost of Goods Sold	0.00	0.00	0.00
f **Gross Profit**	0.00	0.00	0.00

Figure 15.4: Layout editor

Now, we will configure our columns:

1. Click on the header of the column, and we will start with the first column added. Here, we will see the **Date** dialog. We can choose predetermined dates from the dropdown. In this case, I chose **Financial year**.
2. Since I also wanted the prior year, I clicked on the arrow buttons to get the desired year.

Date range

Financial year ▼

1 Jan 2021 - 31 Dec 2021   <   >

Column heading

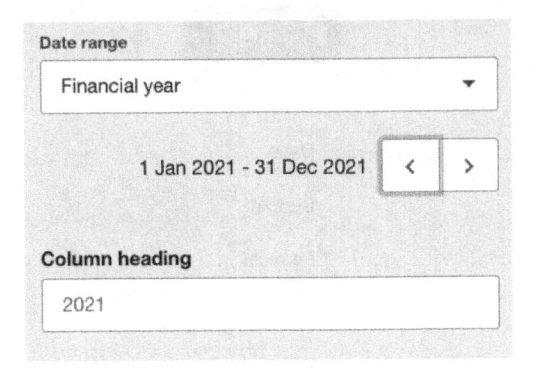

2021

Figure 15.5: Date dialog

3. Now, we will click the top of the **Variance** column to enter the **Variance** dialog screen. We choose the columns using the dropdown to select the columns to compare year over year. If you want to compare multiple years, you can add each of the years you wish to include. In this case, we are comparing the current year with the prior year. You will notice a checkbox under the column selections. If you check this, you can view the variance as a percentage.

4. If you want both percentage and dollars, you will need to add a second variance column.

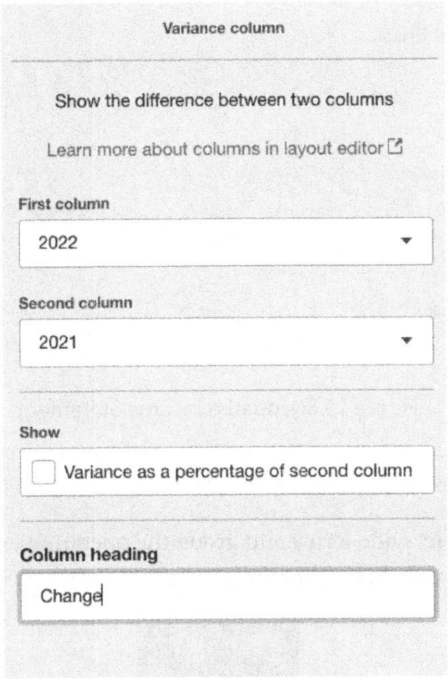

Figure 15.6: Variance dialog

If you see a red highlighted column header in the layout editor, as you see for **Variance** in *Figure 15.4*, it indicates you still have to configure your data or there is an error in the data. The columns and rows are drag-and-drop-style, so if you move a column, you may need to reconfigure it. Columns can only use the data from columns positioned to the left of them.

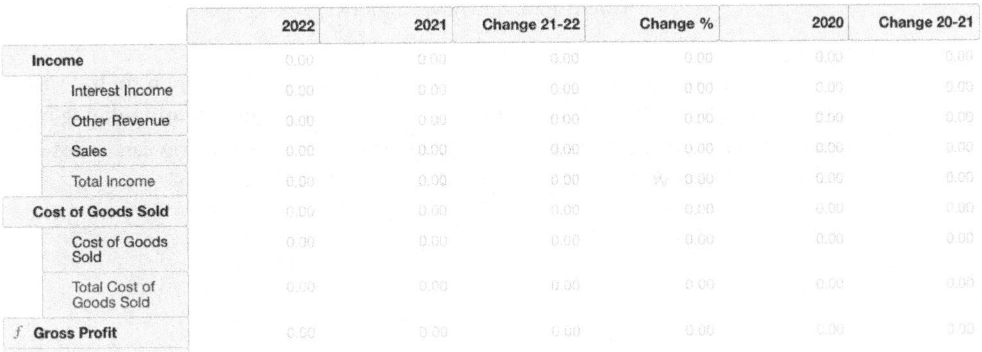

Figure 15.7: Updated layout editor screen after customization

This is what our updated income statement looks like:

Income Statement (Profit and Loss)

Demo Company (US)
For the year ended December 31, 2022

	2022	2021	Change 21-22	Change %	2020	Change 20-21
Income						
Sales	30,623.86	915.34	29,708.52 ↑	3,245.63% ↑	-	915.34 ↑
Total Income	**30,623.86**	**915.34**	**29,708.52**	**3,245.63%**	**-**	**915.34**
Cost of Goods Sold						
Cost of Goods Sold	2,340.00	-	2,340.00 ↑	- —	-	- —
Total Cost of Goods Sold	**2,340.00**	**-**	**2,340.00**	**-**	**-**	**-**
Gross Profit	**28,283.86**	**915.34**	**27,368.52**	**2,989.98%**	**-**	**915.34**

Figure 15.8: Updated Income Statement

We have added columns; now, let's play with the rows.

1. Click **Edit layout** and let's add a row and group the operating expenses into one line. Click on the **add Rows** button and choose **Formula**.

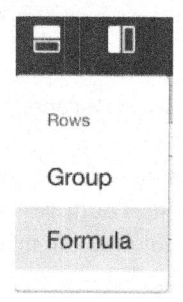

Figure 15.9: Add Rows options

2. The new row is inserted at the bottom of the report; drag it up to where you want it. I will bring it up below **Gross Profit** and then click the row header to open the **Formula** dialog box. We will calculate the gross profit percentage. Using the **Insert** dropdown, you can choose any of the lines or formulas above the row the formula is on.

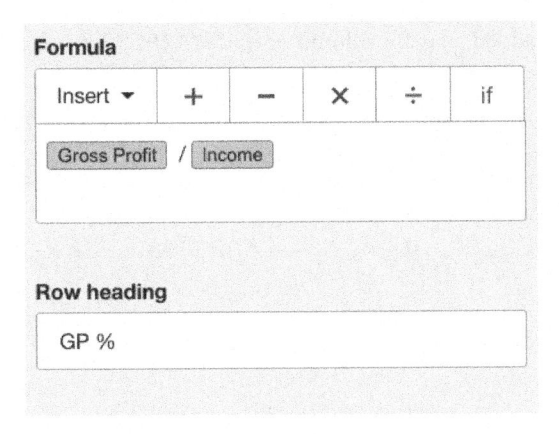

Figure 15.10: Formula dialog box

3. Once the formula is configured, select the expense rows you wish to be included in the group. In this case, we want all of them, so we will click the top expense line, hold down the *Shift* key, and click the last one. Doing so will include all lines within the range.
4. Then, click the **Group selection** button to the right, to open the **Group** dialog. Let's give the row a name and then we can just click the **Group selection** button again to complete the group and move on to the next step.
5. Next, if you want to, you can create rules to include certain accounts by clicking the **Include accounts by code** button. You can use the switch rule feature by clicking the **Move negative balances (switch)** button. I mainly use this to move negatives on the balance sheet – a very helpful feature.

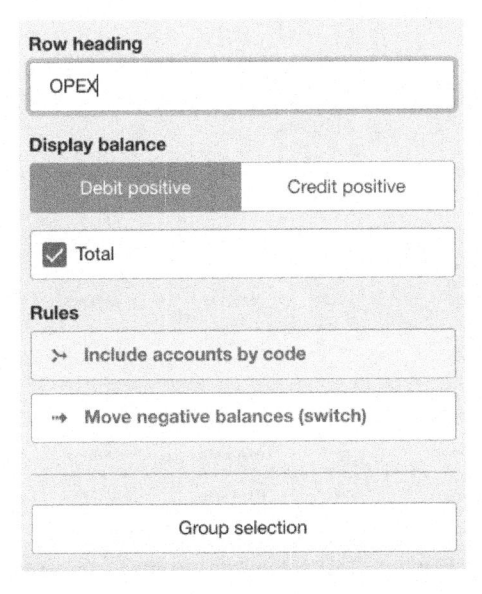

Figure 15.11: Group dialog box

Creating Custom Reports in Xero Using the layout editor

6. If, by chance, you added an extra column or row, just click that column or row to select it and click the *trash* icon to delete it.
7. When your edits are complete, click **Update layout** and view your handy work.

When working with groups, you have the option to see all of the accounts within the group or just the summary. You can set that by clicking on the triangle to the left of the account name.

Figure 15.12: Group showing detail

When it points down, it shows all the details, and when it points to the side, it is in summary.

Figure 15.13: Group showing summary

We can now see the summary information in our income statement:

Income Statement (Profit and Loss)

Demo Company (US)
For the year ended December 31, 2022

	2022	2021	Change 21-22	Change %	2020	Change 20-21
Income						
Sales	30,623.86	915.34	29,708.52 ↑	3,245.63% ↑	-	915.34 ↑
Total Income	30,623.86	915.34	29,708.52	3,245.63%	-	915.34
Cost of Goods Sold						
Cost of Goods Sold	2,340.00	-	2,340.00 ↑	-	-	-
Total Cost of Goods Sold	2,340.00	-	2,340.00	-	-	-
Gross Profit	28,283.86	915.34	27,368.52	2,989.98%	-	915.34
GP %	0.92	1.00	(0.08)	-7.64%	-	1.00
Operating Expenses						
OPEX	39,066.56	185.50	38,881.06 ↑	20,960.14% ↑	-	185.50 ↑
Total Operating Expenses	39,066.56	185.50	38,881.06	20,960.14%	-	185.50
Operating Income	(10,782.70)	729.84	(11,512.54)	-1,577.41%	-	729.84
Net Income	(10,782.70)	729.84	(11,512.54)	-1,577.41%	-	729.84

Figure 15.14: Customized Income Statement

In the layout editor, Xero allows you to add rules to automatically group your accounts to save time editing layouts when new account code is added or edited:

1. Select **Edit Layout.**
2. Create or choose an account group.
3. Select **Include accounts by code** to provide an automation rule based on the account code prefix or range in your chart of accounts.

We have customized the basic report, but there may be a need at some point to build a report from scratch, so we will address that in the next section.

Starting from a blank slate

Previously in this chapter, we modified an *Income Statement* to meet the needs of the client. We can do so for the *Balance Sheet* and other reports as well. Let's say you want to build schedules to run a reconciliation of prepaid expenses, or you want to see all of the merchant clearing accounts in a single schedule; Xero has a blank template to start from.

Let's design a schedule from a blank template:

1. Start by clicking on **Accounting** in the main menu, followed by the **Reports** option below it.
2. In the **Report** search box, enter Blank and choose the blank report from the dropdown.

Figure 15.15: Blank report

3. Start working on the schedule by choosing the date range for your report. I am going to use **Last Month**.
4. Then click **Edit layout**, either at the bottom left or you can use the link in the middle of the report.
5. Click the **Schedule** icon at the top of the screen. A blank schedule (*Figure 15.15*) will appear.

Untitled Report

Demo Company (US)
For the month ended November 30, 2022

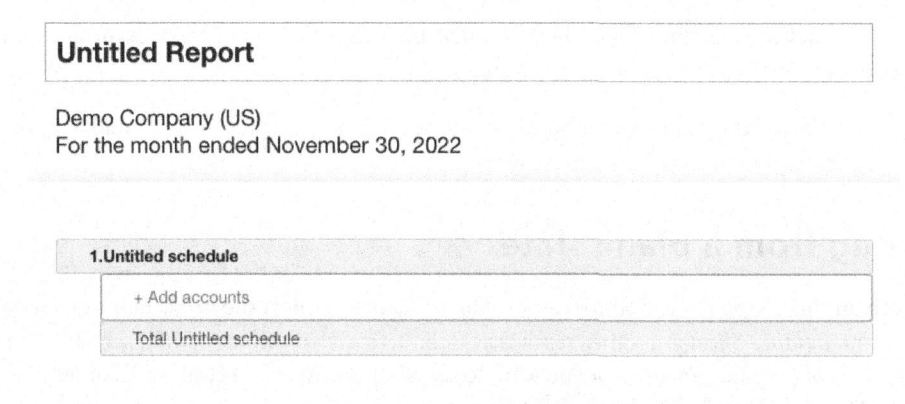

1. Untitled schedule
   + Add accounts
   Total Untitled schedule

Figure 15.16: Blank schedule

6. To add accounts to the schedule, click on + **Add accounts**.
7. Choose the accounts you wish to have on the report.
8. Then, click the **Add Column** icon. Add the columns you need, date ranges, formulas, and so on.
9. Click on the row header and add your own heading.
10. Click on the report title and enter the name of your report.

Untitled Report

Demo Company (US)
For the month ended November 30, 2022

	Nov 2022	Oct 2022	Sep 2022
1. Personnel Related Liabilities	0.00	0.00	0.00
Federal Tax withholding	0.00	0.00	0.00
State Tax withholding	0.00	0.00	0.00
Employee Benefits payable	0.00	0.00	0.00
Employee Deductions payable	0.00	0.00	0.00
Total Personnel Related Liabilities	0.00	0.00	0.00

Figure 15.17: Schedule detail in the layout editor

11. Click **Update layout** when you are finished to view the new report.

Personnel Liabilities

Demo Company (US)
For the month ended November 30, 2022

	Nov 2022	Oct 2022	Sep 2022
1. Personnel Related Liabilities			
Federal Tax withholding	(4,825.00)	(3,300.00)	(1,525.00)
State Tax withholding	(11,025.00)	(7,550.00)	(3,475.00)
Employee Benefits payable	(60,300.00)	(50,300.00)	(37,800.00)
Total Personnel Related Liabilities	**(76,150.00)**	**(61,150.00)**	**(42,800.00)**

Figure 15.18: Completed schedule

You can add any available feature to this report, just as you can to a prebuilt report.

To do that, follow these steps:

1. Go back to the layout editor.
2. Click **Text block**. Add your heading text.
3. In the **Text block** dialog box, you can select **Numbered**, **Standard**, or **None**. **Numbered** will give you a numbered list if you desire, **Standard** will remove the number, and **None** will remove the header. I entered the heading and text shown in *Figure 15.18*.
4. I also added a **Notes** column and linked the note in the column to the note we added to the bottom of the report. You can add as many notes as you need, and each can be linked to a specific line on the report.
5. Click on the *Footer* icon. Type in your footer for your report pages.

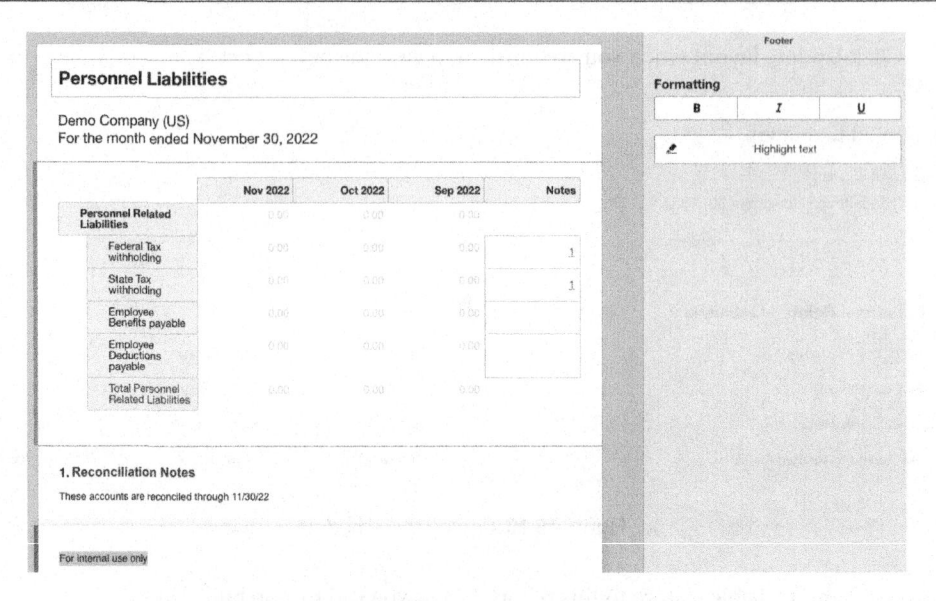

Figure 15.19: Completed schedule and Footer dialog box

6. Any of the text features also allow you to format the text in their respective dialog boxes. Click **Update Layout** when you are finished.

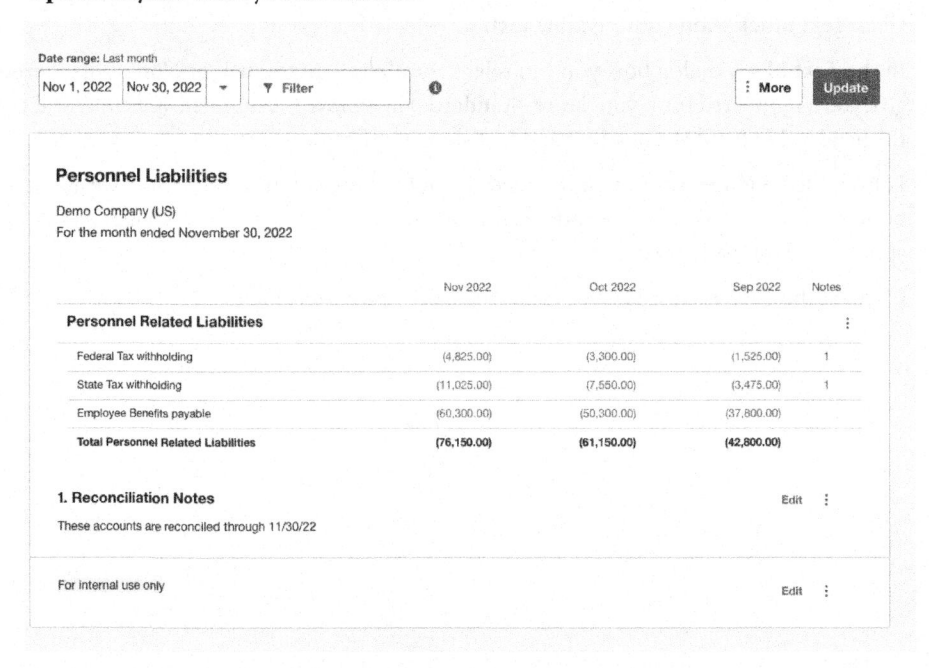

Figure 15.20: Completed schedule

7. You will now see the completed schedule.

As you can see, we have a very powerful tool to create schedules in Xero. In this section, we created a schedule of liabilities. Next, we will save the custom reports so we can reuse them over and over.

Saving your reports

Now that we have created reports that we will use month after month for this company, let's save them to ensure we will always have access to them:

1. Start by clicking the **Save as** button on the lower right of your screen.
2. Click **Custom option** to bring up the **Save** dialog box.
3. Enter the name of your report. I usually do not use the **Make custom report the default** option and remove the check should it be there. I do that in case I need the original report for something else; it makes it easier to use as a jumping-off place the next time you need to customize a basic report.

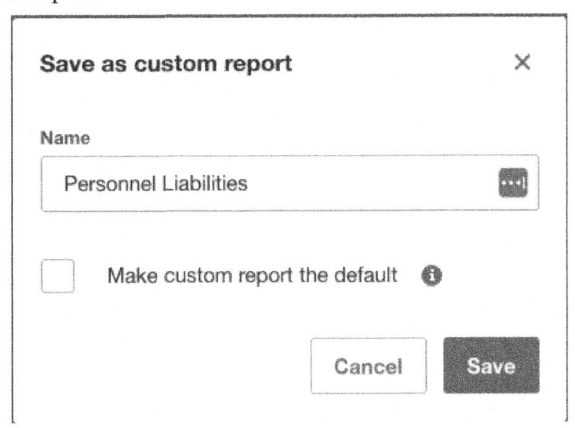

Figure 15.21: Custom report save dialog box

4. Click **Save** and you are through.

We have now saved the custom report, and this brings us to the end of the chapter.

Summary

We have now come full circle. We have set up Xero, entered transactions, used the basic report, and customized the report to our unique needs. As you can see, Xero is a very powerful tool for business owners, accountants, and bookkeepers.

In the next chapter, we will look at Xero HQ, a great tool to help you organize your accounting and bookkeeping business.

Part 5:
For the Advisor

The objective of this section is to tell you about the tools available for Xero Advisors. These would be tools to use to help you build and run your accounting practice, as well as tools that you can apply across all of the clients in your Xero Partner account.

This section comprises the following chapters:

- *Chapter 16, Running Your Practice with Xero HQ*
- *Chapter 17, Exploring Practice-Wide Report Templates*
- *Chapter 18, Exporting Your Data and Reports Out of Xero*
- *Chapter 19, Increasing Your Powers with Apps and Xero*

16
Run Your Practice with Xero HQ

We have covered all the accounting features in Xero. Now, we turn to Xero HQ, which has features that help accounting and bookkeeping professionals run their businesses smoothly. Xero has given you all the tools, such as client management, Explorer, Xero Ask, and the ability to manage your staff. These tools help to build and run an efficient business. We will explore these tools and features throughout this chapter.

In this chapter, we're going to cover the following main topics:

- Adding new clients to Xero and how to connect an existing Xero organization or create a Xero organization
- Using the **Explorer** feature to see the apps, banks, and industries used by your clients
- Making requests safely and securely to clients using **Ask**
- Managing staff

What is Xero HQ?

Xero HQ was introduced a few years ago, replacing **My Xero** as the central location to run your accounting business. It is a light **customer relationship management** (**CRM**) system where you load your clients and their business information, keep notes, manage staff, securely trade information with the client, and gain insights into your clients. We are going to dive in deeper here, showing you just how all this is accomplished.

212 Run Your Practice with Xero HQ

Now that we know what Xero HQ is, let's see what Xero HQ does:

1. To get to Xero HQ, we click the main button in the top-left corner of the Xero window, which shows the Xero company you are currently logged into, followed by the **Xero HQ** option below it:

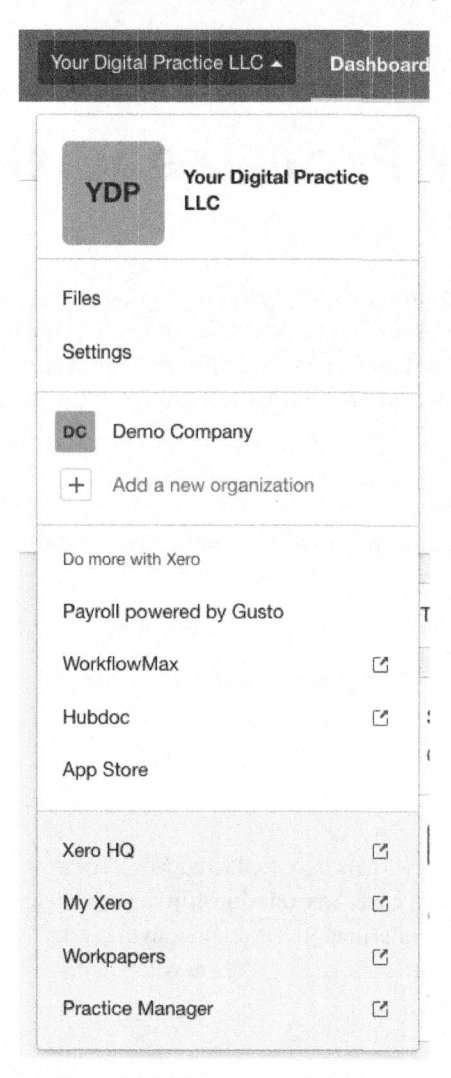

Figure 16.1: Xero accounting menu

2. This will take you to Xero HQ:

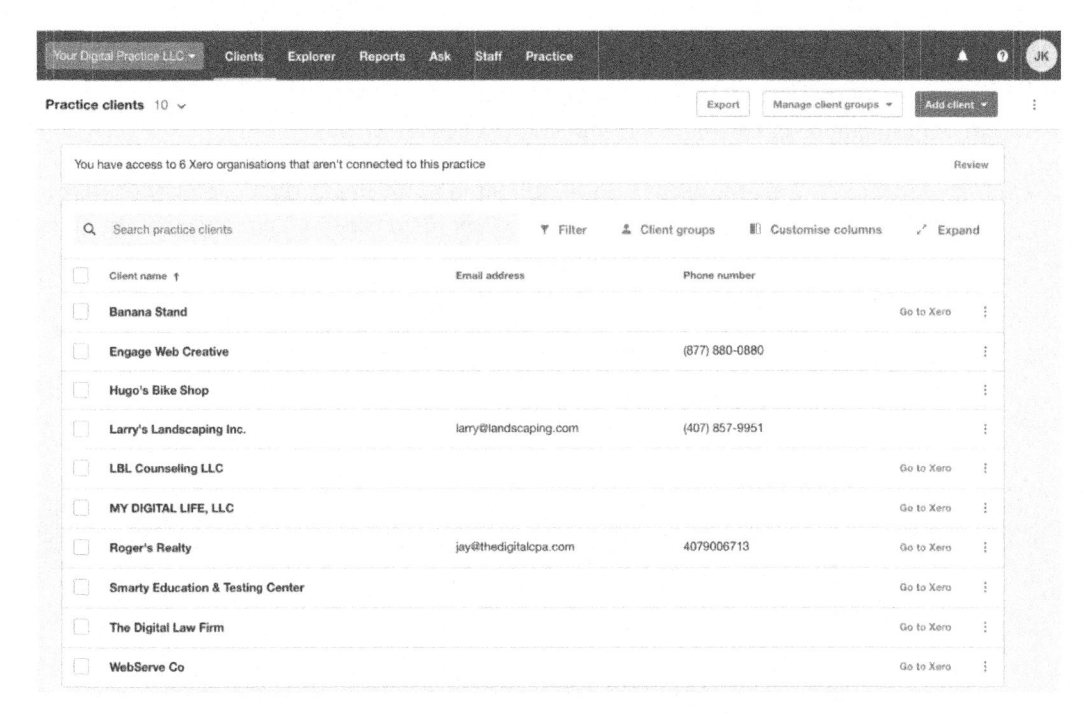

Figure 16.2: Xero HQ main menu

3. As you can see in the preceding figure, in the Xero HQ main menu, we start with a list of our business clients. These are, or at least should be, all of our clients, not just the ones we have connected with on Xero. See, we are already managing our business.

4. As you can see in *Figure 16.2*, the rightmost column will show you whether your client is on Xero, and clicking the **Go to Xero** link will take you right into Xero.

If you look at the top of the Xero HQ main menu, you can see that Xero HQ is composed of six tabs, very similar to the user interface on other features of Xero. The Xero HQ tabs are **Clients**, **Explorer**, **Reports**, **Ask**, **Staff**, and **Practice**.

Let's start exploring Xero HQ.

Clients in Xero HQ

As we said earlier in this chapter, Xero HQ is a light CRM, and that is where you would expect to find your clients and their details.

Let's start our exploration of **Clients** in Xero by adding a new client:

1. We do that by clicking the green **Add client** button in the upper-right corner of the screen (*Figure 16.2*). This will allow us to add a new client or an existing Xero organization. If the client is on Xero already, click the *existing* option.
2. We are going to start from scratch and click **New client**. This will open the **New client** box:

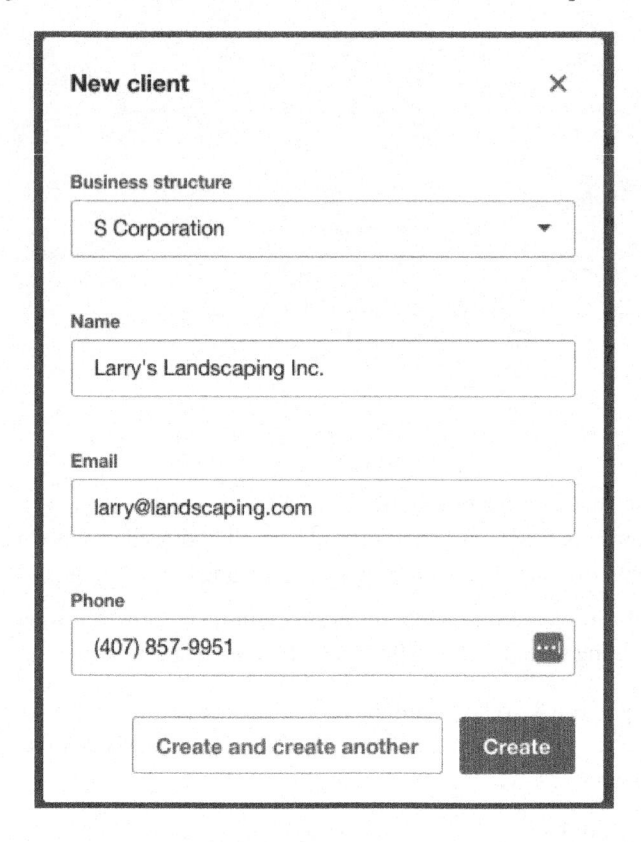

Figure 16.3: New client box

3. We will start creating this new client by adding the business structure. Using the dropdown, choose the entity/tax type of this client. Here, we chose **S Corporation**.
4. Add the **Name**, **Email**, and **Phone** details of this new client.
5. Click the **Create** button. This will take you to the client details screen:

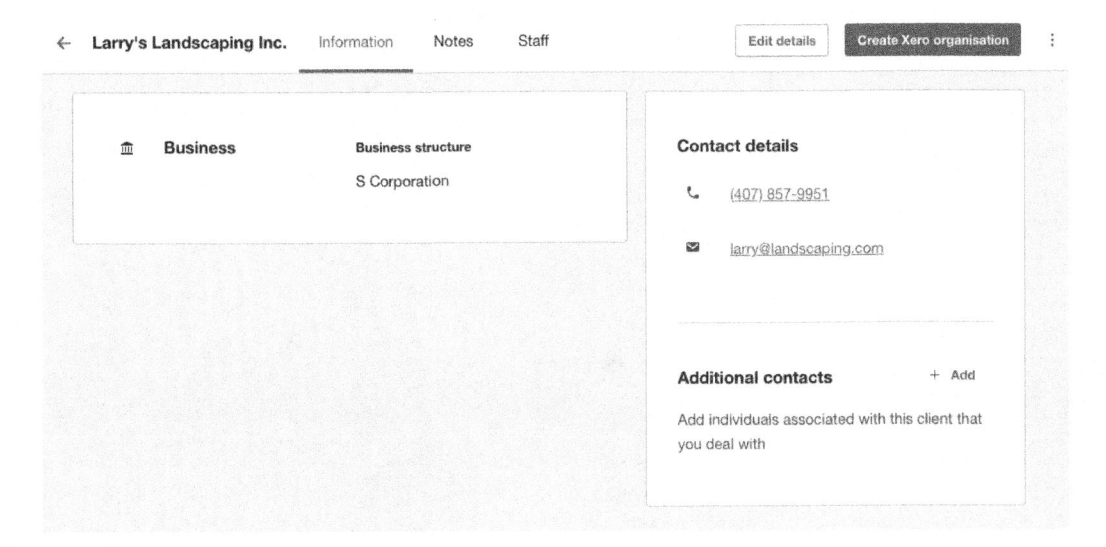

Figure 16.4: Client details screen

6. From here, we can edit the client by clicking the **Edit details** button. This takes you to the main **Client** screen:

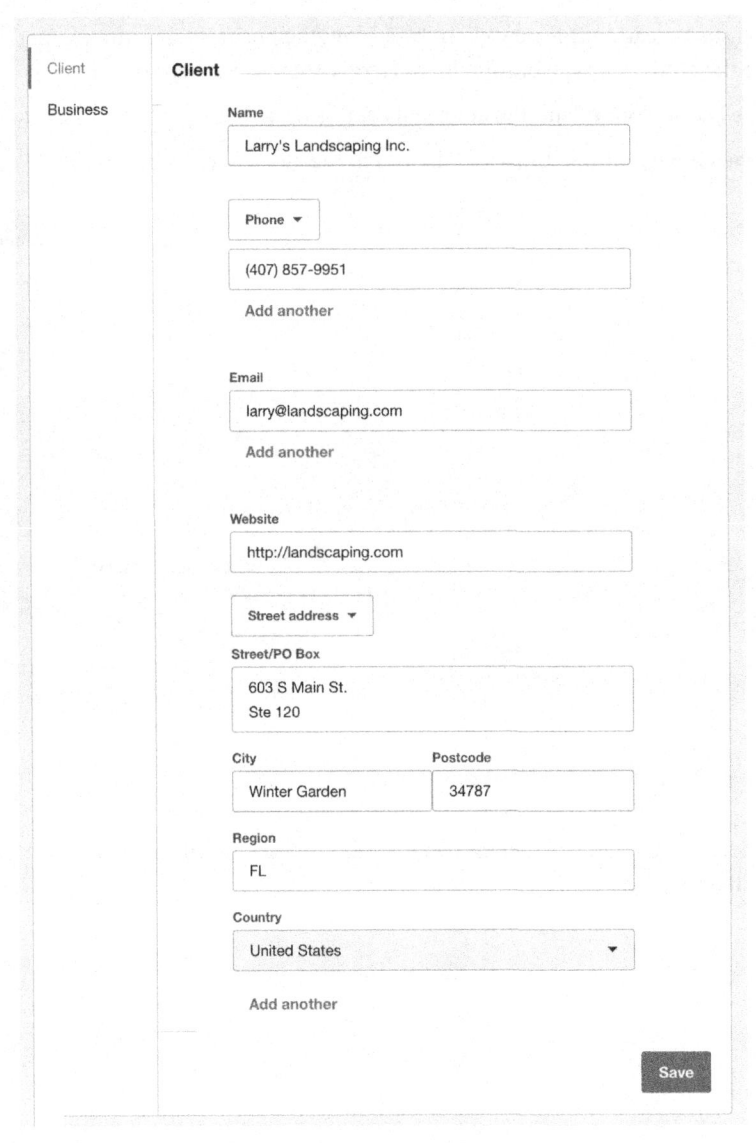

Figure 16.5: Edit client screen

7. As you can see, in the upper-left corner of this screen, there are two tabs: **Client** and **Business**.
8. In the **Client** tab, we can enter the address and other information regarding this client.
9. Clicking **Add another** at the bottom of the screen allows you to add additional addresses, such as post and delivery addresses if different from the mailing address of the client.
10. Let's click on **Business** and look at those details:

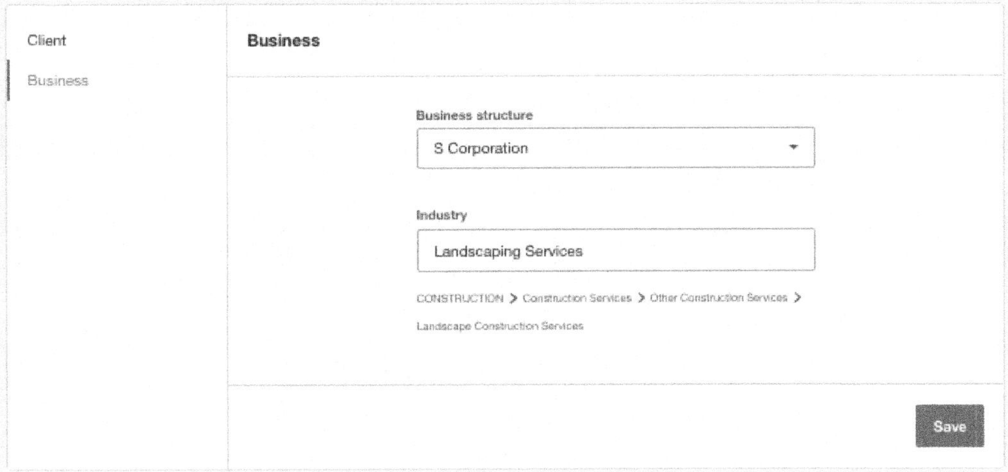

Figure 16.6: Business details screen

If you were not sure of the **Business structure** type, you can edit it here. Just use the dropdown and choose the correct entity type:

- **Corporation**
- **S Corporation**
- **Not for Profit**
- **Partnership**
- **Trust**
- **LLC**
- **Other**

I would suggest you make this the tax entity of the company. This will keep you and your staff in the know and help when it comes to the chart of accounts structure and details when recording specific tax- or equity-related entries.

The other field is **Industry**. Xero has the **North American Industry Classification System (NAICS)** system built in. The NAICS is a classification system of businesses in the US used by many businesses and government departments to track data and trends by specific industries. Just enter the main industry your client is in, and Xero will search the database and give you options to choose from. This is probably one of the most important fields you can complete in Xero HQ. This data is used in the **Explorer** tab details and also used to help other prospective clients in that industry find you when searching for a Xero accountant on the Xero partner advisor directory.

When you are finished editing the client details, click the **Save and Close** button at the top right of the page.

This returns you to the main **Client** screen.

11. As seen in *Figure 16.4*, you can click the + **Add** link to add contacts. Enter the details and click **Save** when you have completed the entry:

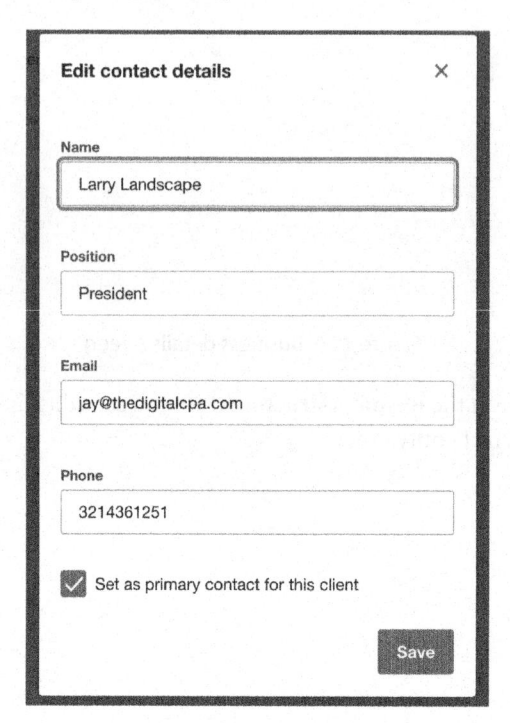

Figure 16.7: Edit contact details screen

This will take you to the updated client details screen:

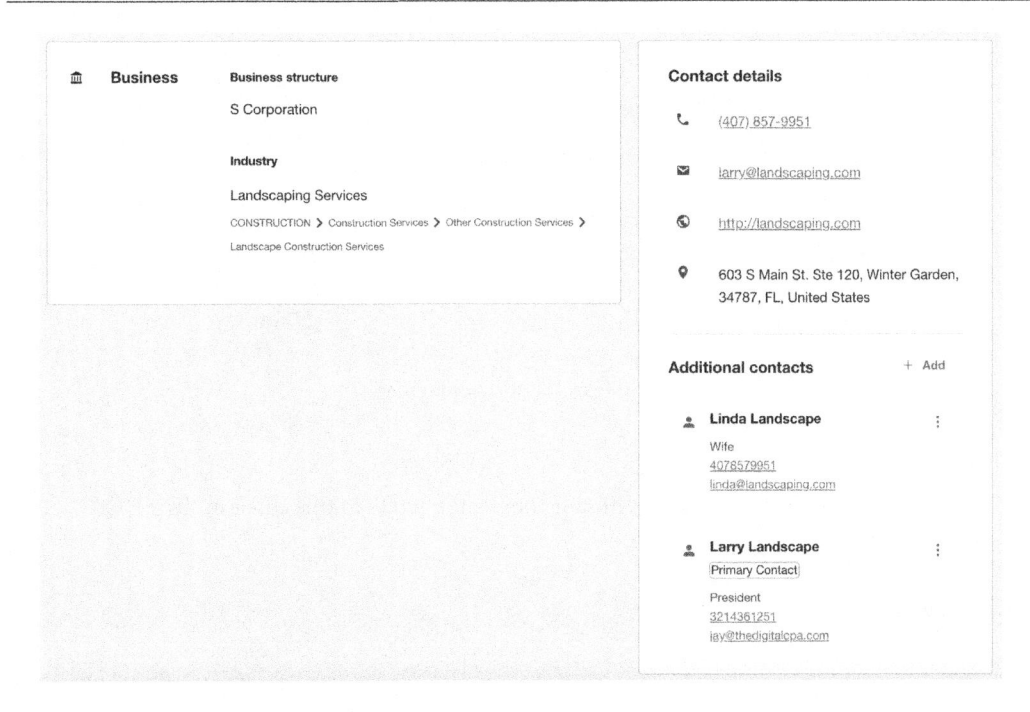

Figure 16.8: Updated client details screen

12. At the top of the client details screen, you can click on **Notes** to go to the **Notes** section of the client details:

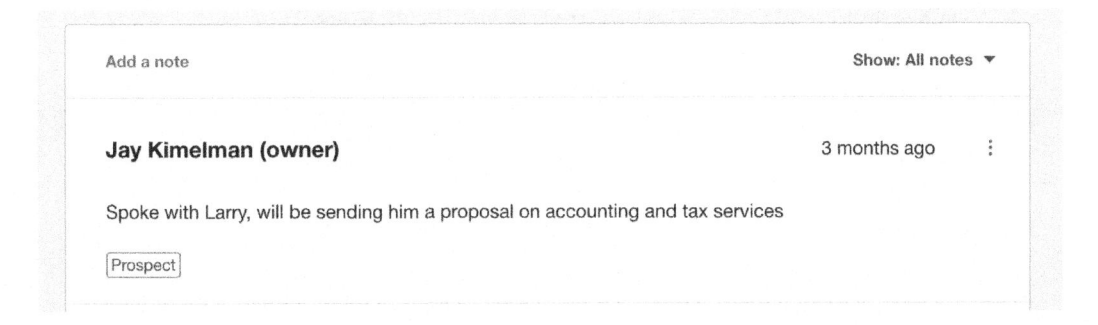

Figure 16.9: Client Notes screen

As you see in *Figure 16.9*, there are details of notes you have made for this specific client, and you can filter your notes by tags associated with a note by clicking **Show: All notes** and choosing a tag.

13. Clicking **Add a note** takes you to a new note screen, allowing you to add information that you feel is relevant to this client or your work with them:

Jay Kimelman (owner)

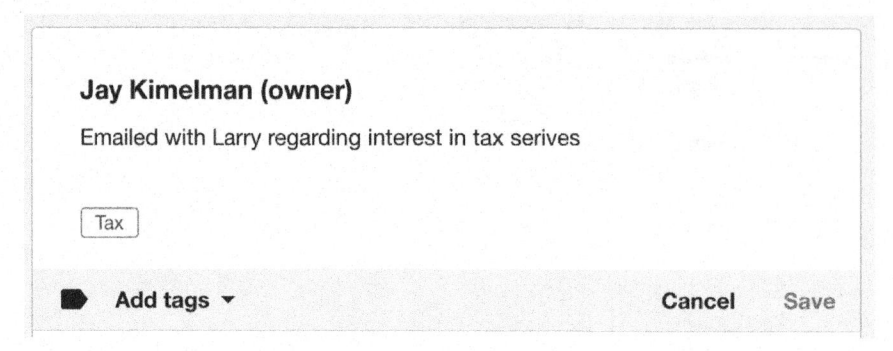

Emailed with Larry regarding interest in tax serives

[Tax]

▶ Add tags ▼   Cancel   Save

Figure 16.10: Add note screen

14. Click **Save** to complete your note.
15. Then, click on the **Staff** tab to maintain your staff's access to this client in Xero HQ:

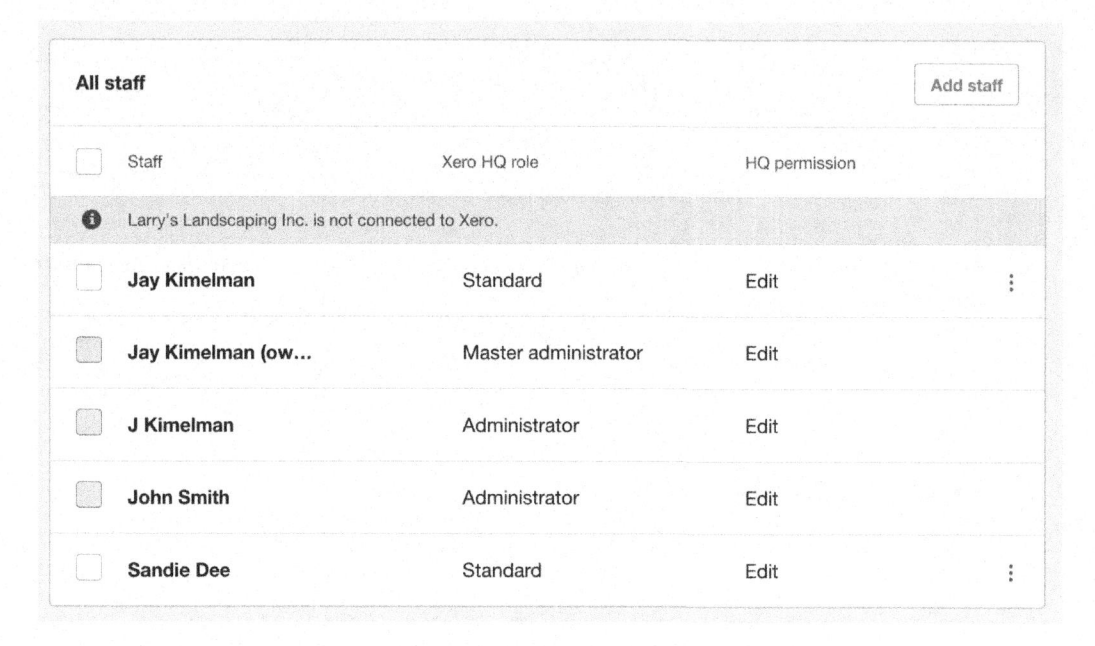

All staff			Add staff
Staff	Xero HQ role	HQ permission	
ⓘ Larry's Landscaping Inc. is not connected to Xero.			
Jay Kimelman	Standard	Edit	⋮
Jay Kimelman (ow…	Master administrator	Edit	
J Kimelman	Administrator	Edit	
John Smith	Administrator	Edit	
Sandie Dee	Standard	Edit	⋮

Figure 16.11: Staff main screen

16. Click the **Add staff** button to add staff to this client:

Figure 16.12: Add staff screen 1 of 2

17. Click the checkbox to select a staff member for this client and click **Next** when done:

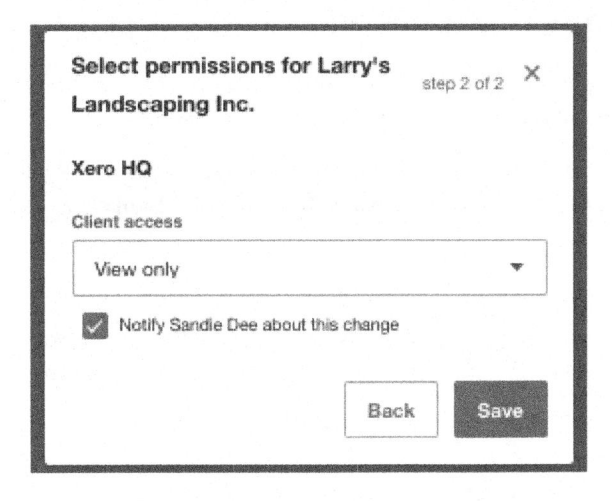

Figure 16.13: Add staff screen 2 of 2

18. This screen gives the staff permissions for this client. The options are **View only** and **Edit**. I suggest you determine what access you want staff to have at this level. If you are a one- or two-person operation, I would probably use **Edit**. If you are a larger organization, I would use **View only** for accounting staff.

19. Click **Save** to complete the process.

> **Note**
> We can customize the client list with a number of columns such as email address, phone number, subscription type, unreconciled bank feeds, industry, financial year, and so on. In addition, you can also create different groups for your listed clients according to your requirements. This grouping helps you keep your clients organized.

We have now completed the review of the client details in Xero HQ. As we continue through this chapter, we will see how this data is used. In the next section, we will see how the data entered is used and displayed in Explorer.

Explorer details in Xero – what is it exactly?

Xero set up the **Explorer** tab to give the accounting practices details about their clients in the area of industry, apps in use, and the banks they have relationships with.

Looking at the top of the **Explorer** tab, you will find four tabs set up exactly like the other features in Xero. Here, we have **COVID-19 support**, **Apps**, **Industry**, and **Banks**:

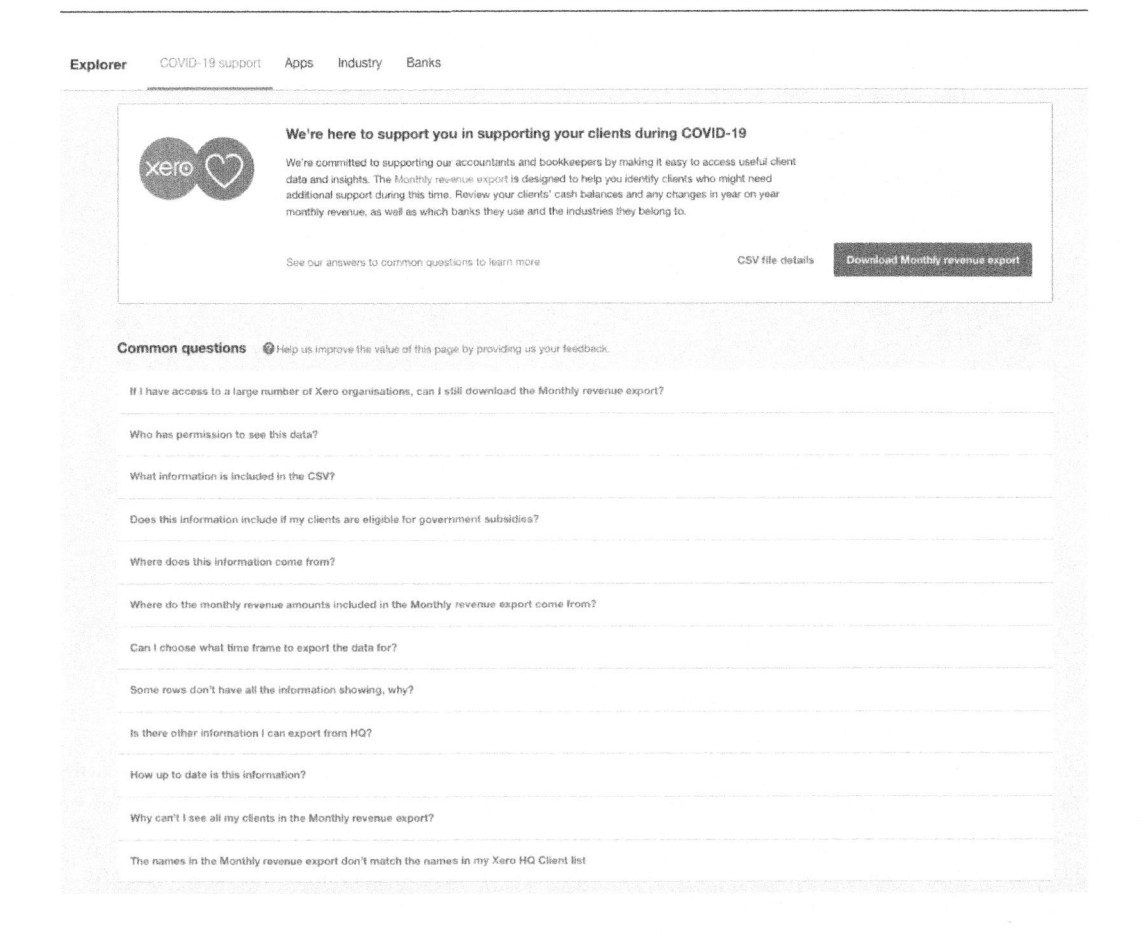

Figure 16.14: Xero HQ Explorer

The **COVID-19 support** tab was built during the pandemic, giving accountants and bookkeepers information they could use to assist their clients. The information is still there and relevant today.

The **Apps** tab gives you insights about the apps in use by your clients:

224   Run Your Practice with Xero HQ

Figure 16.15: Xero HQ Apps

At the top of the page is a graph showing the apps of your clients that are connected to Xero. It shifts to the right in descending order of Xero organizations connected to the specific app. You can click on the app in the graph and Xero HQ will filter the list to show you a list of the clients using that app. This is really important, as it can help you know which of your clients are using this specific app, which, in turn, can help in case of any issue that you may want to be proactive with in the case of a specific client. Some common issues that you may face are a price change coming, an API connection issue, or a major upgrade coming. Now you know exactly who to contact and keep them in the know well in advance.

Figure 16.16: Xero HQ Apps Hubdoc details

The **Industry** tab works in the same way as the **Apps** tab, except it displays your clients by industry or niche. This is very useful when you are planning your marketing strategy or looking at other industries to specialize in. You can filter to the specific industry and see who your client is and whether this is an industry you know and perform well in. You can also use this to stay proactive with your clients in a specific industry. Maybe there is some new legislation or a new tool that will benefit companies in this industry. With the help of the details, you can go on to send communication to these clients and help them plan for the upcoming changes.

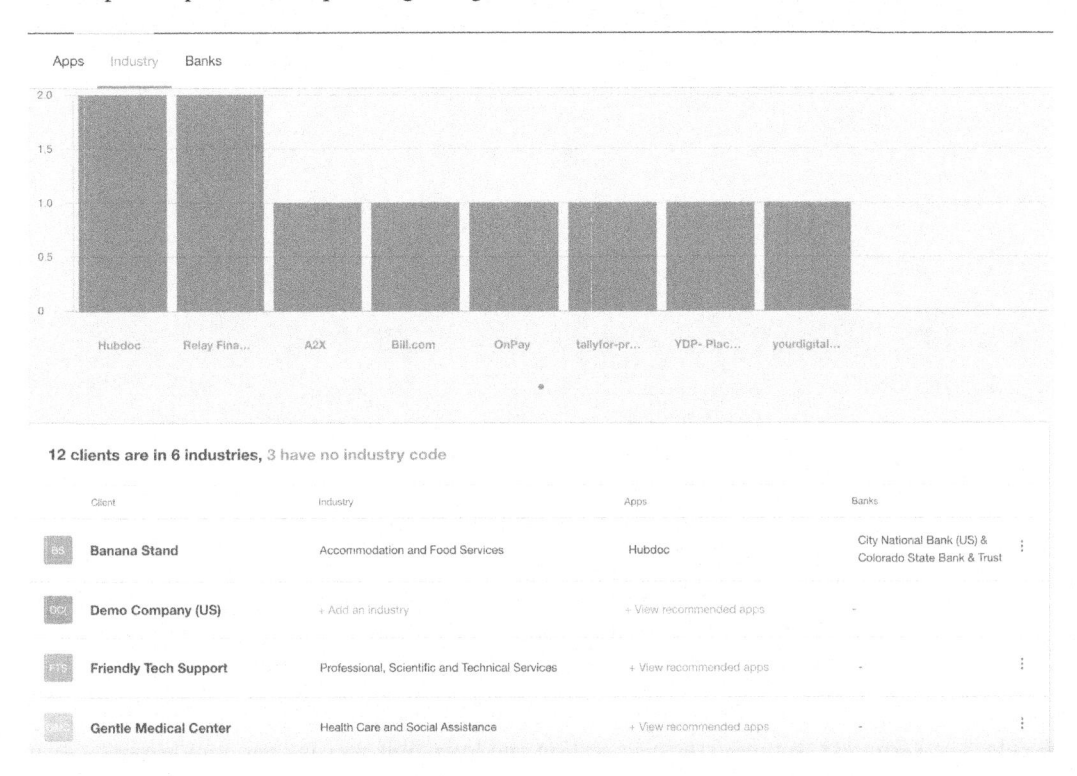

Figure 16.17: Xero HQ Industry details

Just like the tabs we have already covered, the **Banks** tab works the same. Through this tab, you can gain insights into the banks your clients are using. You will be able to guide your clients to better banks for technology, be able to let clients know there may be a bank feed issue due to some change to the bank's online system, and much more.

Figure 16.18: Xero HQ Banks details

You can see the same theme throughout the **Explorer** tab. Xero gives you the tools to be a proactive advisor, allowing you to avoid the traditional reactionary historical response, giving you more proactive means and helping you give your clients information or actionable instructions in advance.

Now that we have insights into the clients and their operations, let's dig in and get operational. We will look at Xero's **Ask** feature in the next section and learn how we can communicate and gather information securely.

What is Ask, you ask?

Ask is a secure tool that allows you and your client to share information and documents back and forth.

Ask has been a very useful tool since its introduction some time back. We can use it to ask our clients specific questions or share documents we need to effectively manage their accounts and transactions.

What is Ask, you ask?   227

To find Ask, from the Xero HQ menu, click on **Ask** at the top of the screen:

Figure 16.19: Ask main screen

As you can see, **Ask** has two tabs: **Queries** (for the exchanges going back and forth with the client) and **Templates** (where you can assemble a standard list of questions to send to your clients).

Onboarding is a perfect topic to have a template set up to expedite communication with a new client. Templates help you build efficiency in your process by having a standard document of requests and questions that you send to most of your new clients.

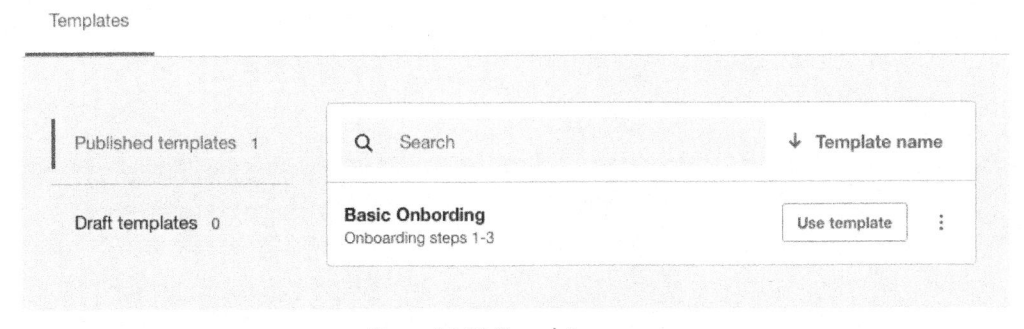

Figure 16.20: Templates screen

Let's learn how to create and use a new template with the help of the **Templates** tab:

1. You can create a new template by clicking the green **New template** button in the upper-right corner of your screen.
2. You can put the template to use by clicking the **Use template** button or you can click the three-dot menu to edit, delete, or copy the template. We are going to click **Edit**. This will bring you to the **Edit template details** screen:

Figure 16.21: Edit template details screen

3. Update the name and the description and click **Save**.
4. Click the name of the template and you will see the details of the requested template.
5. Now, click on the three-dot menu to edit the template questions:

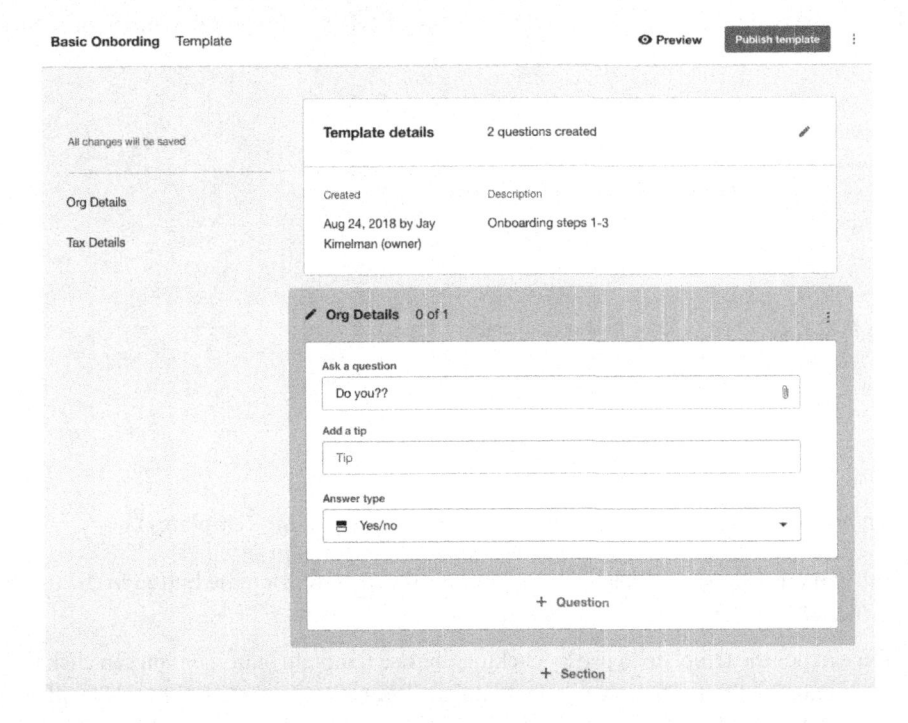

Figure 16.22: Edit template details screen

6. You can see the **Ask** template is broken down into a header and a question section. You can update the header by clicking the pencil icon at the top of the page. This works just like the **Edit template details** section previously, as seen in *Figure 16.21*.
7. The template is broken up into sections, displayed on the left of the screen: **Org Details** and **Tax Details**. You can add sections to the template by clicking + **Section** at the bottom of each section.
8. Click the pencil icon to the left of the section name and enter your section title:

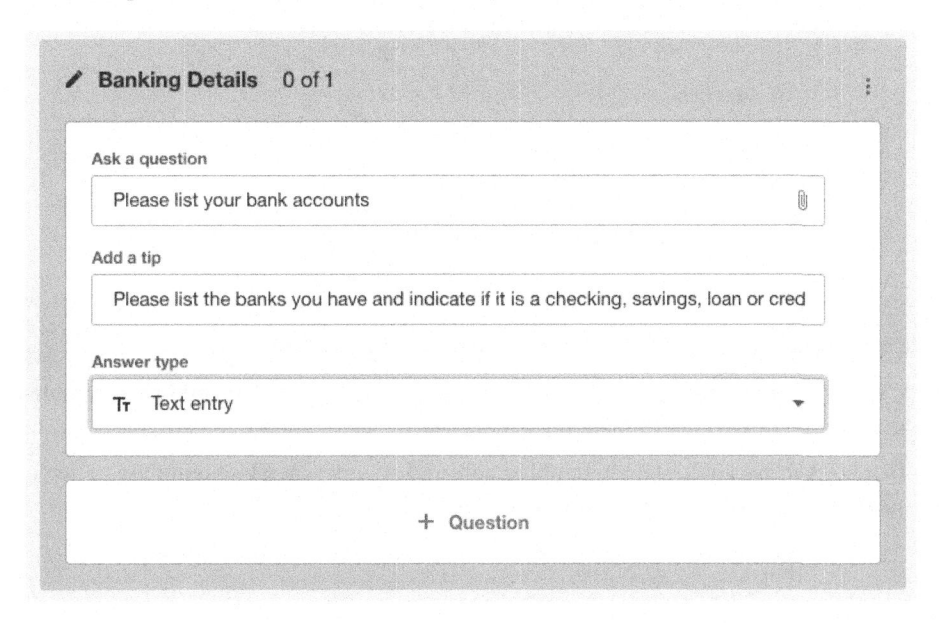

Figure 16.23: Edit template question screen

Ask your question; be specific.

9. Use the **Add a tip** box to add details to your request. **Answer type** will give different options for the client's answers:

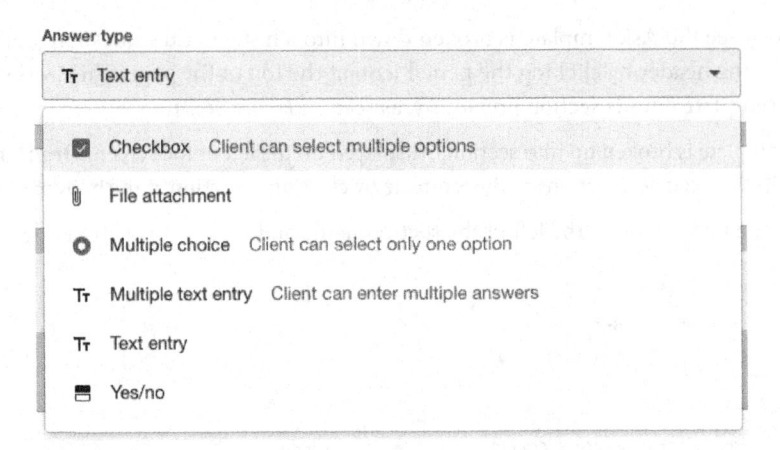

Figure 16.24: Answer type options

Use the appropriate choice for your specific request.

10. Click **+ Question** to add an additional question to this section.
11. When you are through with editing or adding questions, click the **Publish Template** button and confirm by clicking **Publish** once more.
12. That takes us back to the main template screen. Let's now click **Use template** to deploy these questions. This brings up the **New query** box:

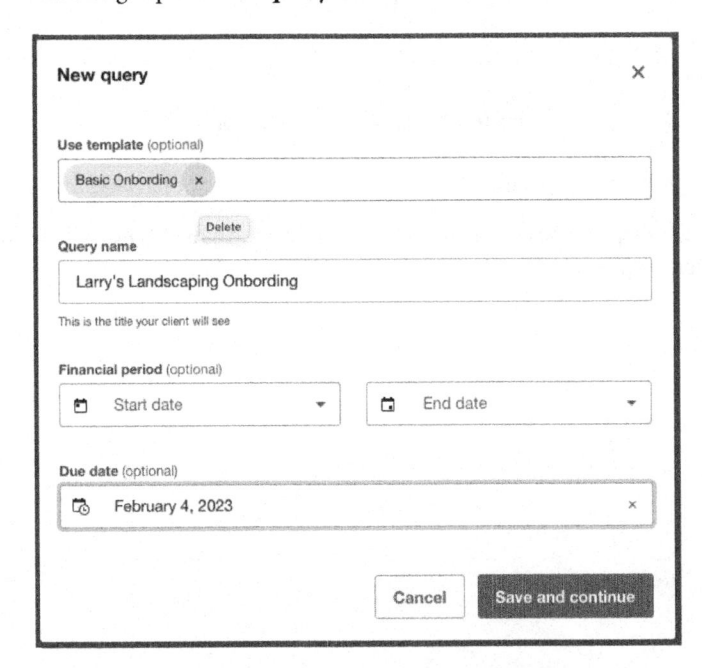

Figure 16.25: New query dialog box

13. Here you can add multiple templates if the case warrants, give the query a name, enter a fiscal period if needed (it is not in this case), and choose a due date. When completed, click **Save and continue**. This will bring you to the **Select recipients** page:

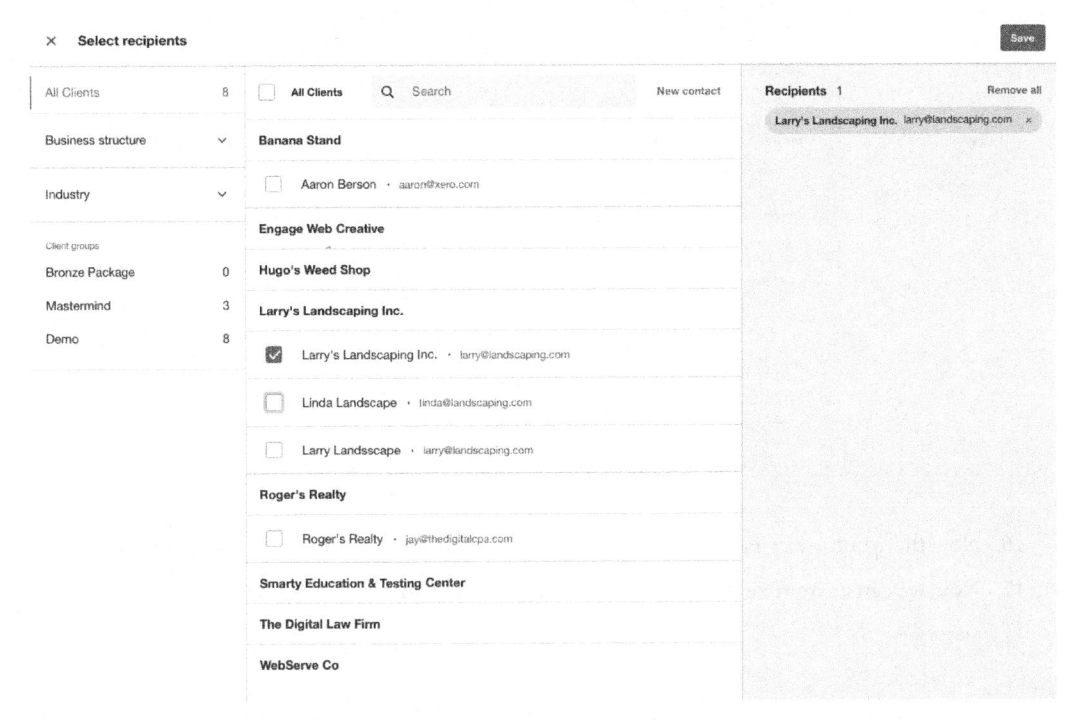

Figure 16.26: Select recipients page

14. Select the contact and client you want to receive this **Ask** query and click **Save**.
15. That will bring you to the query screen, where you can customize the template for your client:

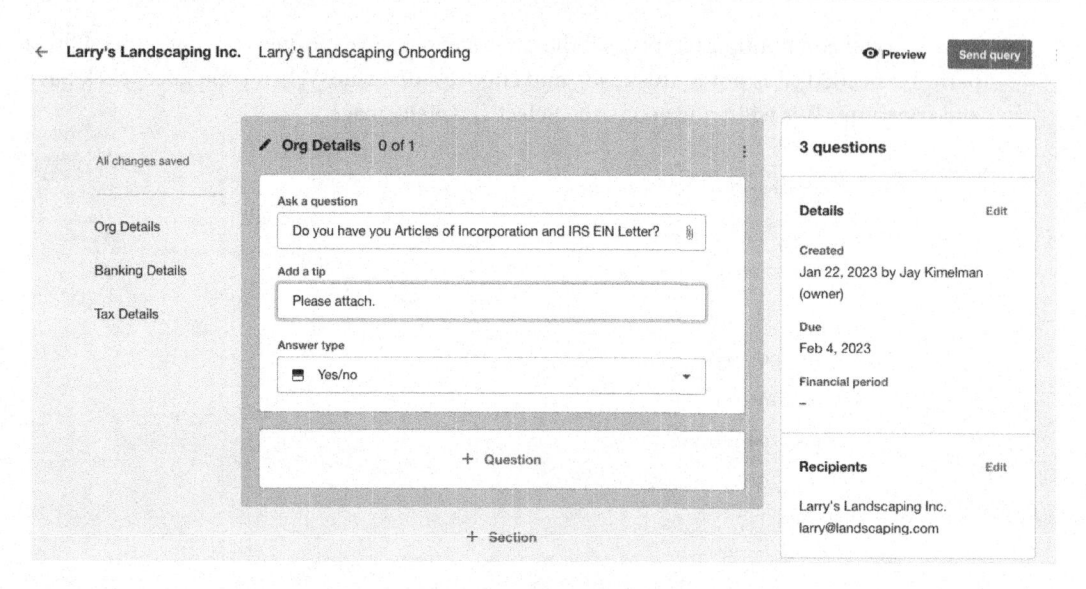

Figure 16.27: Main query screen

16. Now that your query is set up, click **Send query**. This takes you to the messaging screen.
17. Now we can customize the message we will send to get it in the client's hands to complete it:

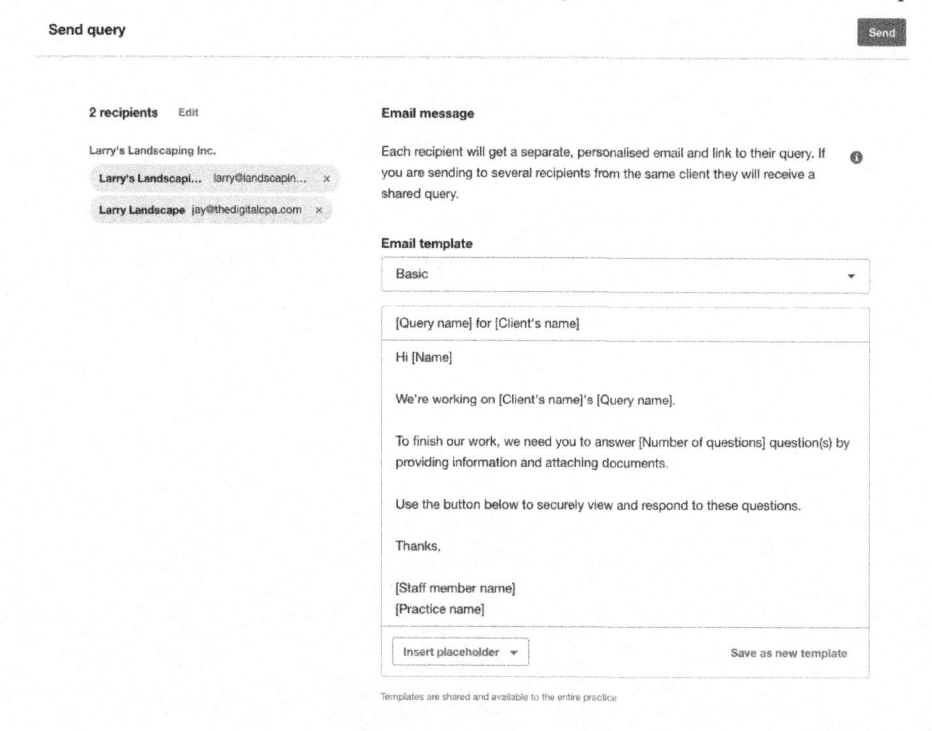

Figure 16.28: Ask email message

18. Choose the email template you wish to use by choosing from the **Email template** dropdown. You can edit the template using placeholder text if necessary, and send or even save it as a new template. When you are ready to send the message, click the **Send** button.

This is the email that is received by the client:

Questions to answer from
Your Digital Practice LLC

Hi Larry Landscape

We're working on Larry's Landscaping Inc.'s Larry's Landscaping Onboarding.

To finish our work, we need you to answer 3 question(s) by providing information and attaching documents.

Use the button below to securely view and respond to these questions.

Thanks,

Jay Kimelman (owner)
Your Digital Practice LLC

Answer questions

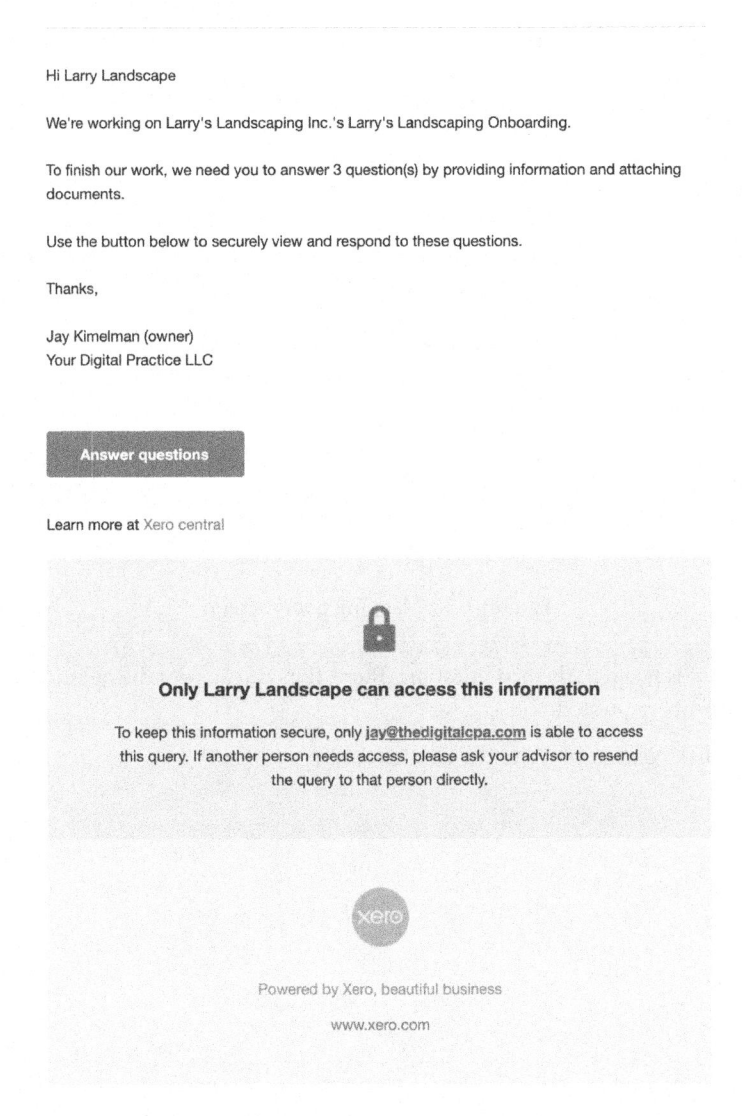

Learn more at Xero central

Only Larry Landscape can access this information

To keep this information secure, only jay@thedigitalcpa.com is able to access this query. If another person needs access, please ask your advisor to resend the query to that person directly.

xero

Powered by Xero, beautiful business

www.xero.com

Figure 16.29: Ask email received

19. The recipient will click **Answer questions** and will be taken to a Xero login screen. Once logged in, they will be at the beginning of your questionnaire. The recipient needs to click **Get started** to begin answering the questions:

Larry's Landscaping Inc.   Larry's Landscaping Onbording • Due February 4, 2023

1. Welcome
2. Org Details
3. Banking Details
4. Tax Details

Your Digital Practice LLC

Hi Jay,
We need you to answer some questions for us

There are 3 questions to answer

You don't have to answer all the questions now
You can leave some questions for now but please answer them all by February 4, 2023

Your responses are automatically saved
Pressing submit will notify your advisor that you've answered

Get started

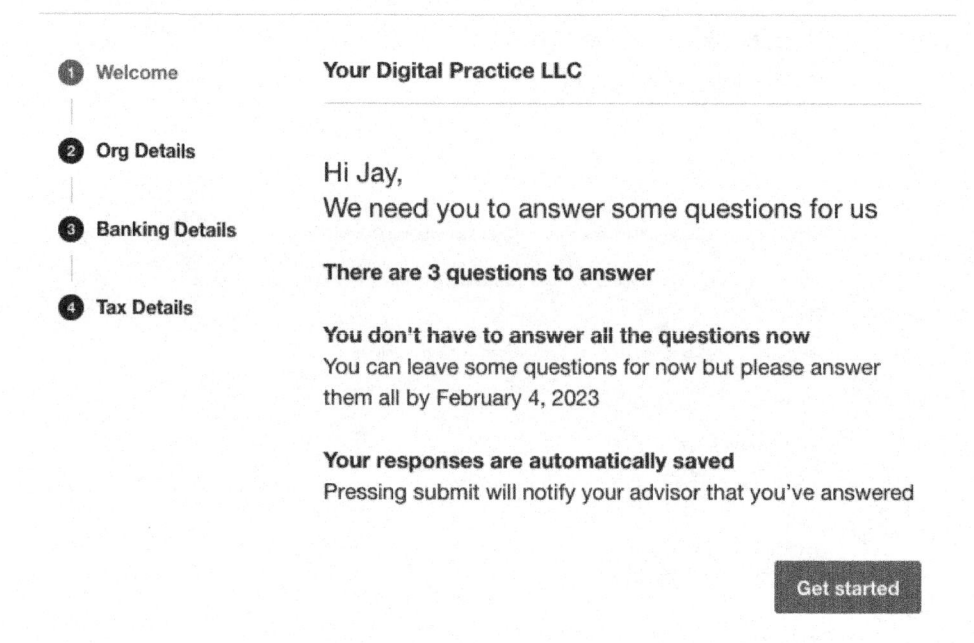

Figure 16.30: Main Ask query screen

20. The recipient is taken to the first question. There, they can answer the question and also upload any documents requested.
21. They can click **Next** to move to the next question:

Org Details 1 question

Do you have your Articles of Incorporation and IRS EIN Letter?

○ Yes   ○ No

📎 Attach files

[Back]   [Next]

Figure 16.31: Ask question screen

22. They can answer the questions until they get to the last question, and then click **Submit**.
23. Back at the accountant side, you can see the status of the request by looking at the **Progress** bar:

Figure 16.32: Ask query status

24. In the right corner of the top line (*Figure 16.32*), you can see that there is a **Progress** status, approximately one-third completed. That will give the sender an idea of where the client is in completing the Ask query. The bottom line shows a completed circle and states **Submitted**, indicating that the client has completed the sender's request. You can click on the client's name or the request name to look at the response:

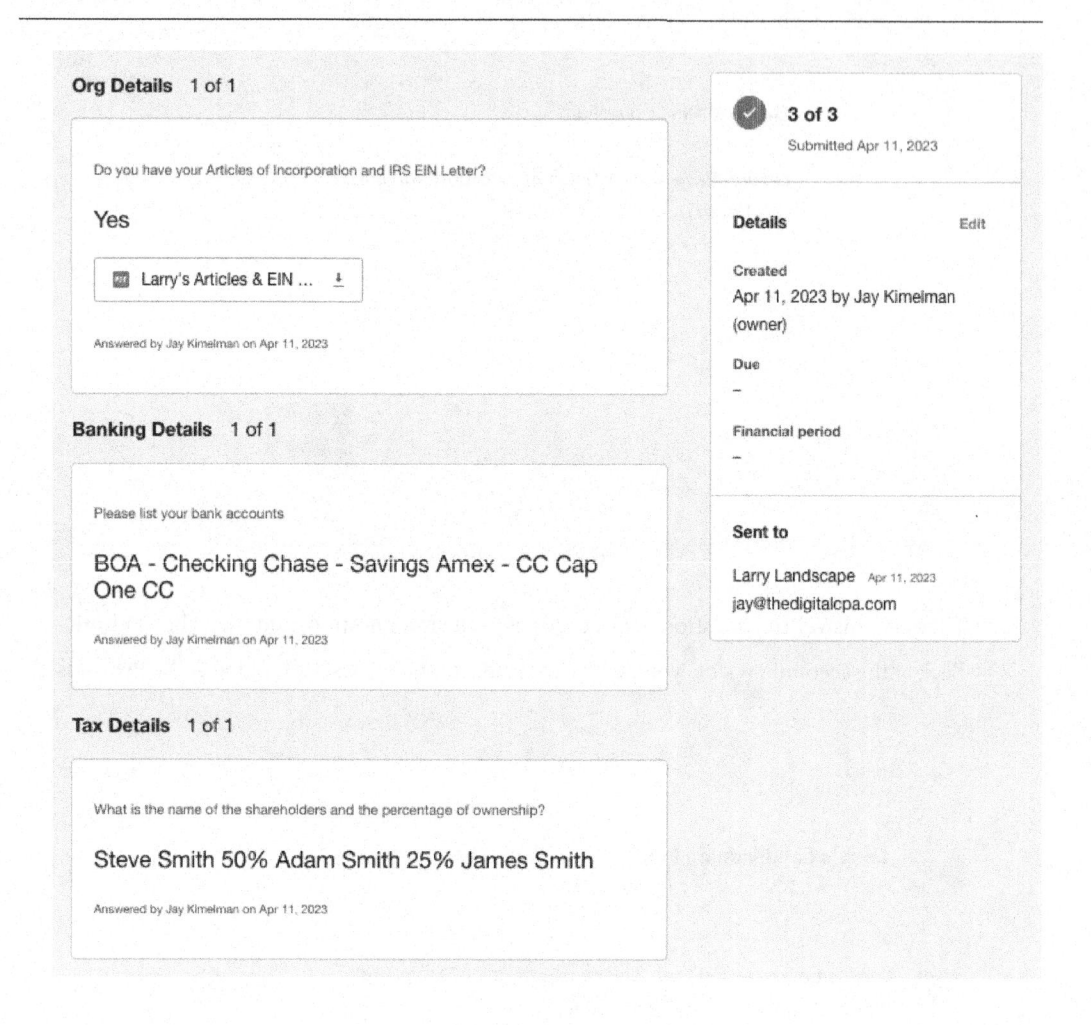

Figure 16.33: Ask submission details

25. You can review the data, download any of the attachments, and so on. You can even ask questions based on the response. To do that, you just have to click **+ Question** below the response just like you did earlier:

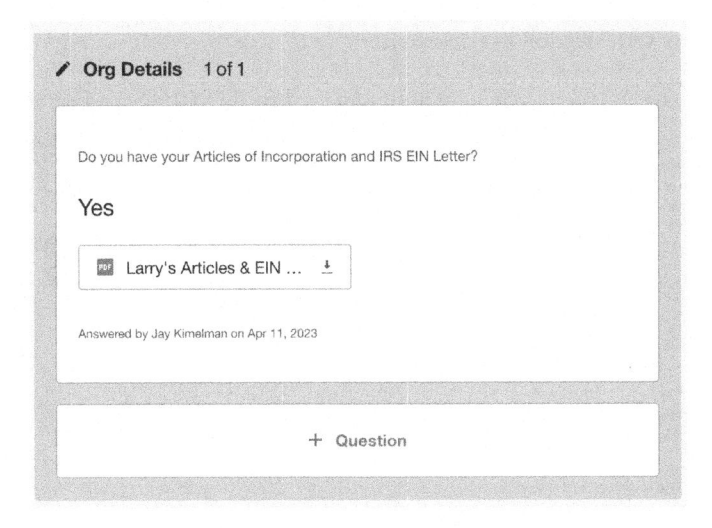

Figure 16.34: Ask additional questions

26. Click **Resend query** when you have completed your response.
27. If you are satisfied with the response, you can click the three-dot icon and choose **Close query**.
28. At that time, you can export the contents of the Ask query. In the three-dot icon, click **Export query**, click the **Export** button, and then the details will be exported in a ZIP file to your computer.

> **Note**
> Just remember, there may be sensitive information in the files you just downloaded. Ensure you store that data securely.

You can see how valuable the **Ask** tool is. It is very powerful and helpful when running your accounting business.

Now that we have the information to work on our new client, in the next section, we will look at managing staff in Xero HQ.

Staff in Xero HQ

Xero HQ is the place for managing your accounting firm or business staff. This is where you can invite people to join your Xero practice and manage the clients they can access.

To work on **Staff** in Xero HQ, follow these steps:

1. From the Xero HQ screen, click on **Staff** and go directly to the Xero HQ **Staff** page:

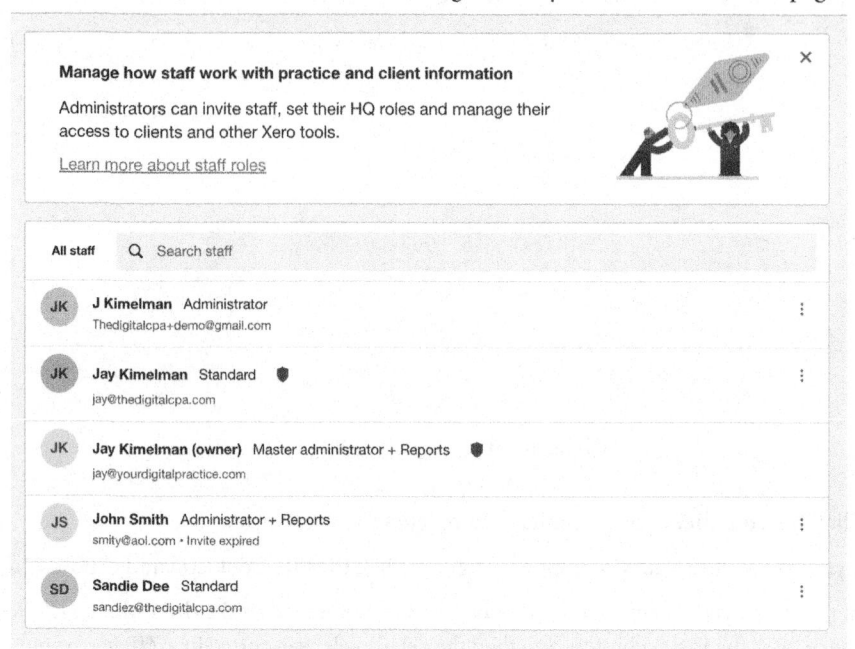

Figure 16.35: Staff main screen

2. Here, you can invite Xero support or export a staff list by clicking on the three-dot menu at the upper right. You can invite a new staff member to your practice by clicking the **Invite staff** button. This will bring up the **Invite staff to Xero HQ** dialog:

Figure 16.36: Invite staff dialog box 1

3. Enter the name and email address of the new staff member and then click **Next**:

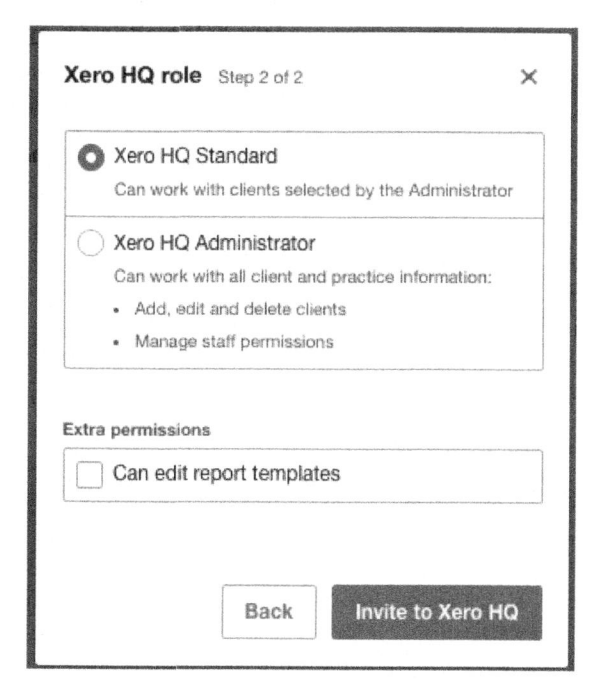

Figure 16.37: Invite staff dialog box 2

4. Choose the appropriate role for this new staff member and click **Invite to Xero HQ**:

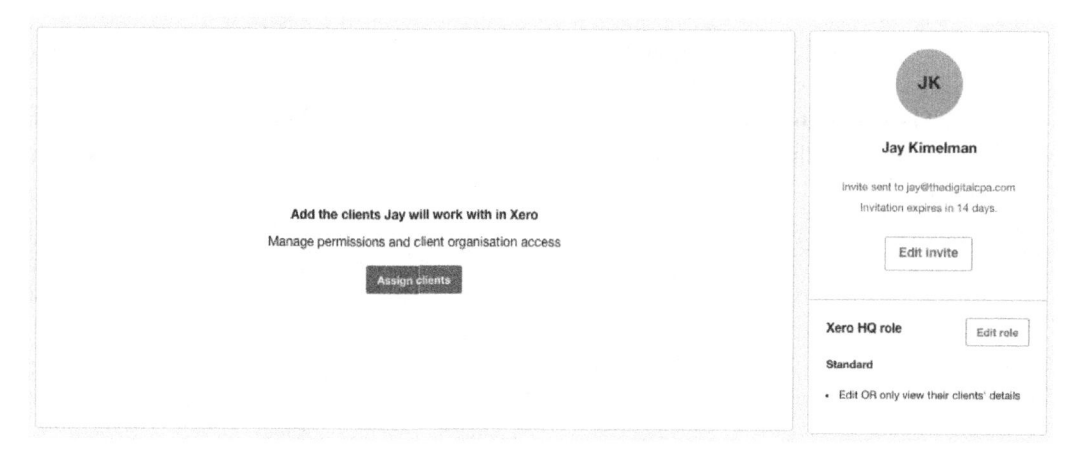

Figure 16.38: Staff details page

5. This will take you to the staff member details page. At this point, the new staff member has no clients, so click the **Assign clients** button to give the new staff member access to clients for work:

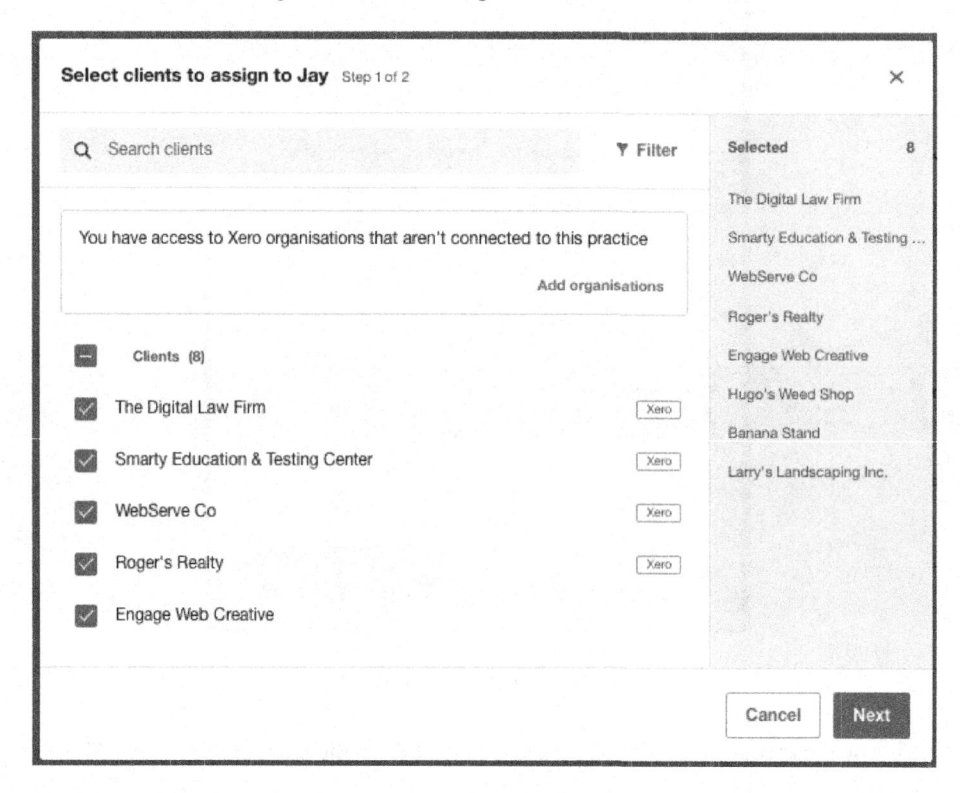

Figure 16.39: Select clients screen

6. The **Select clients to assign to {Name}** screen will come up. Add a checkbox next to each client you want the new staff member to be able to have access to in Xero. Click **Next** when you are finished.

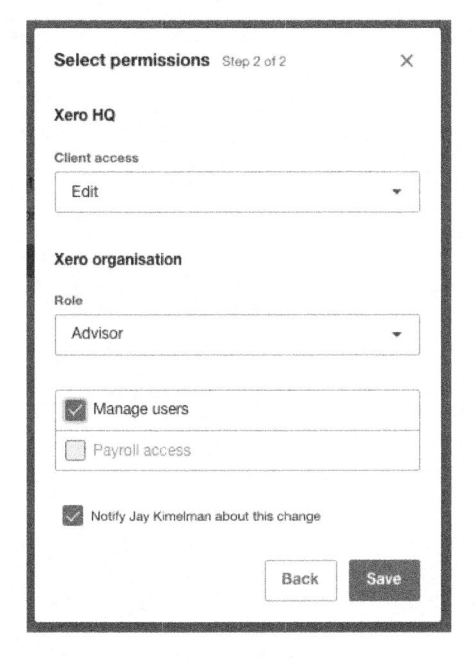

Figure 16.40: Select permissions screen

7. The **Select permissions** box will come next. Make your selections as needed and click **Save**.

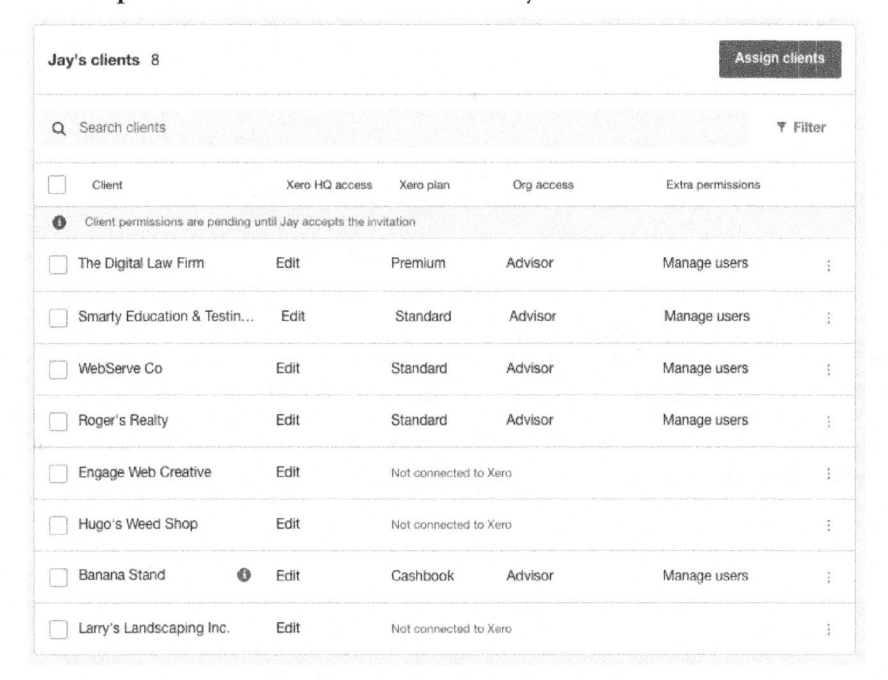

Figure 16.41: Updated staff client assignments

You will now see the new staff member and the clients they are assigned, and the roles assigned for each client.

On the same page as the client assignments are the staff member details:

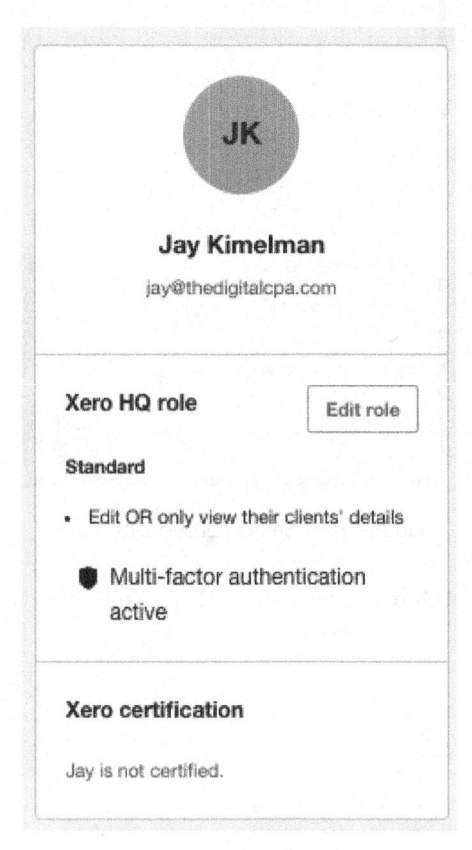

Figure 16.42: Staff member details

From here, you can see the access the staff member has. You can see things like whether they have multi-factor authentication turned on, their Xero certification status, and so on. These are all important details for managing your staff.

We have covered the Xero HQ items that we use to work with clients; now we will look at **Practice**, which gives us tools for working on our business.

Practice

We have covered so much in this chapter on Xero HQ. There is one more area I want to just touch on. That is the **Practice** area. **Practice** gives you information about your Xero business, information on how to build your business, and actionable resources. I am going to just touch on this, as I highly recommend that if you are a Xero partner or are about to become one, you reach out to your Xero rep and have them walk you through this section of Xero HQ. There are many moving pieces to this, and it is best to have the most up-to-date details explained to you by your rep.

I will say that this is important, as it keeps count of your Xero points and gives you an immediate status of your firm's partner level.

The **Practice** overview also gives you details of who your Xero rep is and how to contact them. In addition, the **Partner Resources** section at the bottom of the page is very helpful to those firms just starting out. I highly recommend the **Partner** toolkit, which contains marketing resources and helpful information to help you build your practice.

The last thing I want to touch on in the **Practice** tab is **Advisor Directory**. Once you reach Bronze status, you can add your firm to the advisor directory. Again, I suggest you connect with your Xero account manager to get the most up-to-date details on setting up your directory listing.

We have covered a lot in this chapter. Xero HQ is a very powerful set of tools you can use when working in or on your business. Xero has really added to your toolbox with Xero HQ. Keep in mind that if you wish to use the partner resources, you need to maintain your Xero Advisor certification.

Summary

We have just covered the basics of running your accounting firm in Xero HQ – from adding clients and staff, to securely transferring information and documents, to gaining valuable insights into your client and their business.

In the next chapter, we look at custom reporting again but from the practice-wide reporting tool called **Report Templates**, which gives you a standard reporting tool you can use across multiple clients.

17
Exploring Practice-Wide Report Templates

Report templates are designed to give an accounting practice a firm-wide report template across its clients. Think about the industry vertical or the franchise you are supporting; having a template report will save you time and give you and your client consistency in their reporting. In this chapter, we will discuss how to set up, edit, and use a report template and learn how to utilize report codes to map an existing client to a report template.

In this chapter, we're going to cover the following main topics:

- Building a report template specifically for the practice and their client's needs
- Mapping the chart of accounts to the report codes
- Producing a report for each client using the template

What are Report templates?

Report templates are pre-designed reports that can be customized and applied to any organization across your accounting firm. They are tied to report codes, which are mapped for each Xero company through their chart of accounts. Report templates allow you to have a consistent reporting format for a specific industry, tax type, or even franchise. If you work across multiple regions around the globe, you can create Report templates on a regional basis based on that specific region's requirements.

Let's take a more in-depth look at report templates now that we know what they are.

To find **report templates**, we must head to **Xero HQ**:

1. We can do that by clicking the main button in the top-left corner of the Xero screen. This button shows the Xero company you are currently logged in to, followed by the **Xero HQ** option below it:

246　Exploring Practice-Wide Report Templates

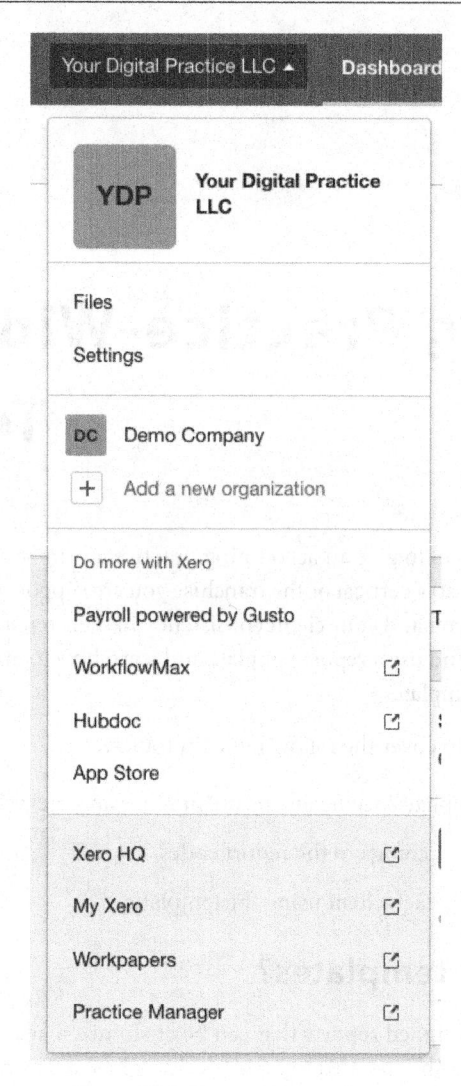

Figure 17.1: Xero main user menu

What are Report templates? 247

2. Clicking on the **Xero HQ** option will take you to the **Xero HQ** main menu:

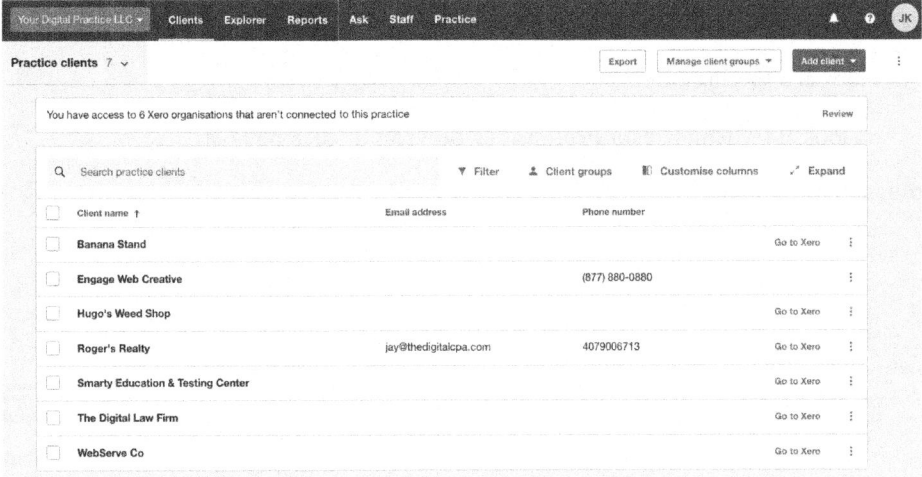

Figure 17.2: Xero HQ main menu

3. Look for **Reports** at the top of the **Xero HQ** main page and click it.

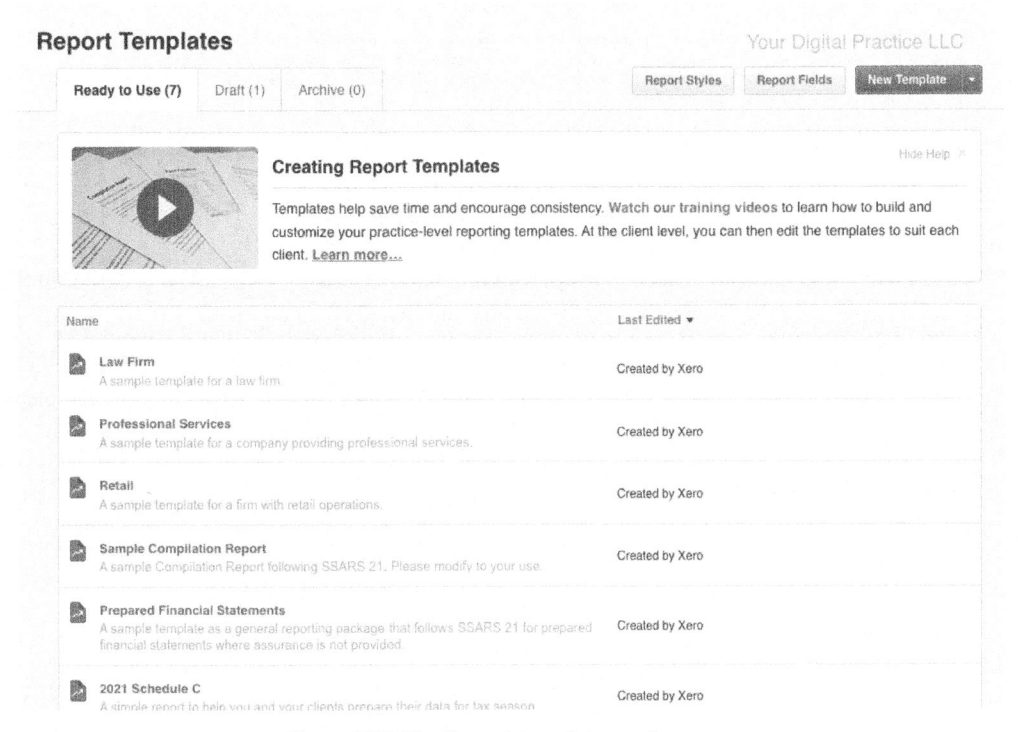

Figure 17.3: The Report templates main screen

As you can see, on this page, several report packs were created by Xero.

This is how you can find Report templates.

Now, let's look at a specific one:

1. Let's look at the template for **Professional Services** by clicking on it.

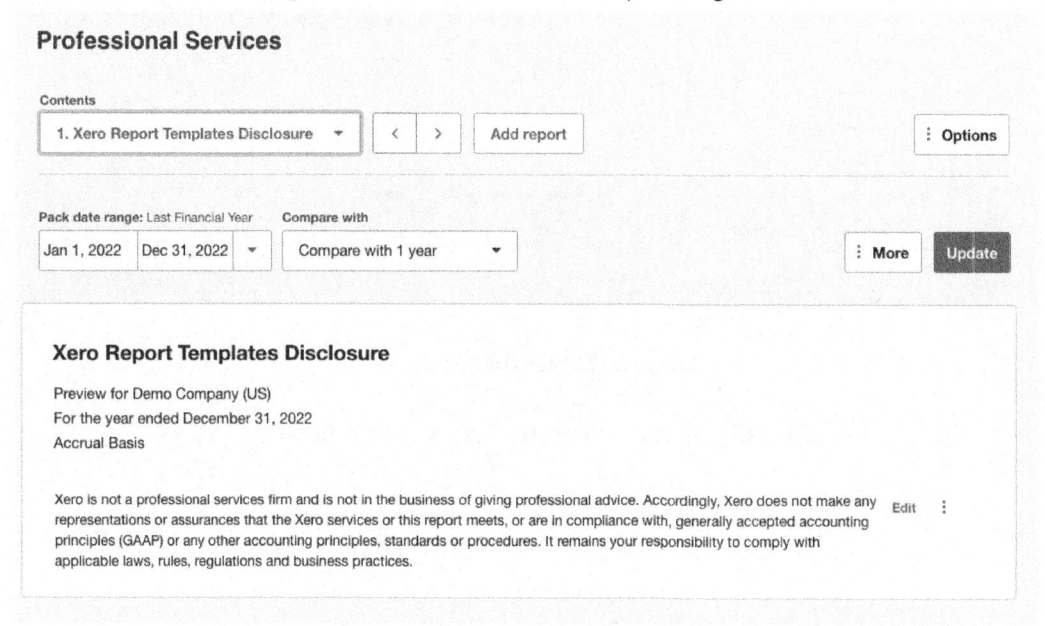

Figure 17.4: Professional Services

You will notice the same controls you saw in the main reports that we looked at earlier in this book, except for the **Contents** drop-down box and the adjacent controls.

2. Here, you can add a report to the template by clicking the **Add report** button. This will bring up the **Add report** dialog and show you the reports you have already added to other templates:

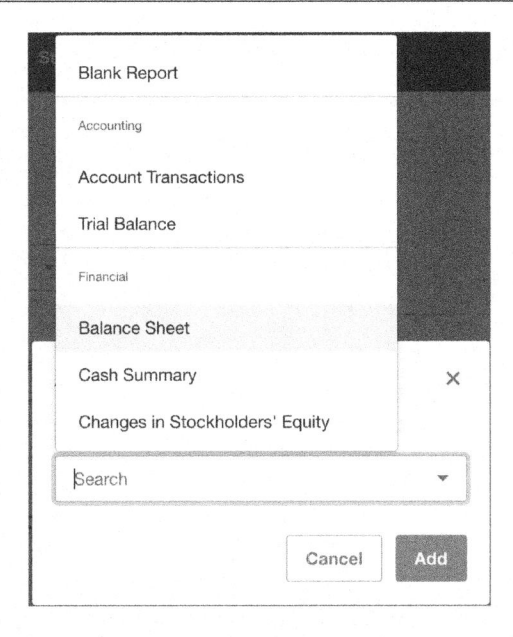

Figure 17.5: Report templates – the Add report screen

3. Just choose a report by scrolling through the list of reports available and click the **Add** button when you find one. You can use the arrow buttons to scroll through the reports, use the dropdown to select the report you want to view, or change their order:

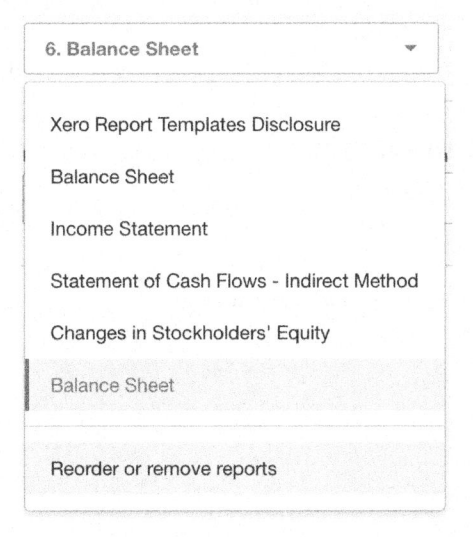

Figure 17.6: Report templates selection screen

4. You will need to click **Reorder or remove reports** to rearrange the report order or delete a report:

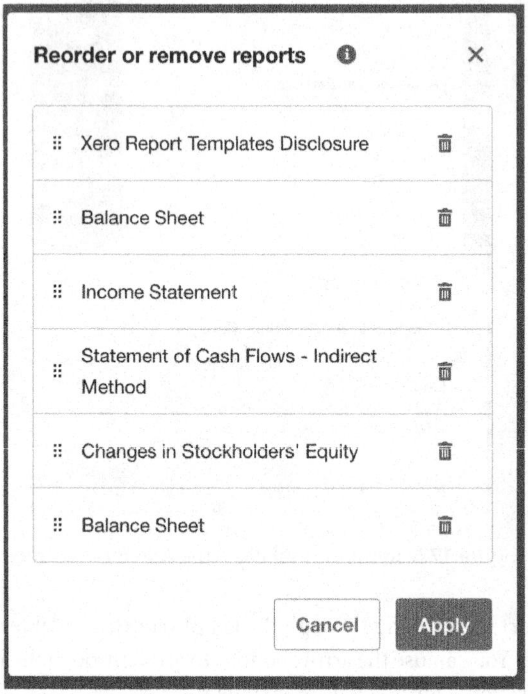

Figure 17.7: Report templates – the Reorder or remove reports screen

Now that we have created a Report template, let's look at how we can edit it to our specific needs.

Editing Report templates

You can edit a Report template in the same way we learned how to edit the report layout of regular reports, as we discussed in *Chapter 15*:

1. Click **Edit layout** and enter the **Layout Editor** area:

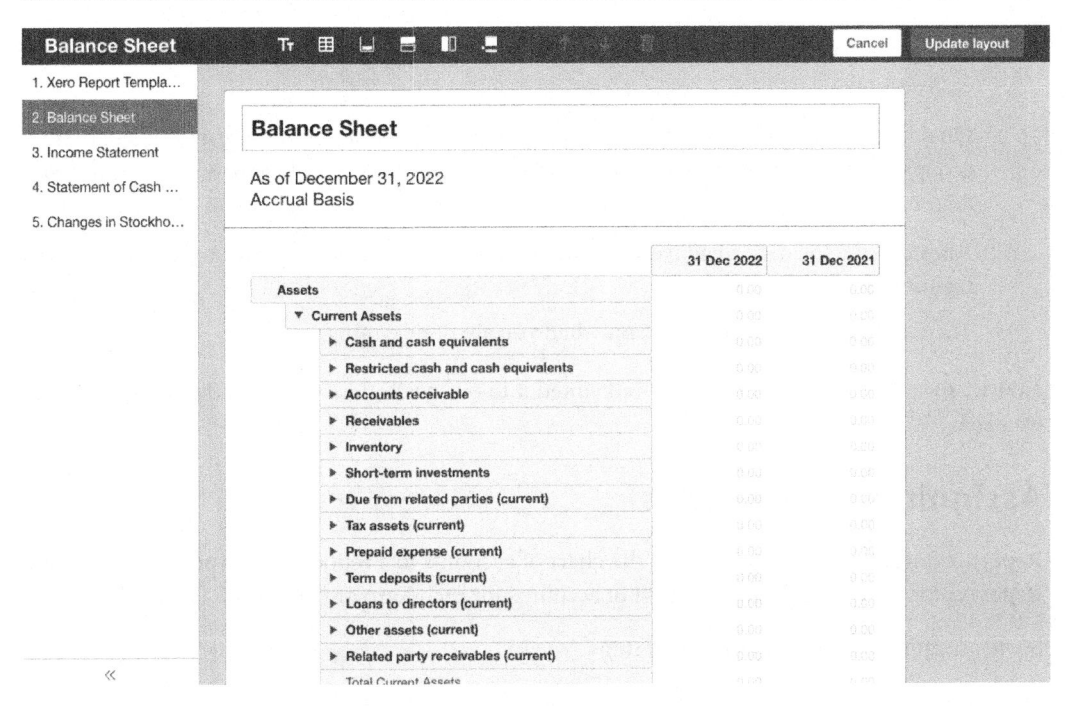

Figure 17.8: Report templates – Layout Editor

You will notice the same controls at the top of the page that we had in the custom report layout editor, as discussed in *Chapter 15*. The main difference is that you can edit all of the reports in the template by clicking the report name in the leftmost column to go to that specific report:

Figure 17.9: Cash and cash equivalents

2. In this case, I clicked on the arrow icon next to **Cash and cash equivalents** to expand the cash section.

   On doing so, you will notice that there is no specific chart of accounts here, only groups. These groups are associated with **report codes**, which we will address in the next section. You format your report how you want it to look and then you map the report codes to the chart of accounts.

3. After making the desired adjustments to the report layouts, you just have to click the **Update layout** button.

4. Then, click the **Ready to use** button when you are done editing.

Now that we have the report template and edited it to our needs, let's map it so that we get the data we need.

Assigning report codes

Report codes are codes used to assign the chart of accounts to a report line in the report template. Report codes are embedded in the chart of accounts for each Xero organization.

So, to assign report codes, follow these steps:

1. Go back to your favorite Xero company and click on **Settings**, followed by **Advanced Accounting settings**.

2. Next, click on **Report Codes**.

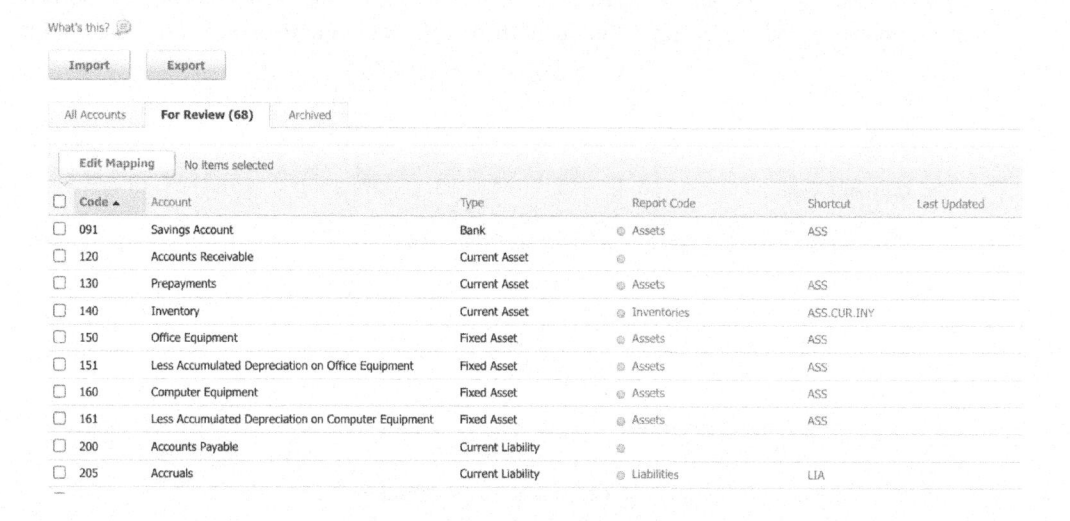

Code	Account	Type	Report Code	Shortcut	Last Updated
091	Savings Account	Bank	Assets	ASS	
120	Accounts Receivable	Current Asset			
130	Prepayments	Current Asset	Assets	ASS	
140	Inventory	Current Asset	Inventories	ASS.CUR.INY	
150	Office Equipment	Fixed Asset	Assets	ASS	
151	Less Accumulated Depreciation on Office Equipment	Fixed Asset	Assets	ASS	
160	Computer Equipment	Fixed Asset	Assets	ASS	
161	Less Accumulated Depreciation on Computer Equipment	Fixed Asset	Assets	ASS	
200	Accounts Payable	Current Liability			
205	Accruals	Current Liability	Liabilities	LIA	

Figure 17.10: The Report Codes main screen

Assigning report codes | 253

3. Here, you will see three tabs, similar to the other sections in Xero. We are in the **For Review** tab, as these are codes that have not yet been assigned a detailed code and must be set, allowing the code to be mapped to lines in the report template. As shown in *Figure 17.10*, your chart of accounts will have an associated account **type**, along with a **report code and a shortcut** code.

4. By looking at the report codes, you will see that the demo company is mapped to the highest level. Let's correctly map **Savings Account** to its proper report code. Click on **Assets** next to **Code 091 Savings Account**.

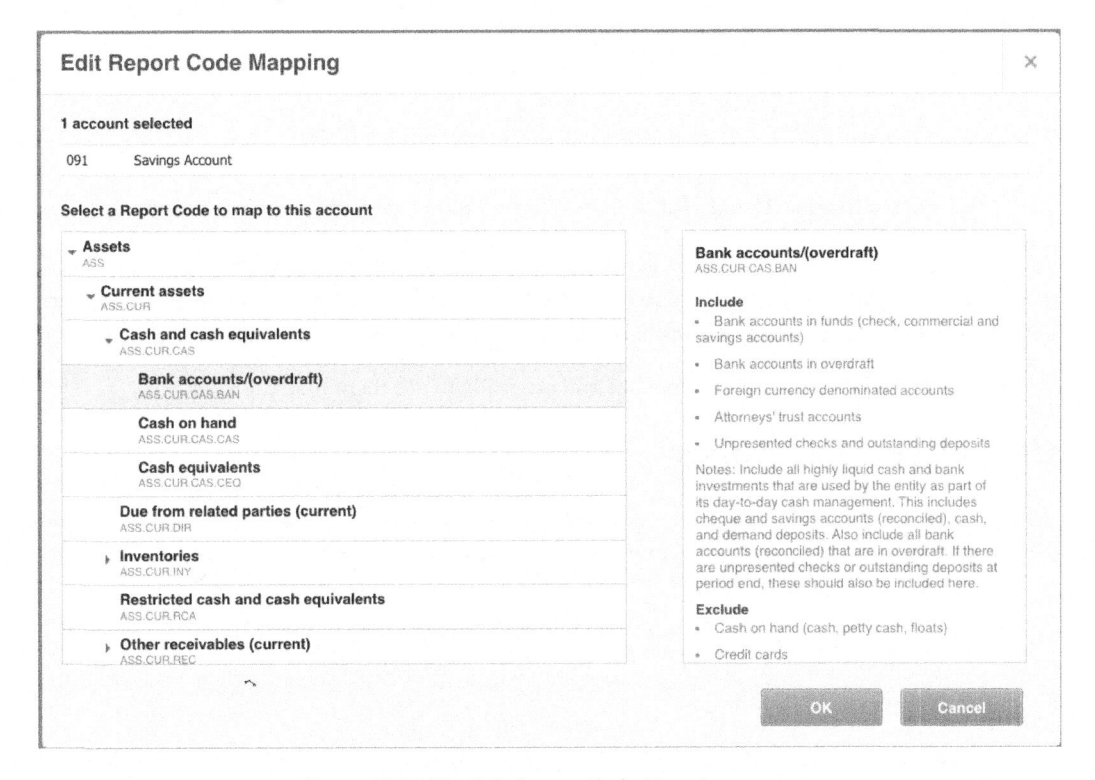

Figure 17.11: The Edit Report Code Mapping screen

5. You will be brought to the **Edit Report Code Mapping** screen. We have drilled down into the **Assets** section by clicking the arrow to the left of the selection.

6. Then, we went down a couple of levels into **Cash and cash equivalents** and chose **Bank accounts/(overdraft)**. You can see that the code for bank accounts is **ASS.CUR.CAS.BAN**.

7. Once you are satisfied that you have the correct report code, click the **OK** button. This will take you back to the **All Accounts** tab:

254   Exploring Practice-Wide Report Templates

Figure 17.12: The All Accounts tab

8. You will see that the **ASS.CUR.CAS.BAN** code is showing for the savings account.

You must repeat this process to map the entire chart of accounts. After doing this several times, you can try to export the chart of accounts and map the fields in Excel and then import them back into Xero. All of this is done very similarly to the chart of accounts process we discussed way back in *Chapter 3*.

We now have mapped-out Report templates and are ready to put them to use.

Using Report templates

When you are ready to use the Report templates in a specific Xero company, this is what you can do:

1. Head to the **Reports** menu and click on **Advisor**:

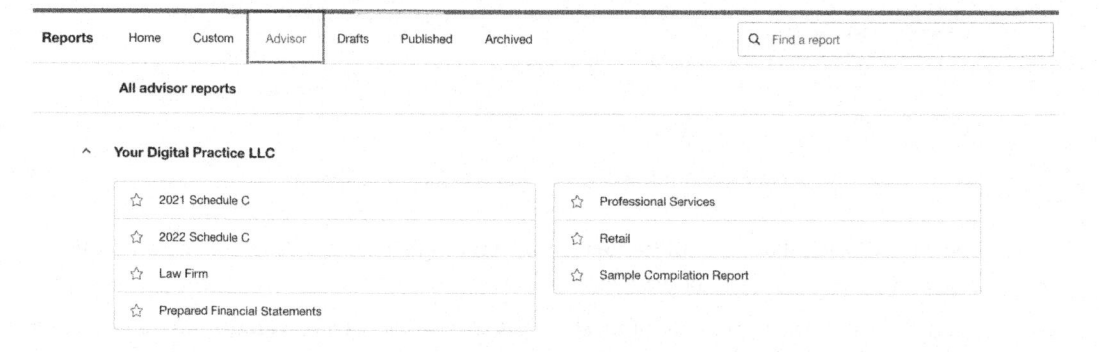

Figure 17.13: The Advisor reports screen

2. Choose the template you wish to use; I have selected **Professional Services**. This is the same **Professional Services** template we edited earlier in this chapter:

Balance Sheet		
Preview for Demo Company (US)		
As of December 31, 2022		
Accrual Basis		
	Dec 31, 2022	Dec 31, 2021
Assets		
Current Assets		
Cash and cash equivalents	15,000.00	-
Total Current Assets	**15,000.00**	**-**
Non-Current Assets		
Other assets (non-current)	15,572.79	4,630.98
Total Non-Current Assets	**15,572.79**	**4,630.98**
Total Assets	**30,572.79**	**4,630.98**
Liabilities and Equity		

Figure 17.14: Balance Sheet from the Professional Services template

3. Under **Cash and cash equivalents**, you will see the amount from the savings account.

Again, this can be a time-consuming process. So, you can also choose to use a chart of accounts template that has been mapped, and it will be much simpler the next time you do this.

Summary

We have covered a lot in this chapter. We covered how to create and edit a report template and then how to map the report codes to the chart of accounts. We now have reports we can apply to specific industries or vertical niches we work with. This saves time and is a great way to add consistency to your practice.

In the next chapter, we will look at getting your data out of Xero.

18
Exporting Your Data and Reports Out of Xero

We have been on a Xero journey, from setup to transactions to reporting. Now it is time to get that data and reporting out of Xero to use in your business or firm. We will look at exporting reports and data in multiple formats, as well as some tools to help you and your clients. This is all with the aim of helping you work more efficiently. You might ask, *Why do I need to export my data*? For the answer, think of things such as external reporting, financial modeling, or even just tax preparation or planning.

In this chapter, we're going to cover the following main topics:

- Exporting Xero reports
- Exporting your accounting data
- Helping the sole proprietor with the Schedule C report
- Trial Balance apps

Exporting Xero reports to expand their role

Many accountants and business owners know and love Excel, and it is their go-to tool. They might want to create a budget, a cash flow projection, or even perform some analysis. Yes, there are apps for most of that, but we are creatures of habit and go to what we know. Xero makes it super easy to export reports. As we explored in *Chapter 13*, Xero will export reports as a PDF or in spreadsheet formats for Excel and Google Sheets.

Let's have a quick refresher. To get to a report, click on the **Accounting** menu option, followed by **Reports** to go to the **Reports** main menu to choose a report, or you can click on one of your favorited reports right on the **Accounting** menu.

Exporting Your Data and Reports Out of Xero

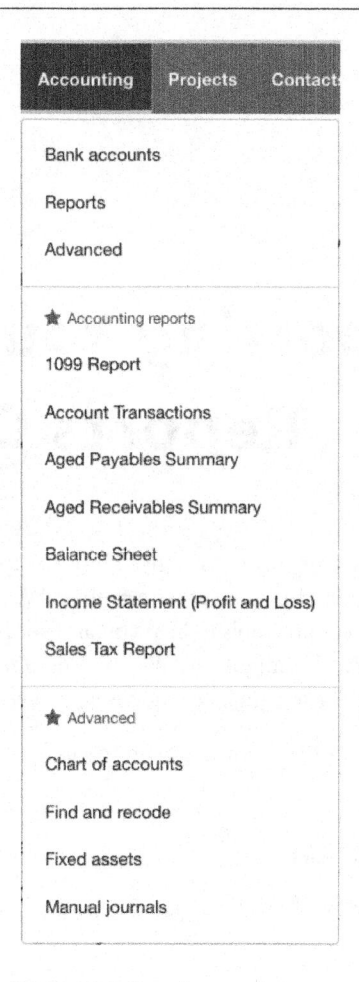

Figure 18.1: Xero Accounting menu

In our case, we opened the **Income Statement (Profit and Loss)** report and we will look at the **Export** options at the lower right of the screen (*Figure 18.2*).

Figure 18.2: Xero report Export options

Here, you can choose from the **PDF**, **Styled PDF**, **Excel**, or **Google Sheets** options. No matter the choice you make, Xero will export your report in the selected format, and it is ready for your use. Every report in Xero functions in exactly the same way.

Exporting accounting data to make your life easy

There are many reasons to export your data: tax prep, safeguarding, or even an audit. In the case that you are having a financial audit, you may want to limit the data you give to your auditors. You can accomplish that by using the date picker, only exporting the exact dates under audit, and filtering the accounts you are providing. You can save the general ledger data by year, by selecting the **Account Transactions** report, selecting the time frame, and exporting as we explained previously.

The more probable reason is that you want to export the data and upload it into your tax software. Xero makes it very easy for you as well:

1. Click on the **Accounting** menu and choose the **Advanced** option. This will take you to the **Advanced accounting** settings screen.
2. Click on the **Export accounting data** option.

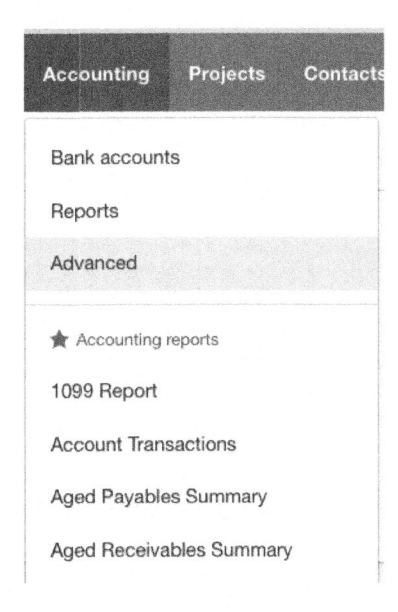

Figure 18.3: Accounting menu

This takes you to the **Export accounting data** screen where you can select the system to which you want to export your data.

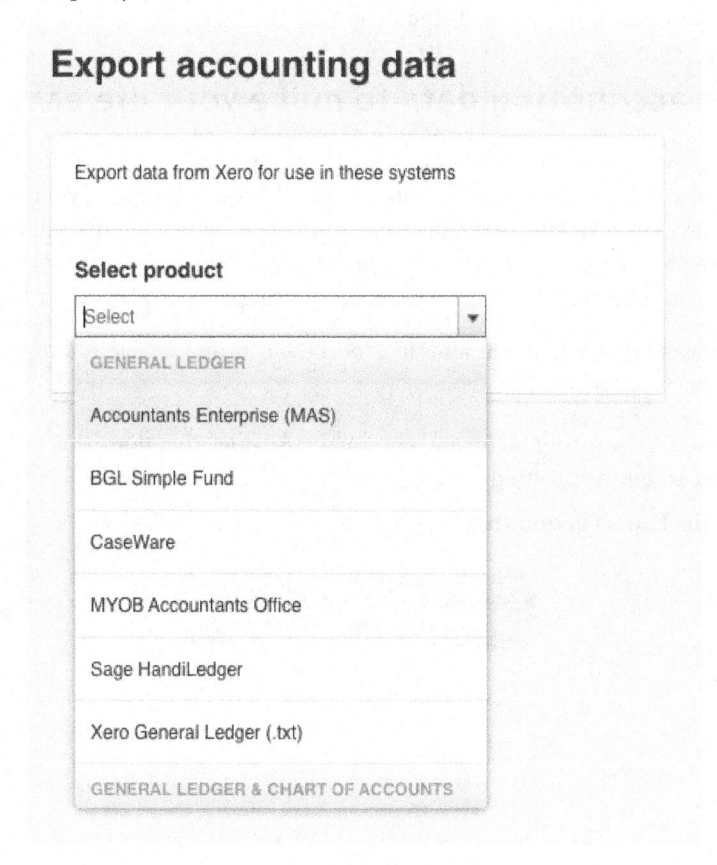

Figure 18.4: Export accounting data screen

3. There are many products to export to. Click the **Select product** dropdown to find your destination software.

   Here is the list of accounting and tax software you can export to along with the data and the formats:

Accounting product	Export file and format		
	General ledger	Chart of accounts	Trial balance
Accountants Enterprise (MAS)	MYE		
APS Accounting (XPA)	TXT	TXT	
BGL Simple Fund	CSV		
CaseWare	TXT		
CCH Accounts Production			CSV
CCH Per Tax			TXT
CCH Prosystem fx Engagement			CSV
Forbes Accounts			CSV
Intuit ProSeries			DBF
IRIS	CSV		CSV
Keytime			CSV
Lacerte Tax			CSV
MYOB Accountants Office	MYE		
Sage HandiLedger	CSV		
TaxACT			CSV
TaxCalc			CSV
Thomson Reuters' Accounting CS (UltraTax)			XLSX
Thomson Reuters' Workpapers CS (UltraTax)			XLSX

Figure 18.5: Accounting software products that Xero can export to (source: Xero Central)

4. From the list in the **Select product** dropdown, select your destination and period for your export. Xero will show you the document and filename, along with the **Download** button.

5. When you are ready to export, click the **Download** button.

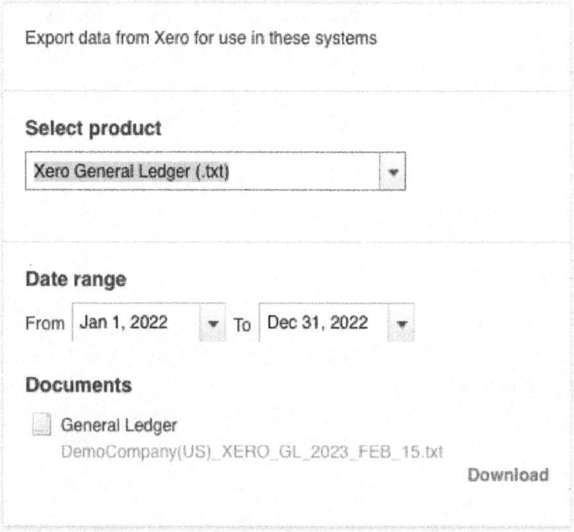

Figure 18.6: Select product download screen

The file you requested, will be downloaded to your computer and ready to use.

Next, we turn to the **Schedule C** report, a very helpful report for sole proprietors who wish to do their own tax return preparation.

The Schedule C report for sole proprietors

There is a completely different tax form for sole proprietors, and it is called **Schedule C**. If your business is an LLC and you are the only member, well, you too are taxed on your Schedule C, and this report may be a huge help for you. The Schedule C report in Xero is available as a report template. You remember them, right? We just covered report templates in *Chapter 17*.

The Schedule C report for sole proprietors   263

Head over to the report templates by clicking on **Accounting**, then **Reports**, and selecting the **Advisor** tab.

Figure 18.7: Advisor reports menu

Select the **Schedule C** report; in this case, **2022 Schedule C**. Recall from *Chapter 17*, how to map the chart of accounts to the reporting code to generate the report from the template.

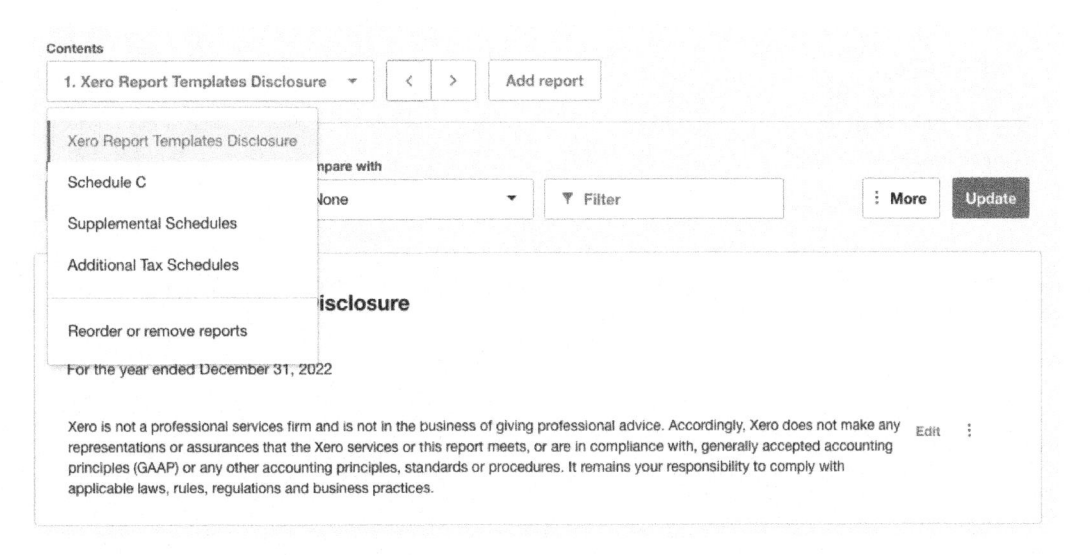

Figure 18.8: Schedule C report template contents

You can see from *Figure 18.8* that the **Schedule C** template has four components: the disclosure, which you can see in the preceding figure, the **Schedule C** form, **Supplemental Schedules**, and **Additional Tax Schedules**.

Select the page you wish to view by selecting the page from the **Contents** dropdown.

The **Schedule C** report is just like any other report in Xero. It is formatted like the Schedule C form that is part of the 1040 filing to the Internal Revenue Service.

Schedule C

Demo Company (US)
For the year ended December 31, 2023

	2023	2022	DIFF	% CHANGE
Schedule C				
Part I Income				
1 Gross receipts or sales	24,948.77	6,590.43	18,358.34	73.58%
Gross Income	24,948.77	6,590.43	18,358.34	73.58%
Part II Expenses				
8 Advertising	10,453.75	-	10,453.75	100.00%
17 Legal and professional services	87.00	-	87.00	100.00%
18 Office expense	119.08	-	119.08	100.00%
20 Rent or lease				
b Other business property	3,543.75	-	3,543.75	100.00%
21 Repairs and maintenance	1,133.06	-	1,133.06	100.00%
27a Other expenses (from line 48)				
Telephone & Internet	145.87	-	145.87	100.00%
Total 27a Other expenses (from line 48)	**145.87**	**-**	**145.87**	**100.00%**
28 Total exp before exp for business use of home	15,482.51	-	15,482.51	100.00%
29 Tentative profit or (loss)	9,466.26	6,590.43	2,875.83	30.38%
Part V Other Expenses				
General Expenses	115.20	-	115.20	100.00%
Telephone & Internet	91.74	-	91.74	100.00%
Total Part V Other Expenses	**206.94**	**-**	**206.94**	**100.00%**

This report is not a tax form and should be used in conjunction with tax software to prepare your forms and filings.

Figure 18.9: Schedule C report

You can see that the Schedule C report resembles Schedule C in your tax return, but as the disclaimer at the bottom states, it is *not* a fileable tax form. The data must be transferred from the report by entering the data into your tax return for filing.

Supplemental Schedules are helpful to capture your mileage deduction as well as the *office-in-home* deduction. This gives you the total picture of the taxable income of your business. Keep in mind that the office-in-home calculation is based on $5 per square foot and is the safe harbor option. I do prefer the safe harbor method; you can reach me on Twitter someday and ask me why.

Supplemental Schedules

Demo Company (US)
For the year ended December 31, 2023

	2023
Supplemental Schedules	
Mileage Schedule for 1/1-6/30/2022	
Business miles @ $0.585/mile for 1/1 - 6/30	1,531.00
Mileage expense for 1/1 - 6/30/2022	895.64
Mileage Schedule for 7/1-12/31/2022	
Business miles @ $0.625/mile for 7/1 - 12/31	1,278.00
Mileage expense for 7/1 - 12/31/2022	798.75
Total mileage expense for 2022	1,694.39
Home Office Usage Schedule - Simplified Method	
Square footage of home office @ $5/sq. ft.	
Square footage of home office	175.00
Total Square footage of home office @ $5/sq. ft.	**175.00**
Deduction per square foot	5.00
Home Office Deduction - Simplified Method	875.00

Figure 18.10: Supplemental Schedules

Additional Tax Schedules can be of use; most importantly, at the bottom is your income to be reported on your tax return – again, giving you a picture of your business income and the possible tax liability you may face.

Additional Tax Schedules

Demo Company (US)
For the year ended December 31, 2023

	2023	2022	DIFF	% CHANGE
Schedule 1				
	2023	2022	DIFF	% CHANGE
Schedule A				
	2023	2022	DIFF	% CHANGE
Schedule B				
	2023	2022	DIFF	% CHANGE
Meals & Entertainment				
M&E subject to 50% limitation	-	-	-	-
	2023	2022	DIFF	% CHANGE
Book to Sch C income (before tax adjustments) reconciliation:				
Book income	(15,695.89)	5,626.83	(21,322.72)	-378.95%
Sch C income	(15,695.89)	5,626.83	(21,322.72)	-378.95%

Figure 18.11: Additional Tax Schedules

As you can see, the Schedule C report is very powerful and gives the sole proprietor a lot of great information. Xero had made this a priority over the years, knowing the problem sole proprietors face in obtaining the information they need regarding the profitability of their business (especially come tax time) and offering this solution.

Continuing on the tax theme, in the next section, we will look at tools to make tax preparation easier for tax professionals.

Using Trial Balance apps to make tax time easier

While we are talking about reports and exports for tax and other apps, I figured I would introduce the topic of apps. Our next chapter is all about apps and connecting apps to Xero, but Trial Balance apps fit right here in this discussion, which is a great primer on why we use them.

As a firm owner and a CPA, I prepared many tax returns of varying complexity over the years. That return input takes a lot of time, energy, and strong eyes. So, back when Xero introduced report templates, I was excited, as I could create templates that matched the order of the input of my tax software, making that data entry easier.

Well, it got even easier with the Trial Balance software I am about to tell you about.

I first found the *Regroup tax* app; it connected to Xero, or you could import your trial balance or income statement and balance sheet. Once imported, you could map your trial balance to the tax return and *Regroup* would export an import file.

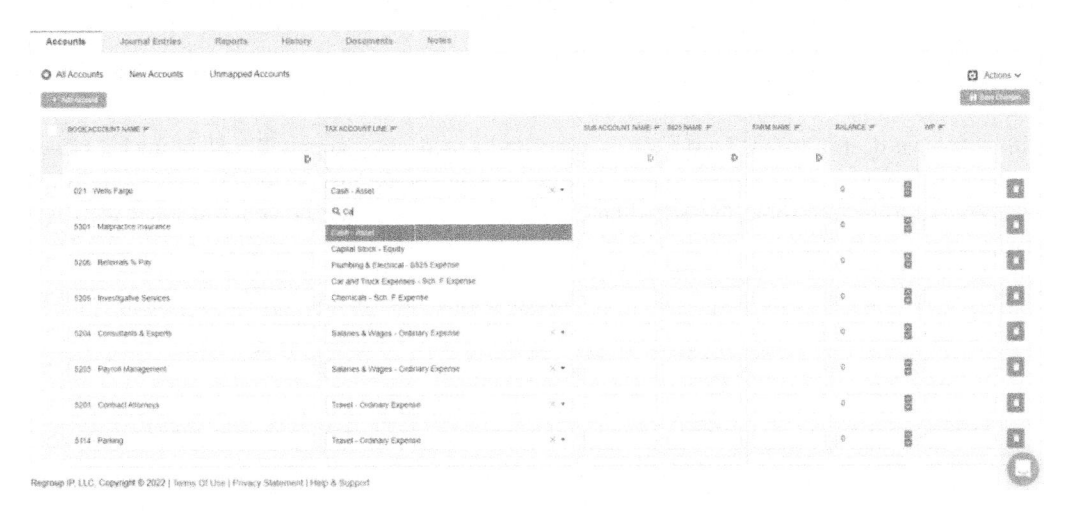

Figure 18.12: Regroup tax dashboard

This was a great method for building efficiency in your tax prep. But that efficiency got a supercharge from a newcomer in the Trial Balance space, *Tallyfor*. This connected to Xero or you could upload your trial balance data as well.

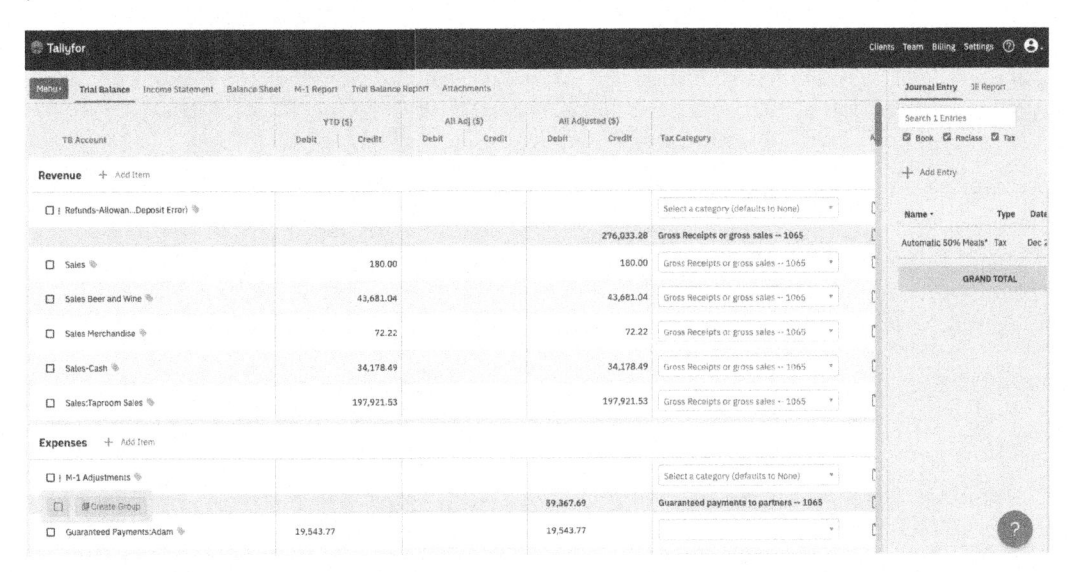

Figure 18.13: Tallyfor dashboard

Tallyfor upped the efficiency by connecting to the popular tax software and pushing the data directly into the software, saving you time to perform a more thorough review or more time advising your client.

So, as you can see, Xero has you covered in the export game, whether it is reports or apps.

Summary

This chapter is dear to me, as I am a tax preparer and a recovering appaholic. All of my bases were covered by these topics. So, export your reports to Excel or Google Sheets, export the data in a format you can import to your tools, use Schedule C for your sole props, and up your efficiency with Trial Balance apps.

In the next chapter, we dive deep into apps – how to connect them, and how to find them. I did say I was an appaholic, right?

19
Increasing Your Powers with Apps and Xero

Throughout this book, I have given you tips on becoming more efficient in your use of Xero so that you will have more time for what is important. This chapter is no different. This is where it all comes together: we'll look at the great efficiency improvements we get by using apps and how we connect the apps to Xero, and I'll share some of the apps I have used and love.

In this chapter, we're going to cover the following main topics:

- Why do we want to use apps?
- How we connect apps to our Xero companies
- Some of my favorite apps

What are apps that are built for Xero?

Xero on its own is a powerful tool in the small to medium-sized business and accounting worlds. Add a few properly vetted and placed apps, and Xero is now supercharged and an efficient, well-oiled machine.

I like to put apps in two categories, internal or foundational apps and external or your client-side deliverable apps.

To get an idea of the apps available to Xero users, you should head to the Xero App Store at `Apps.Xero.Com`.

Here, you can see the hundreds of apps built and approved for use with Xero.

> **Note**
> You can search the App Store by app function, the industries they serve, and by collections, which are Xero staff picks, featured apps, and the like.

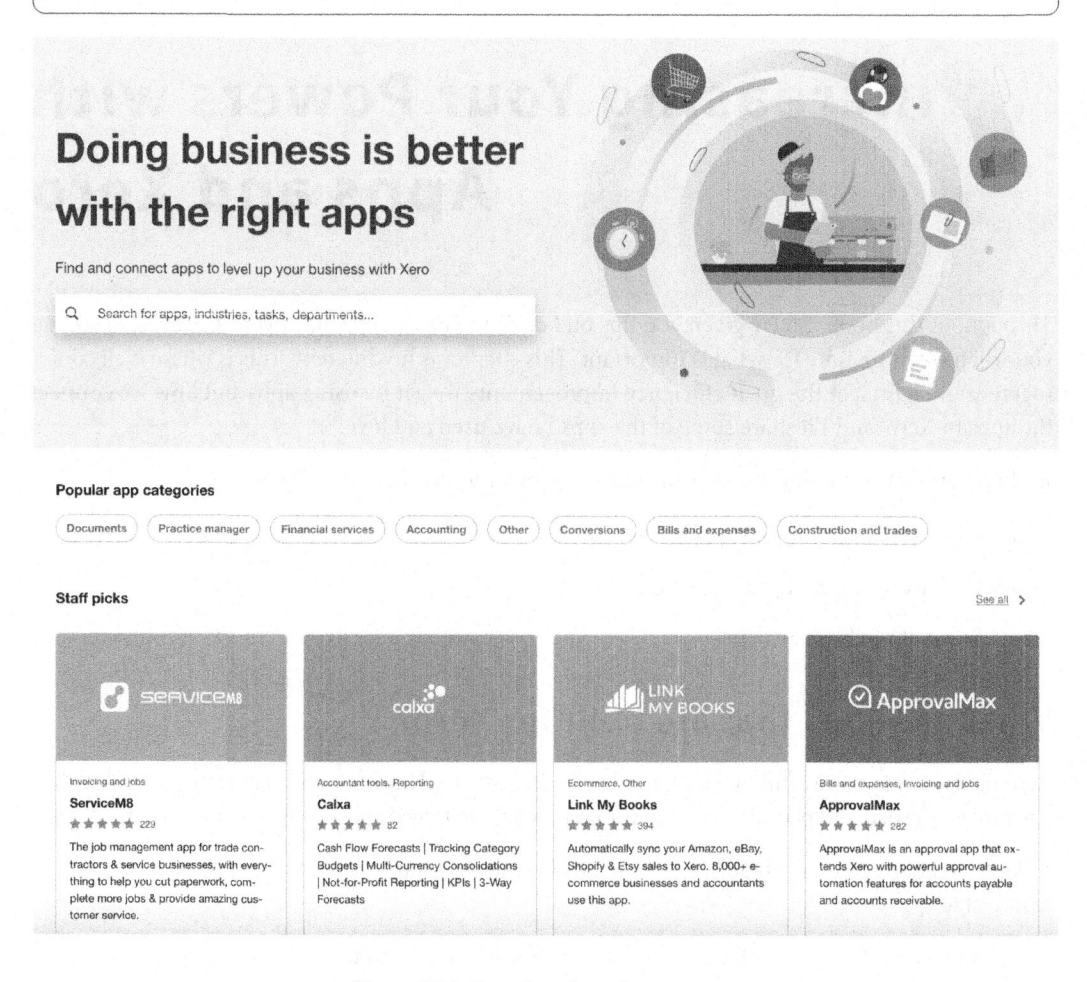

Figure 19.1: Xero App Store home page

As you can see in *Figure 19.1*, you can search for specific apps, industries, tasks, and departments. You can click on **Popular app categories** such as **Time tracking, Payroll HR, Payments, Inventory, Reporting**, and **CRM**. At the bottom of the page, you can see a list of **Staff picks**. If you click **See all** on the right side, it will show all apps in that category.

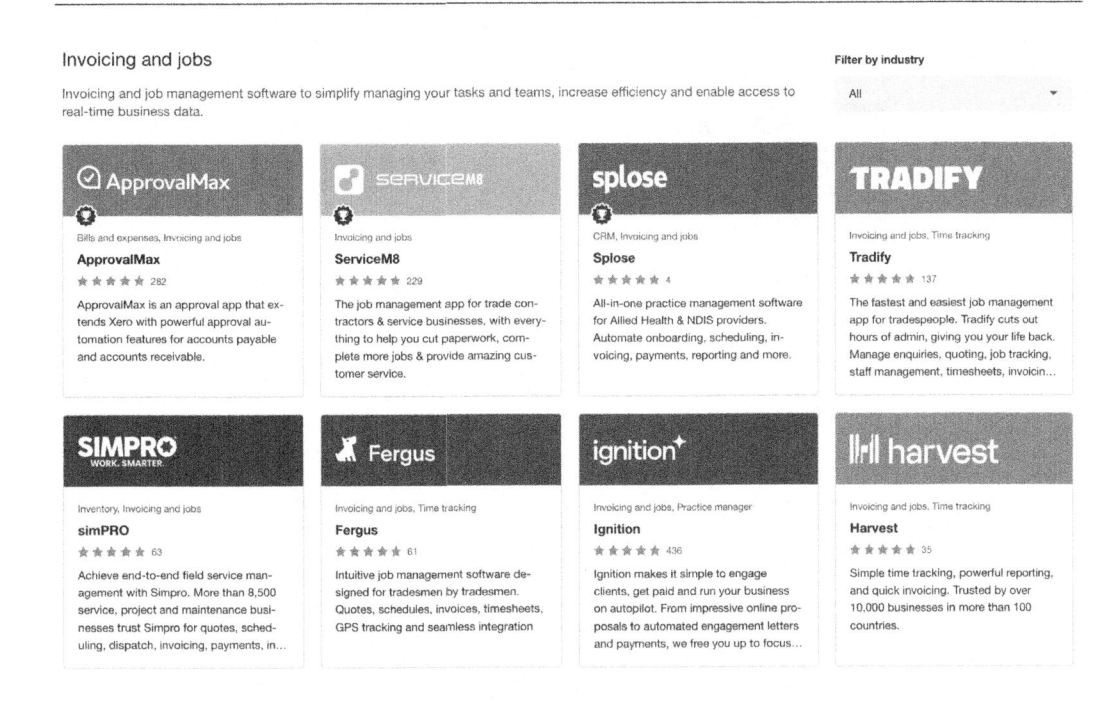

Figure 19.2: Xero invoicing and jobs apps

As you can see in *Figure 19.2*, I searched for invoicing and jobs apps. You can see a display of those apps on the screen. I am going to select **Ignition**, which is one of the oldest apps in my tech stack.

272 Increasing Your Powers with Apps and Xero

Home > Invoicing and jobs

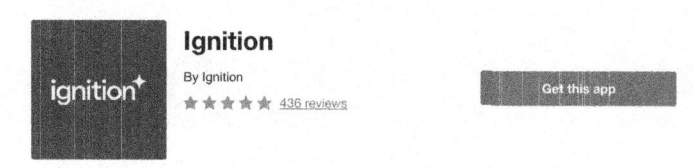

Ignition
By Ignition
★ ★ ★ ★ ★ 436 reviews

[Get this app]

Ignition makes it simple to engage clients, get paid and run your business on autopilot. From impressive online proposals to automated engagement letters and payments, we free you up to focus on what matters most.

Overview | Getting started | Reviews | Additional info

Overview

Ignition is a client engagement and commerce platform for professional services businesses to streamline how they engage clients and get paid.

Over 5,000 businesses such as accounting and bookkeeping firms use Ignition to help them grow, be more efficient, and create win-win client relationships.

With Ignition, you can easily win new business with impressive digital proposals, engage new and existing clients with a clear scope of work, and get paid on time by automating payment collection - all in one place.

Ignition also connects with leading apps to run your business on autopilot and automate time-consuming tasks, such as client onboarding or invoicing. That means less admin and more time for clients.

Ignition + Xero

Ignition takes care of your client, invoice, payment and reconciliation processes once your proposal is accepted—creating your clients in Xero, marking their invoices as paid and even reconciling payments. What's not to love?

And when Ignition and Xero Practice Manager unite, the results are outstanding. Import your client records, automatically create new jobs once a proposal is accepted, and sync updated client information.

Expand your team's productivity, keep them motivated to do their best work, and streamline workflows, budgets and milestones. It's power at your fingertips.

Features you'll love

- Ignition creates a new client record in Xero or matches it with one that already exists. So no duplicate records.
- Each service line in your Ignition proposal is translated to a line item on the invoice. Now that's a real life-saver.
- Flexible fee schedules. On acceptance. Recurring. And on completion.
- Gain deeper business insights by categorizing your revenue data from invoices generated in Ignition.

Figure 19.3: Ignition App Xero App Store profile

When you click on the app, you get to see a bit about the app, such as how it works and how it interacts with Xero. Make sure you check the ratings of the app you are interested in and read the user reviews and the feedback of the apps posted on the Xero App Store. I recommend you compare the ratings and reviews to other similar apps.

> **Note**
> If you click the **Get this app** button at the top of the page, it will take you right to the app to sign up. Xero has made it super simple.

Now let's talk about why we want to use apps.

Why use apps with Xero?

As we explained in the previous chapter, using the trial balance app saved a ton of time when exporting and performing data entry in Xero. That is what we want to do. We want to have the tools we use to communicate with each other and perform mundane mindless tasks such as data entry. Data entry is so mindless it is frequently riddled with errors. Using an app to perform data entry will ensure our data is consistent across the platform. In addition, using an app such as A2X Accounting to record our e-commerce transactions removes the manual tasks from our team and posts the details to Xero in a consistent, timely manner. This gives the business owner, our client, timely information and makes our processes more efficient and our lives easier. There are many apps in the Xero ecosystem. As I said earlier, there are foundational apps that we can use to perform functions across our business, ensuring we are set up and have efficient processes for scaling. Then there are the external apps that we use with our clients to deliver the best client experience we can. These apps might be specific to the clients' industries, or they may help in other ways, such as by adding cash flow advisory services.

Connecting apps to Xero

Xero has made it easy to connect apps to its platform. To explain the process, we will walk you through an example. In this example, we will be connecting Xero to the Hubdoc app. This process is very similar to most apps you will connect to Xero.

1. Start by going to the app's settings or integrations page and look for a link or button that allows you to connect to Xero.

Accounting Integrations

Deliver new Hubdoc documents to your accounting platform.

xero   Connect

Figure 19.4: Hubdoc button for connecting to Xero

2. Click the **Connect** button or link and you will be taken to the access screen.
3. Use the **Select an organization** dropdown to find your company name and select it, as seen in *Figure 19.5*.

xero

Hubdoc wants access to:

Your Digital Practice LLC ▼

Organisation data

Your Digital Practice LLC
View and manage your:
- File library
- Organisation settings
- Attachments
- Business transactions
- Contacts

By allowing access, you agree to the transfer of your data between Xero and this application in accordance with Xero's Terms of use and the application provider's terms of use and privacy policy.

You can disconnect at any time by going to Connected apps in your Xero settings.

Allow access

Figure 19.5: App access authorization screen

4. Click the **Allow access** button to complete the process.

Some apps will require further setup, such as chart of accounts mapping and feature settings, like in inventory apps. Just follow the prompts and the instructions set by the app developers.

When you are using an app that imports a tremendous number of transactions into Xero, I like to test the connection and the data setup by connecting first to the demo company and testing the integration. Testing in the demo company allows me to see the results of the imports, ensuring all the setup was done correctly and the app is functioning exactly as I expect it to. After you have tested it, all you need to do is to connect to your actual company and let it rip. Now that we've seen how to connect Xero to an app, let's talk about some of my favorite apps.

What apps should I use with Xero?

We've talked about efficiency and preventing data entry errors (which is why we use apps) and how to connect apps, but now we are going to talk about some of my favorite apps. I did mention I am a recovering appaholic?

Let's look at the foundational apps first. They are apps that help you take a sales lead through your sales process and make them a client. The list of foundational apps also includes the apps you use across every client in your practice.

So, my foundational tech stack starts with my website and the forms used to collect data from the prospective lead. This then connects the lead and adds them to my CRM. I have used Hubspot, Salesforce, and Microsoft Dynamics, all of which connect to the lead capture forms on my website. We connect these apps with Zapier, a no-code tool designed to connect apps that do not have a native API connection. Zapier is used through the workflow when there are no direct connections.

From the lead, when it is ready to become a client, we transfer the data to the proposal software. I use Ignition and Pandadoc for this. We want to ensure the data is consistent, so these connections enforce that for us. When the new client executes the proposal, the data is transferred to Xero, where billing takes place now. All that without really lifting a finger. Well, you do have to add the services to the proposal after performing sales or discovery calls with the prospective client. The actual time spent in the process outside of the calls with the prospective client is minimal.

From here, we want to onboard our new client. We can automate this with the help of a number of tools to collect data and properly onboard your new client. I have used Typeform, Asana, Notion, and Active Collab for this.

Now we can look at the client delivery side of the business. I have spent the last few years in the e-commerce and inventory space. I have implemented several apps many times for many clients. Some of my favorites, depending on the client's needs, are A2X Accounting, Dear Systems, and Unleashed Inventory. Some of the other favorite apps I have implemented and used are Helm for short-term cash flow; Syft for reporting and analyzing data; Spotlight, Futrli, Fathom, Etani, and Reach for reporting; Shogo for POS integration; and Loft 47 for real estate.

Most of the apps in the Xero App Store offer free trials. I recommend that you use those free trials. Anyone that has heard me speak about apps and app selection knows that I recommend abusing that trial. Use it, use it a lot, ask for an extension if you need to, or even create a new trial. But test out the apps and compare them to similar apps in their space.

Find out which features work best in the app you wish to use, and which features are better in the competitors' apps. Reach out to the teams at each app and ask them the questions you need. Ask them for a road map. Are there features you must have in order to use their app? Is it in the development pipeline? When is it expected to be released? Can you be a part of the beta? These are all questions you should be asking. With that said, keep an eye on similar apps even if you are not using them. Know when new features are coming and ask the support or sales team at the app you are using when they are implementing a similar feature.

I could go on for hours here about different apps, what they are best at, how to vet them, and how to stay ahead in the apps space, but connect with me on social media and we can have that conversation.

Summary

Apps are integral to building efficiency in the accounting process. In this chapter, we have talked about why we use apps, how we connect them to Xero, and the apps I use and love in my processes every day.

We have now taken Xero full circle, from setup to using apps to make your workflow more efficient. As you can see, Xero is the ultimate hub for the tools you use to run your business or accounting firm. Take advantage of the efficiency of Xero's built-in features and then supercharge those features with the integration of a few very well-placed apps.

And with the end of this chapter, we have reached the end of this book. If you have read it all the way through from start to finish, now go back and use this book to guide you as you go step by step setting up Xero, recording transactions, running reports, etc... and most importantly, run your business, generate income, and increase your profits. Use Xero to keep you in the know!

Index

A

accounting data
  exporting 259-262
Accounts Payable (AP) 109
  bills, processing 114-117
Analytics 185
Analytics Plus 185
application programming interface (API) 10
artificial intelligence (AI) 79
assets
  adding, to Xero 143-145
  depreciation, running 145-147
  disposing 147-149

B

bank feed 69-73
  balancing 19-22
  Direct feeds 10
  need for 9, 10
  setting up 11-19
  time 56
  Yodlee feeds 10
bank reconciliation process 82, 84
bank rules
  setting up 76-79

bank statement
  importing 73-76
basic report
  customizing 197-202
beginning balances 46, 47
  data entry, with conversion balances 56
  importing 47
  importing, with chart of accounts 48-55
bill payment 118-122
blank template
  schedule, designing 203-207
Business snapshot 190, 192

C

capital asset 139
Cashbook plan 6
cash coding 56, 81, 82
chart of accounts (COA) 23-29
  importing 30-32
  used, for importing beginning balances 48-55
  viewing 33
conversion balances
  for data entry 56
customer relationship management (CRM) 211

D

data
  converting 57
depreciation 142
Direct feeds 10

E

Employer Identification Number (EIN) 38
Established plan
  Xero Expenses 5
  Xero Projects 5

F

Find & Recode
  basics 161-163
  mistakes, correcting 166-169
fixed assets 139
  exploring 139-142
Fresh Start (FS) 45
  usage scenarios 45, 46

G

general ledger (G/L) 151

H

Hubdoc 5

I

Internal Revenue Service (IRS) 139
invoices
  options 97
  setting up 88-92

invoices, options
  Add Credit Note Options 100
  Copy to Options 99
  Edit Options 100
  Repeat option 98
  sharing 101-103
  Void on Invoice Options 99

J

JetConvert
  conversion, initiating with 59
  conversion, preparing 58
  QBDT file, converting 60-62
  QBDT file, preparing 58
  QBO file, converting 62-64
  QBO file, preparing 59
  used, for automating Xero conversion 58

L

layout editor
  exploring 195-197
Ledger plan 6
long-term asset 139

M

manual journal 151
  creating 153-157
  fields 154, 155
  importing 159, 160
  options 156
  overview 153
  Xero rules, creating 152

Index

O

opportunities
  quoting 92-97

P

Products and services option 85-88
Purchase Orders (POs) 109
  exploring 109-114
purchase process
  processing 114-117

Q

QBDT file
  converting 60-62
  preparing 58
QBO file
  converting 62-64
  preparing 59
QuickBooks Desktop (QBDT) 58
QuickBooks Online (QBO) 58
Quotes menu option 92-97

R

repeating journal entry 157, 158
  fields 158, 159
report codes
  assigning 252-254
reports
  saving 207
  saving, in Xero 183
report templates 245-250
  editing 250-252
  using 254, 255

S

Schedule C report 262
  for sole proprietors 262-266
Short-Term Cash Flow (STCF) 185
  projection 186-190

T

tracking categories 34
  setting up 34-36
Trial Balance apps
  using, for tax preparation 266-268

X

Xero 3, 4
  assets, adding to 143-145
  payment 103, 104
  payment, applying from bank feed 104-107
  reporting in 173-182
  reports, saving 183
  using 79-81
Xero Accounting mobile app 123, 124
  battle, on different operating systems 135
  features 124
Xero Accounting mobile app, features
  banking 127-129
  invoicing 129-133
  mobile dashboard 124-127
  payable feature 133, 134
Xero apps
  building 269-273
  connecting to 273, 275
  need for 275, 276
  using 273

Xero business subscription plans 4
   comparison 4, 5
   Early plan 4
   Established plan 5
   Growing plan 4
Xero conversion
   automating, with JetConvert 58
Xero Expenses 5
Xero HQ 211, 213
   Ask feature 226-237
   clients 214-222
   exploring 222-226
   Practice tab 243
   Staff main screen 237-242
Xero partner subscription plans 6
   comparison 6
Xero Projects 5
Xero reports
   exporting 257, 258
Xero search tool 163-166
Xero settings
   financial settings 43, 44
   need for 24
   organizational details 36-39
   running 36
   subscription and billing 42
   user, adding 39-42

Y

Yodlee feeds 10

‹packt›

www.packtpub.com

Subscribe to our online digital library for full access to over 7,000 books and videos, as well as industry leading tools to help you plan your personal development and advance your career. For more information, please visit our website.

Why subscribe?

- Spend less time learning and more time coding with practical eBooks and Videos from over 4,000 industry professionals
- Improve your learning with Skill Plans built especially for you
- Get a free eBook or video every month
- Fully searchable for easy access to vital information
- Copy and paste, print, and bookmark content

Did you know that Packt offers eBook versions of every book published, with PDF and ePub files available? You can upgrade to the eBook version at `packtpub.com` and as a print book customer, you are entitled to a discount on the eBook copy. Get in touch with us at `customercare@packtpub.com` for more details.

At `www.packtpub.com`, you can also read a collection of free technical articles, sign up for a range of free newsletters, and receive exclusive discounts and offers on Packt books and eBooks.

Other Books You May Enjoy

If you enjoyed this book, you may be interested in these other books by Packt:

Mastering QuickBooks® 2023 - Fourth Edition

Crystalynn Shelton

ISBN: 978-1-80324-363-4

- Set up your QuickBooks company file, migrate data to QBO, and customize QBO for your business
- Tackle bookkeeping concepts and the typical US bookkeeping and financial accounting cycle
- Track everything from billable and non-billable time to expenses and profit
- Generate key financial reports for accounts, customers, jobs, and invoice items
- Understand the complete QuickBooks payroll process and track payments made to 1099 contractors
- Discover QBO's newest features, such as recording upfront deposits on estimates, the simplified business view navigation menu, and improvements to bank reconciliations

Professional Tips and Workarounds for QuickBooks Online

Ashley Beetson

ISBN: 978-1-80181-037-1

- Discover how to correctly set up QuickBooks Online with opening balances
- Adapt QuickBooks Online to meet specific industry needs, from manufacturing and retail using inventory to helping lawyers and property agents handle client funds
- Get the most out of features such as Projects and Multicurrency
- Review reports within QuickBooks Online, understand why errors occur, and learn how to resolve them
- Get to grips with key accounting principles and concepts tailored for bookkeeping and accounting beginners
- Find out how the audit trail works and explore all of the information it holds

Packt is searching for authors like you

If you're interested in becoming an author for Packt, please visit `authors.packtpub.com` and apply today. We have worked with thousands of developers and tech professionals, just like you, to help them share their insight with the global tech community. You can make a general application, apply for a specific hot topic that we are recruiting an author for, or submit your own idea.

Hi!

I am Jay Kimelman, author of *Efficient Accounting with Xero*. I really hope you enjoyed reading this book and found it useful for increasing your productivity and efficiency in performing your businesses accounting or the accounting for your clients.It would really help me (and other potential readers!) if you could leave a review on Amazon sharing your thoughts on this book.

Go to the link below or scan the QR code to leave your review:

https://packt.link/r/1801812209

Your review will help us to understand what's worked well in this book, and what could be improved upon for future editions, so it really is appreciated.

Best wishes,

Jay Kimelman

Download a free PDF copy of this book

Thanks for purchasing this book!

Do you like to read on the go but are unable to carry your print books everywhere?

Is your eBook purchase not compatible with the device of your choice?

Don't worry, now with every Packt book you get a DRM-free PDF version of that book at no cost.

Read anywhere, any place, on any device. Search, copy, and paste code from your favorite technical books directly into your application.

The perks don't stop there, you can get exclusive access to discounts, newsletters, and great free content in your inbox daily

Follow these simple steps to get the benefits:

1. Scan the QR code or visit the link below

`https://packt.link/free-ebook/9781801812207`

2. Submit your proof of purchase
3. That's it! We'll send your free PDF and other benefits to your email directly

Made in the USA
Las Vegas, NV
10 August 2023